EVIDENCE SERIES

SHEPARD'S EXPERT

AND SCIENTIFIC

EVIDENCE

QUARTERLY

VOLUME 1   Spring, 1994   NUMBER 4

Editors:

Bert Black
Weinberg and Green
Baltimore, Maryland

Marc S. Klein
Sills Cummis Zuckerman Radin
Tischman Epstein & Gross
Newark, New Jersey

Stephen A. Brunette
Shepard's/McGraw-Hill, Inc.
Colorado Springs, Colorado

SHEPARD'S/McGRAW-HILL, INC.
P.O. Box 35300
Colorado Springs, Colorado 80935-3530

ESE1
5700
ISBN 0-07-172254-5

CONTENTS

WORTH READING

BOOK REVIEWS

Introduction to the Spring Issue

With this issue, our fourth, we complete the first year of Shepard's Expert and Scientific Evidence Quarterly (*SESEQ*). In the past year we have examined a range of issues — many deriving from the Supreme Court's landmark decision in *Daubert v. Merrell Dow Pharmaceuticals*, Inc.[1] —in the broad and dynamic fields of expert and scientific evidence.

In this issue of *SESEQ*, we focus on many issues at the frontiers of practice and procedure. These include, among others, developments in discovery, hearings *in limine*, ethics, medical and scientific research, the use and abuse of hearsay, and collateral estoppel. We also present, of course, our regular features, including a survey of recent decisions in these fields, recent articles in these fields, and reviews of selected books in these fields.

What Lies Ahead?

Our next two issues will focus on two vital areas concerning expert and scientific evidence.

In the Summer 1994 issue, we will focus on expert and scientific evidence in the domain of environmental regulation. Note that we will primarily focus on *regulatory science* (as opposed to scientific evidence in a toxic tort action). The two areas are similar, since both involve "science," but they are often subject to different criteria of relevance and credibility.

In the Fall 1994 issue, we will focus on *social and behavioral science*. Evidence based on psychological syndromes and profiles, repressed memories, hypnotically refreshed recollections, and survey research, to name a few, are coming into court with increasing frequency. Many have suggested that *Daubert's* "scientific validity" requirement will have a tremendous impact on this type of evidence. We will publish the views of leading experts in these fields on these issues.

Why You Should Subscribe

You should subscribe to *SESEQ* (if you have not yet done so already) or continue your subscription (if you are currently on-board).

The case for our publication is compelling. Expert and scientific evidence — in one form or another — is used (or abused) in a majority of civil and criminal cases. It can, and often does, make or break the case.

Our publication is unique. We have followed the coverage of these issues in other generic publications, particularly those focusing on "toxic torts" or

---

[1] 113 S.Ct. 2786, 125 L. Ed.2d 469 (decided June 28, 1993).

"product liability" or "criminal law." The coverage is often spotty, and the analyses are often misleading or superficial. *SESEQ* does not suffer from these flaws.

Given the critical importance of this area, and the revolution that is now taking place (largely as a result of *Daubert*), *SESEQ* should be at the top of your reading list.

Would You Like to Contribute?

We want to hear from you. If you would like to contribute an article for publication in *SESEQ*, or you have any suggestions for topical areas that we should cover, please do not hesitate to call one of us.

BERT BLACK
MARC S. KLEIN
STEPHEN A. BRUNETTE

RECENT DEVELOPMENTS

Significant Recent Cases on Expert and Scientific Evidence

Stephen A. Brunette
and
Stephen F. Lynch

I. Introduction

This article provides an update on federal and state court interpretations of *Daubert*[1] and discusses significant rulings on the admissibility of evidence in such areas as battered person syndromes,[2] causation,[3] DNA identification,[4] economic injury,[5] hypnotically refreshed memory,[6] injury or disability,[7] intoxication,[8] photogrammetry,[9] some expert evidence issues in product liability cases,[10] and various types of survey research evidence.[11] Rulings concerning whether expert testimony is necessary to assist the trier of fact,[12] the qualifications of experts,[13] the factual bases of expert testimony,[14] and some practice and procedure issues affecting expert and scientific evidence[15] are also discussed.

II. *Daubert* Update

Federal and state courts continue to provide new meaning to the language of *Daubert*. Federal courts are, of course, "fleshing out" the federal rules of evidence; state courts, by comparison, are showing remarkable creativity in determining the effect of *Daubert* on state law.

A. *Daubert* in Federal Courts

During the period covered by this review, federal courts have relied on *Daubert* to adopt a gatekeeping role to exclude evidence, to sharpen the focus on a witness's reasoning or methodology rather than on the witness's conclusions, to justify a flexible approach to expert evidence, to uphold a pre-*Daubert* evidentiary ruling that was found to be consistent with *Daubert*, and for other, nondeterminative reasons.

---

[1] Section II.
[2] Section III.A.1.
[3] Section III.A.2.
[4] Section III.A.3.
[5] Section III.A.4.
[6] Section III.A.5.
[7] Section III.A.6.
[8] Section III.A.7.
[9] Section III.A.8.
[10] Section III.A.9.
[11] Section III.A.10.
[12] Section IV.
[13] Section V.
[14] Section VI.
[15] Section VII.

A *Daubert/DeLuca/Downing* Analysis in the Third Circuit

In a product liability action in *Wade-Greaux v. Whitehall Laboratories, Inc.*,[16] the District Court for the Virgin Islands granted summary judgment in favor of the defendant after an extensive pre-trial "*Downing* hearing" which resulted in exclusion of the plaintiff's evidence of causation.[17] The court invoked the *Daubert*,[18] *DeLuca*,[19] and *Downing*[20] triumvirate to support key components of its rulings under Fed. R. Evid. 702, 703, and 403, observing that "*Downing*, *DeLuca* and *Daubert* have identified several factors to be considered when evaluating the reliability and soundness of a particular methodology."[21]

Gatekeeping Function

In *McLendon v. Georgia Kaolin Co.*,[22] the court assumed a gatekeeping role under *Daubert* and excluded testimony of an unqualified witness. The court acknowledged that cross-examination and the presentation of contrary evidence may be appropriate means of attacking a witness's qualifications in some instances, but it relied more heavily on *Daubert*'s observation that these safeguards are sufficient only when the testimony meets the other requirements of Rule 702. The court concluded that although cross-examination would expose the witness's lack of qualifications in this case, the likelihood that the jury would consider the witness's qualifications was outweighed by the risk that the witness's testimony would prejudice and mislead the jury.[23] *Compare United States v. Sepulveda*[24] [when it became apparent during trial that expert was not qualified, court exercised gatekeeping function in halting testimony in progress and instructing jury to ignore expert's opinion].

Focus on Methodology, Not on Conclusions

In a RICO action, the court in *Davis v. Southern Bell Telephone & Telegraph Co.*[25] applied *Daubert*'s distinction between methodology and conclusions in admitting survey research evidence. The plaintiffs offered the evidence to show that purchasers of the defendant's services misunderstood the nature of those services, and that the defendant employed deceptive marketing and sales techniques. In ruling on a motion to strike affidavits of

---

[16] Civ. No. 30/1988 (D. V.I., Mar. 3, 1994) (1994 WL 80840).

[17] See section III.A.2 for a discussion of the evidentiary rulings.

[18] 113 S.Ct. 1786 (1993).

[19] DeLuca *ex rel* DeLuca v. Merrell Dow Pharmaceuticals, Inc., 911 F.2d 941 (3d Cir. 1990), *on remand*, 791 F Supp 1042 (D. N.J. 1992), *aff'd*, 6 F.3d 778 (3d Cir. 1993).

[20] United States v. Downing, 753 F.2d 1224 (3d Cir. 1985).

[21] *Wade-Greaux*, 1994 WL 80840, at *37.

[22] 841 F. Supp 415 (M.D. Ga. 1994).

[23] See sections V and VI for discussions of the witness's qualifications and testimony.

[24] ____ F.3d ____ , 1993 WL 516354, No. 92-1362 (1st Cir. Dec. 20, 1993).

[25] No. 89-2839-CIV (S.D. Fla. Feb. 1, 1994) (1994 WL 88981).

the plaintiffs' survey research evidence, the court ruled the survey evidence admissible under *Daubert*. An affidavit submitted by one of the witnesses involved in the survey research — a professor and an "expert in the psychology of influence and persuasion"[26] — identified the principles upon which the research was based. At an evidentiary hearing, the witness testified that each of the principles stated in the affidavit had been tested, had been discussed in the peer-reviewed literature in the field of social psychology, and had achieved general acceptance in the witness's field. Copies of pertinent literature were submitted to support the witness's testimony. The court observed that the defendant did not challenge the validity of the principles relied upon by the witness during the hearing, but, instead, questioned the witness as to why he did not perform an independent scientific experiment to test whether the defendant's sales and marketing techniques were misleading. While acknowledging that this line of questioning may have some bearing on the reliability of the witness's conclusions, the court ruled that it was not relevant to a determination of the scientific validity of the witness's principles and methodology under Fed. R. Evid. 702.[27] *Compare O'Conner v. Commonwealth Edison Co.*,[28] [opinion of physician as to what radiation-induced cataracts "look like" was inadmissible where witness had not followed diagnostic procedures specified in medical literature, and one article relied upon by witness actually refuted his claim that radiation-induced cataracts could be distinguished from other cataracts through observation].

Flexible Inquiry

In *Flores v. Puerto Rico Telephone Co.*,[29] an action alleging discrimination on the basis of physical handicap, the defendant filed a motion in limine to exclude the testimony of the plaintiff's medical expert — an ophthalmologist — concerning the plaintiff's secondary angle closure glaucoma and the relationship between stress and intraocular pressure. The defendant argued that the witness was not a specialist in glaucoma, so his opinion was not scientifically reliable. The court allowed the evidence and cited *Daubert* to support the propositions that an expert is permitted wide latitude in offering opinions because of "an assumption that an expert's opinion will have a reliable basis in the knowledge and experience of his discipline;"[30] that the 702 inquiry is a flexible one; that the absence of medical literature on a subject does not require a finding that testimony is not scientific knowledge, since knowledge applies to "any body of known facts or to any body of ideas

---

[26] *Id.* 1994 WL 88981, at *3.

[27] *Id.* at *3-4.

[28] ____ F.3d ____ , 1994 WL 3794 (7th Cir. Jan. 7, 1994).

[29] Civ. No. 89-1697 (D. P.R. Jan. 19, 1994) (1994 WL 52570).

[30] *Id.* 1994 WL 52570, at *1.

inferred from such facts or accepted as truths on good grounds;"[31] and that cross-examination, presentation of contrary evidence, and careful instruction on the burden of proof are the appropriate means of attacking the witness's testimony.[32]

Applicable Only to Scientific Evidence

The Second Circuit noted that because *Daubert* deals specifically with scientific evidence, not all expert testimony, there was no requirement for the testimony of an accountant who prepared a payroll review to meet the *Daubert* burden of reliability. *Tamarin v. Adam Caterers.*[33]

Pre-*Daubert* Rulings Unaffected If Consistent with *Daubert*

In *Borawick v. Shay*,[34] the plaintiff argued that pre-*Daubert* evidentiary rulings that had excluded post-hypnotic memories of childhood sexual abuse should be reviewed in light of *Daubert*. The court ruled that the evidentiary rulings were not affected by *Daubert*'s rejection of *Frye* and interpretation of Fed. R. Evid. 702, for the reason that the rulings had been made under Second Circuit precedent which had already rejected *Frye* and interpreted Rule 702 in a manner consistent with *Daubert*.

Unique Uses of *Daubert*

A Magistrate Judge relied on *Daubert* to deny a defense motion for a Rule 35 dental examination of a plaintiff, to explore a possible relationship between tooth enamel defects and cerebral palsy, in *Dodd-Anderson v. Stevens*.[35] The court conducted an extensive review of the medical literature submitted by the defendant and concluded that the literature may suggest a higher prevalence of enamel defects in children with cerebral palsy, but it does not establish the causal link that the defendant sought to explore. The court cited *Daubert* to support its denial of the motion, for the reason that the defendant's theory did not meet *Daubert*'s requirement of scientific validity, and thus relevance and reliability.

Other Citations to *Daubert*

— *United States v. Ridlehuber*[36] [*Daubert* cited by dissent for propositions that Rule 402 is the "baseline" of the Federal Rules of Evidence and that the standard of relevance under Rule 401 is liberal].

---

[31] *Id.*, citing *Daubert*, 113 S.Ct. at 2795.

[32] *Id.* 1994 WL 52570, at *2.

[33] ____ F.3d ____ , 1993 WL 535877, No. 93-7634 (2d Cir. Dec. 27, 1993).

[34] 842 F. Supp. 1501 (D. Conn. 1994).

[35] Nos. 92-1015-MLB, 92-1016-MLB (D. Kan. Jan. 5, 1994) (1994 WL 26922).

[36] No. 92-8296, ____ F.3d ____ , 1993 WL 536874 (5th Cir. Dec. 29, 1993).

—United States v. Quinn[37] [Ninth Circuit relied on *Daubert* to affirm admissibility of "photogrammetry" evidence to estimate height of bank robber based on surveillance photographs taken during robbery].[38]

—Wilson v. Merrell Dow Pharmaceuticals, Inc.[39] [remanded for consideration in light of *Daubert*].

B. State Court Reactions to *Daubert*

State courts have provided a range of interpretations of *Daubert*. Some have simply adopted or rejected *Daubert*, others have crafted permutations of *Frye*, *Daubert*, *Downing*, and state rules or case law. If *Frye* provided a metaphorical hook for state courts to hang a hat on, *Daubert* has provided them with a hat check room.

Daubert Applied

West Virginia adopted *Daubert* in its entirety, and elevated Justice Blackmun's four "general observations" to the status of essential components of a judicial assessment of scientific evidence, in *Wilt v. Buracker*.[40] The court ruled that *Daubert's* analysis of Rule 702 should be followed in analyzing the admissibility of scientific evidence under W. V. R. Evid. 702, and applied this reasoning to exclude an economist's calculations of "hedonic damages."[41]

In *State v. Hofer*,[42] the **South Dakota** Supreme Court cited *Daubert's* rejection of *Frye* for the proposition that "general acceptance in the scientific community is no longer required"[43] and adopted *Daubert's* requirement that trial judges assure that expert testimony rests on a reliable foundation, is relevant to the case, and is based on scientifically valid principles.[44] Under this standard, the court found that the scientific principles underlying the intoxilyzer breath test are "beyond scientific dispute,"[45] and that the defendant's concerns over the assumptions and procedures for implementing the test go to the weight, not the admissibility, of intoxilyzer test results. The defendant had argued that the test's assumptions were not generally accepted in the scientific community.

---

[37] Nos. 92-10452, 92-10509 (9th Cir. Mar. 17, 1994) (1994 WL 82048).
[38] See section III.A.8 for a discussion of the photogrammetry evidence.
[39] No. 90-5257, ____ F.3d ____ (9th Cir. Mar. 10, 1994) (1994 WL 73253).
[40] No. 21708 (W. Va. Sup. Ct. App. Dec. 13, 1993) (1993 WL 517042).
[41] See section III.A.4 for a discussion of the hedonic damage issue.
[42] No. 18107-A-RAM (S.D. Sup. Ct. Feb. 23, 1994) (1994 WL 53756).
[43] *Id.* 1994 WL 53756, at *2.
[44] *Id.*
[45] *Id.*

Daubert seems to be firmly entrenched in **Louisiana**. In *Clement v. Griffin*,[46] a Louisiana Appellate Court relied on the state Supreme Court's adoption of *Daubert* in *State v. Foret*[47] and ruled the testimony of an engineer as to an alleged manufacturing defect in a tire[48] inadmissible, under the newly proclaimed *"Daubert/Foret"* standard.[49] In *Williams v. General Motors Corporation*,[50] the *Daubert/Foret* standard was invoked to support a dissenting opinion that an engineering expert's surprise testimony at trial, consisting of a new theory of an alleged manufacturing defect, should have been excluded on grounds that the witness had not performed any tests or examinations to support the new theory.[51]

Daubert Accommodated by *Frye*/702 Standard

In *State v. Riker*,[52] the Supreme Court of **Washington** noted that *Daubert* had held the *Frye* standard inapplicable under the Federal Rules of Evidence but ruled that Washington courts would "continue to adhere to the view that the *Frye* analysis is a threshold inquiry to be considered in determining the admissibility of evidence under ER 702."[53] In addition to incorporating *Frye* in Rule 702, the court adopted a unique approach in finding that "many of the 'general observations' made by Justice Blackmun in the majority opinion [in *Daubert*] may be of use to trial judges in making the threshold *Frye* determination."[54]

The *Riker* court then applied these criteria in a *Frye*/702 analysis. Under the *Frye* analysis, the court inquired "(1) whether the underlying theory is generally accepted in the scientific community and (2) whether there are techniques, experiments, or studies utilizing that theory which are capable of producing reliable results and are generally accepted in the scientific community."[55] The court stated that the core concern of a *Frye* analysis is whether the evidence is based on "established scientific methodology," which includes both a generally accepted theory, and a "valid technique" to

---

[46] Nos. 91-CA-1664, 92-CA-1001, 93-CA-0591, 93-CA-0592, 93-CA-0593, 93-CA-0594, 93-CA-0595, 93-CA-0596, 93-CA-0597 (La. App. Mar. 3, 1994) (1994 WL 65134).

[47] 628 So.2d 1116 (La. 1993). See the discussion of *State v. Foret* in 1(3) SESEQ 379, 396-97 (Winter 1994).

[48] See the discussion of this issue in section III.A.9.

[49] *Clement*, 1994 WL 65134, at *10.

[50] No. 93-CA-0287 (La. Ct. App. Feb. 11, 1994) (1994 WL 42511).

[51] *Id.* 1994 WL 42511, at *14. See section III.A.9 for a discussion of the evidentiary issues raised by the dissent.

[52] 1994 WL 61683 (Wash. Mar. 3, 1994) (No. 58970-4).

[53] *Id.* at *12-13, n.1.

[54] Citing *Daubert*, 113 S.Ct. at 2796-98.

[55] 1994 WL 61683, at *4. Citing State v. Cauthron, 120 Wash. 2d 879, 885, 846 P.2d 502 (1993). *See also* State v. Cissne, 72 Wash. App. 677, 865 P.2d 564 (1994) [decided before *Riker*; court decided that until state supreme court abandoned *Frye* and interpreted ER 702 as interpreted by *Daubert*, it was bound by *Cauthron*].

implement the theory.[56] Under this standard, the court found the "battered person syndrome theory" to be generally accepted and admissible, under the first prong of its *Frye* analysis, in cases where the batterer and the victim are in a long-term relationship — such as a father/son, husband/wife, or long-term romantic relationship — but that the evidence was inadmissible in this case, under the second prong of the *Frye* analysis, because there were no studies to support the extension of the battered woman syndrome to a relationship which was "brief, business-oriented, and without any history of physical abuse."[57] The court quoted *Daubert*'s observations that "scientific validity for one purpose is not necessarily scientific validity for other, unrelated purposes,"[58] and that "scientists typically distinguish between 'validity' (does the principle support what it purports to show?) and 'reliability' (does application of the principle produce consistent results?)"[59] and concluded: "Similarly, the *gatekeeping function of Frye* requires both an accepted theory and a reliable method of applying that theory to the facts of the case."[60] Under the Rule 702 analysis, the court concluded that the same lack of scientific studies that required exclusion of the evidence under *Frye* required exclusion under 702, because there was an inadequate foundation for establishing probative value of the battered woman syndrome outside the context of a battering relationship.[61]

Frye Applied; *Daubert* Ignored or Rejected

In *People v. Webb*,[62] the Supreme Court of California declined to reexamine *People v. Kelly*[63] in light of *Daubert*. The defendant challenged the admissibility of fingerprint evidence, arguing that the chemical and laser process that was used to reveal the defendant's fingerprint on a piece of duct tape was not generally accepted as reliable in the scientific community. The witness — a "latent print analyst" employed for many years by a state crime laboratory — explained the manner in which he had placed the tape in an enclosed tank, exposed it to heat, superglue, and dye, and then photographed the item through an orange filter, with the help of a laser beam. The result was a photographic image of a fingerprint that the witness compared with the sample print provided by the defendant and found that the two had thirteen points of similarity and no dissimilarities. Slides and photographs of each stage of the chemical and laser process were introduced into evidence; the court concluded that "[t]he reliability of the laser procedure in producing an

---

[56] *Id.*

[57] *Id.* See section III.A.1 for a discussion of the evidentiary issues in the case.

[58] *Id.*, citing *Daubert* at 113 S.Ct 2796.

[59] 1994 WL 61683, at *6, citing *Daubert* at 113 S.Ct 2795, n.9.

[60] 1994 WL 61683, at *6 (emphasis added).

[61] *Id.* at *7.

[62] 6 Cal. 4th 494, 862 P.2d 779, 24 Cal. Rptr. 2d 779 (1993).

[63] 17 Cal. 3d 24, 130 Cal. Rptr. 144, 549 P.2d 1240 (1976).

image commonly recognizable only as a human fingerprint was manifest at trial."[64] The defendant offered no expert testimony to rebut the fingerprint evidence.

The court concluded that the method of revealing the fingerprint and the comparison of the fingerprint with that of the defendant were both sufficiently established that a *Kelly/Frye* inquiry regarding the trustworthiness of novel scientific evidence was unnecessary. Because it concluded that *Kelly* was inapplicable to the case before it, the court felt no need to reexamine *Kelly* in light of *Daubert* in this case.

See also *In re Clara B.*,[65] a child dependency proceeding in which the court declined to review a challenge to expert testimony that had not been challenged at trial and simply noted, without discussion, that *Daubert* had questioned *Frye*.[66]

In *State v. Hodgson*,[67] the Supreme Court of **Minnesota** declined to address the question of "what impact *Daubert* should or will have in Minnesota"[68] and ruled bite-mark evidence admissible without the need for a *Frye* hearing after concluding that bite-mark evidence is "not a novel or emerging type of evidence."[69] See also *State v. Bauer*,[70] in which the Minnesota Court of Appeals applied a *Frye* analysis and noted that the state supreme court was the proper forum to determine whether *Daubert* will have any impact on the *Frye* standard in Minnesota.

In *Bass v. Florida Department of Law Enforcement*,[71] the concurring opinion in a wrongful discharge case cited the state supreme court's ruling in *Flanagan v. State*[72] — that **Florida** would continue to follow *Frye* — and noted that radioimmunoassay analysis of human hair as a test for cocaine use is generally accepted in the scientific community and is therefore admissible under *Frye*.

In *People v. Watson*,[73] an **Illinois** Appellate Court observed that *Daubert* had rejected *Frye* but ruled that *Daubert* did not apply to state court proceedings. The court concluded that it would continue to apply *Frye* "until such time as our supreme court ceases to recognize the *Frye* test as the applicable standard for admitting novel scientific evidence in this state."[74]

---

64 24 Cal. Rptr. 2d at 798.

65 20 Cal. App. 4th 988, 25 Cal. Rptr. 2d 56 (1993).

66 *Id.* at 1000, 25 Cal. Rptr. 2d at 62.

67 No. C5-93-222 (Minn. Feb. 11, 1994) (1994 WL 37808).

68 *Id.* 1994 WL 37808, at *3.

69 *Id.*

70 No. C8-93-1073 (Minn. Ct. App. Feb. 15, 1994) (1994 WL 42240).

71 627 So.2d 1321 (Fla. Dist. Ct. App. 1993).

72 ____ So. 2d ____ (Fla. 1993).

73 No. 1-91-1351 (Ill. App. Jan. 28, 1994) (1994 WL 30084).

74 *Id.*

Compare People v. Bynum[75] [citing *Daubert* for proposition that foundation proof concerning use of mechanical or electronic device is necessary under Rule 703 to assure that scientific evidence, including expert scientific testimony based on use of such device, is relevant and reliable].

Daubert Mentioned, But Not Discussed

In *City of Fargo v. McLaughlin*,[76] the **North Dakota** Supreme Court applied — without articulating — "the *Frye* standard"[77] to determine the admissibility of police officer testimony concerning horizontal gaze nystagmus (HGN) test results. The court also noted, without explanation: (1) the text of N.D. R. Evid. 702; (2) the holding in *Daubert* that *Frye* was superseded by Fed. R. Evid. 702; and (3) that Montana and Oregon courts had ruled HGN test results admissible under their respective versions of Rule 702.[78]

In *Commonwealth v. Smith*,[79] a **Massachusetts** appellate court cited *Daubert* for the proposition that evidence —such as retrograde extrapolation from alcohol test results — should be based on "a scientifically acceptable or reliable method."[80] The court noted that *Daubert* was based on Fed. R. Evid. 702 but had "enlarged on the 'generally accepted in the scientific community' standard for admissibility of scientific evidence which had initially been articulated in *Frye*."[81] As to whether *Daubert* would be followed in Massachusetts, the court said: "Rule 702 of the Proposed Massachusetts Rules of Evidence is identical [to Federal Rule 702], but neither in this case nor any that has come to our attention has the issue been argued whether the *Daubert* approach should be grafted onto Massachusetts practice."[82]

In *State v. Cephas*,[83] a workers' compensation claim based on mental injury caused by job-related stress, the **Delaware** Supreme Court cited *Daubert* for the proposition that the validity of the controversial scientific evidence that supports such a claim can be tested through vigorous cross-examination.[84]

In *Paxton v. State*,[85] the **Oklahoma** Court of Criminal Appeals noted *Daubert*'s holding that *Frye* had been superseded by the Federal Rules of Evidence, and observed that state case law that held polygraph evidence

---

[75] No. 1-92-1176 (Ill. App. Feb. 4, 1994) (1994 WL 30178).

[76] Crim. No. 930130 (N.D. Sup. Ct. Feb. 23, 1994) (1994 WL 51963).

[77] *Id.* 1994 WL 51963, at *5.

[78] *Id.* at *8, n.2.

[79] 35 Mass. App. Ct. 655, 624 N.E.2d 604 (1993).

[80] *Id.* at 662, 624 N.E.2d at 609.

[81] *Id.* n.9.

[82] *Id.*

[83] 1994 WL 17029 (Del. Jan. 20, 1994).

[84] *Id.* at *8.

[85] 867 P.2d 1309 (Okla. Crim. App. 1993).

inadmissible was based in part on *Frye,* but ruled the evidence was properly excluded in this case because the trial court was presented with no evidence to overcome the presumption of unreliability of the evidence.[86]

The **Colorado** Court of Appeals cited *Daubert* in *Grogan v. Taylor*[87] for the proposition that an expert witness is permitted "wide latitude" in offering opinions. Nonetheless, the court ruled inadmissible expert testimony by an attorney concerning the meaning of a statute of limitations, on grounds the testimony usurped the function of the jury.

III. Scientific, Technical, or Specialized Knowledge

A. Validity of Reasoning or Methodology

1. Battered Person Syndromes

In *State v. Riker,*[88] the defendant in a prosecution for delivery and possession of cocaine raised a defense of duress and offered testimony on the battered woman syndrome to support the defense by showing that her apprehension of immediate harm from a police informant was reasonable. The informant had made several purchases of cocaine from the defendant and had allegedly threatened harm to the defendant's sister if the cocaine sales were not made, but there was no intimate relationship between the defendant and the informant.

The defendant offered expert testimony that the battered woman syndrome is a type of post-traumatic stress syndrome, in which a woman exhibits "learned helplessness" as a result of a pattern of repeated threats, fears, coercions, and physical violence, and that the defendant was a battered woman at the time she was arrested. The expert witness admitted that use of the battered woman syndrome to explain conduct in the absence of an intimate relationship between a victim and a batterer was novel — but testified that the defendant was unable to separate her relationship with the informant from her prior abusive relationships with significant men in her life. The trial court ruled the testimony inadmissible on grounds that it would not help the trier of fact and was not necessary for the defense of duress.

The state Supreme Court noted that it had previously ruled such testimony admissible in self-defense cases to show that the defendant's conduct was reasonable, because such testimony helps the jury to understand how severe abuse, in the context of a battering relationship, can affect the victim's perceptions and reactions. The court ruled that the testimony was properly excluded in this case of first impression, however, because it was offered to explain conduct outside of a battering relationship. The court did

---

[86] *Id.* at 1323.

[87] No. 92CA1298 (Colo. Ct. App. Feb. 10, 1994) (1993 WL 524131).

[88] 1994 WL 61683 (Wash. Mar. 3, 1994) (No. 58970-4).

not question the general acceptance of the battered woman syndrome in the context of a battering relationship, but based its exclusion of the testimony on the finding that extension of the battered woman syndrome to a relationship that was "brief, business-oriented, and without any history of physical abuse"[89] was not generally accepted in the scientific community. The court found neither scientific literature nor legal precedent for extending use of battered woman syndrome evidence to explain conduct outside of a battering relationship.

One dissenting justice would have admitted the testimony because it was offered only to assist the jury in determining whether the defendant's apprehension of harm was reasonable, given the effect of past abuse on the defendant's perception of harm. The dissent argued that the purpose of testimony concerning battered person syndrome is to inform the jury of the effects of severe abuse on a victim's state of mind in general, and the perception of danger in particular, and that the absence of an intimate relationship between the defendant and the informant was immaterial to a determination of whether the defendant's perceptions of danger were distorted by past abuse. The dissent relied on testimony of the proffered expert witness to the effect that "the effects of abuse on the human psyche cannot be so neatly compartmentalized."[90]

2. Causation

In *Wade-Greaux v. Whitehall Laboratories, Inc.*,[91] an action alleging that birth defects were caused by a mother's use of Primatene tablets and Primatene mist during pregnancy, the court granted summary judgment in favor of the defendant after an extensive pre-trial "*Downing* hearing" which resulted in exclusion of the plaintiff's medical and scientific evidence of causation. Invoking *Daubert*,[92] *DeLuca*,[93] and *Downing*,[94] the court required the witnesses to address both general causation — defined by the court as "whether the agent at issue is capable of causing birth defects in humans at therapeutic dose levels"[95] — and specific causation — defined by the court as "whether that agent caused the particular malformations found in this particular plaintiff."[96] Based on the evidence adduced through the testimony of four causation witness for the plaintiff, and four for the defendant, the court made extensive and detailed findings of fact concerning: the incidence and causes of birth defects; the drugs at issue; the science of teratology, and

---

[89] *Id.* at *4.

[90] *Id.* at *11.

[91] Civ. No. 30/1988 (D. V.I. Mar. 3, 1994) (1994 WL 80840).

[92] 113 S.Ct. 1786 (1993).

[93] DeLuca *ex rel* DeLuca v Merrell Dow Pharmaceuticals, Inc., 911 F.2d 941 (3d Cir. 1990), *on remand*, 791 F Supp 1042 (D. N.J. 1992), *aff'd*, 6 F.3d 778 (3d Cir. 1993).

[94] United States v. Downing, 753 F.2d 1224 (3d Cir. 1985).

[95] *Wade-Greaux,* 1994 WL 80840, at *1.

[96] *Id.*

methodologies for determining general causation (human teratogenicity) through the use of epidemiology, and in vivo and in vitro animal studies; and specific problems with the methodologies and data used by all experts to establish opinions on general causation, including findings concerning the scientific validity of studies on which they relied. The court asserted its duty as a gatekeeper to assure that expert testimony is relevant and reliable, and ruled the plaintiff's evidence inadmissible under Fed. R. Evid. 702, 703, and 403.

Under Fed. R. Evid. 702, the court addressed the validity of the methodologies employed by the plaintiff's witnesses, observing that "*Downing, DeLuca* and *Daubert* have identified several factors to be considered when evaluating the reliability and soundness of a particular methodology."[97] Specifically, the court considered the novelty of the methodologies and their relation to methodologies accepted by the relevant scientific community, the existence of a specialized literature, nonjudicial uses of the methodologies, the frequency of erroneous results, and the qualifications and professional stature of the witnesses. Under these criteria, the court concluded that the methodologies employed by the plaintiff's experts were contrary to methodologies generally accepted by the scientific community of teratologists, in that they were not based on human epidemiological studies of the drug in question; that none of the witnesses had identified any specialized literature that endorsed their respective methodologies; that none of their methodologies had been put to any use outside of the courtroom; that the witnesses' techniques of extrapolating from animal data to human experience, and relying on anecdotal human data contained in Drug Experience Reports, and conjecture regarding possible effects of human therapeutic doses, were highly likely to produce erroneous results; and that although the plaintiff's experts may have been qualified in their particular fields of specialization — including pediatric subacute critical care, internal medicine, clinical pharmacology, pediatric pathology, cell biology, and physical chemistry — none were qualified in human teratology.[98]

The plaintiff's evidence was also inadmissible under Fed. R. Evid. 703, for the reason that "each of the plaintiff's experts relied upon data not reasonably relied upon by teratologists in drawing ultimate conclusions about whether an agent is a human teratogen."[99] This conclusion was based on findings that the epidemiological studies relied on by the witnesses did not involve ingredients contained in the defendant's product, that anecdotal human data contain inherent biases, and that animal data are unreliable predictors of causation in humans.[100]

---

[97] *Id.* at *37.

[98] *Id.* at *35-42.

[99] *Id.* at *43.

[100] *Id.* at *42-45.

Finally, the court ruled that expert opinions that therapeutic doses of the defendant's product were teratogenic would confuse, mislead, and overwhelm the jury, and were therefore inadmissible under Fed. R. Evid. 403.

In *O'Conner v. Commonwealth Edison Co.*,[101] the plaintiff's treating physician testified that the plaintiff's cataracts were caused by exposure to radiation, and that he could distinguish between radiation-induced cataracts and other cataracts merely by observation. The district court ruled the testimony inadmissible and granted the defendants' motion for summary judgment; the plaintiff argued that his expert should not have been excluded merely because he was a "lone voice" on the issue of distinguishing radiation-caused cataracts by observation. The court of appeals relied on *Daubert* in ruling that the witness's testimony was not scientific knowledge within the meaning of Fed. R. Evid. 702, for the reason that the witness's claim that he could tell what radiation-induced cataracts "look like" was not supported by any of the journals or other sources on which the witness relied. In fact, one of the articles cited by the witness refuted the witness's claim that it is possible to distinguish radiation-induced cataracts from other cataracts through observation, and outlined the proper steps to determine whether a patient's cataracts were caused by radiation — but the witness had not followed those steps.

In *Thomas v. FAG Bearings Corporation*,[102] a class action by residents of two communities against a manufacturer for alleged groundwater contamination, the defendant filed third-party complaints against other corporations which maintained facilities near the communities. The third-party defendants filed motions for summary judgment on grounds that the defendant's evidence of causation was inadmissible or insufficient. The defendant's evidence consisted of the opinion of a hydrogeologist that a "general groundwater contaminant pathway" ran under or near the third-party defendants' sites and toward the plaintiffs' communities. The witness admitted that he did not know whether the pathway in fact ran from any third-party defendant's site to the communities, nor whether any contaminant had in fact migrated from any third-party defendant's site to the communities' drinking water wells; the witness testified that extensive testing would have to be done to collect data to establish such a causal relationship.

The court ruled the testimony inadmissible for the reason that it lacked scientific certainty on basic issues, including the identity of the source of the contamination, the specific contaminant pathways, and whether any of the third-party defendants were the source of the contaminants. The court reasoned that although the witness could testify that groundwater pathways are generally recognized in the scientific community, an opinion about causation at a particular site must have a factual basis. Testimony that every third-party defendant is a potential contributor does not establish a causal

---

[101]   ____ F.3d ____ , 1994 WL 3794 (7th Cir. Jan. 7, 1994).
[102] No. 92-5070-CV-SW-8 (W.D. Mo. Feb. 10, 1994) (1994 WL 65307).

link and is therefore not admissible. Summary judgment was granted in favor of the third-party defendants.

3. DNA Identification

In *People v. Watson*,[103] the court observed that although the structure of DNA was discovered more than 40 years ago, the application of DNA technology to forensic sciences is relatively recent, and that DNA evidence is, therefore, precisely the type of evidence that *Frye* was intended to address. The court found that both the theory underlying DNA profiling and the matching technique employed by the FBI in this case[104] are generally accepted in that community. The court considered the defendant's complaints concerning the testing procedures — including failure to replicate test results, imprecise measurements, lack of adequate proficiency testing, absence of uniform standards governing forensic DNA typing, risks of band shifting, and the danger of false positives — to go to the weight of the evidence, but not to its admissibility.

The court did not, however, consider the statistical methods employed by the FBI for calculating the possibility of a random match to be generally accepted in the relevant scientific community of population geneticists. The court remanded the case for a determination of whether the modified ceiling principle, recommended in the National Research Council's report on DNA evidence, is generally accepted in the relevant scientific community, and, if so, for a determination of an appropriate estimate of the probability of a random match between the defendant's DNA and the DNA specimen taken from the victim's body.[105]

In *State v. Bauer*,[106] the Court of Appeals of Minnesota reaffirmed that DNA testing is a generally accepted scientific technique under the state's *Frye* standard,[107] but that a *Frye* hearing may be necessary to establish that the DNA tests in a particular case were conducted in accordance with appropriate laboratory standards.[108]

Relevant Scientific Community

In the course of determining whether DNA evidence is generally accepted in the scientific community, the court in *People v. Watson*[109] first concluded

---

[103] No. 1-91-1351 (Ill. App. Jan. 28, 1994) (1994 WL 30084).

[104] The restriction fragment length polymorphism (RFLP) technique. *See id.* 1994 WL 30084, at *1-6, for the court's description of the technique.

[105] *Id.* at *11-16.

[106] No. C8-93-1073 (Minn. App. Feb. 15, 1994) (1994 WL 42240).

[107] *Id.* 1994 WL 42240, at *3 [relying on State v. Schwartz, 447 N.W.2d 422 (Minn. 1989)].

[108] *Id.* at *3.

[109] No. 1-91-1351 (Ill. App. Jan. 28, 1994) (1994 WL 30084).

that the relevant scientific community includes molecular biologists, population geneticists, and forensic scientists who work with DNA evidence. The court refused to limit the definition of the relevant scientific community to the community of forensic scientists, for the reason that forensic DNA evidence involves innovative principles or procedures that are derived from molecular biology and population genetics, and that application of these principles and procedures is relatively recent so the level of expertise in the forensic science community may be limited.[110]

4. Economic Injury

Hedonic Damages

In *Wilt v. Buracker*,[111] the Supreme Court of Appeals of West Virginia relied on *Daubert* to rule that damages for loss of enjoyment of life — also known as *hedonic damages* — may be considered by the jury as an element of general damages but may not be put into evidence as the result of expert testimony by a psychologist and an economic calculation by an economist.[112] The economist's calculations began with a "benchmark whole-life value" of $2.5 million that is the same for every human life, as determined by averaging economic values arrived at through more than 50 "willingness-to-pay" studies. The witness then subtracted from this amount an average value of $800,000, referred to as the "economic machine," which represented the value of the person's average lifetime earnings, to leave a average value of $1.7 million as the loss of enjoyment of life value of the average American. The psychologist testified, based on "loss-of-enjoyment-of-life tests" he had devised, that the plaintiff had suffered a 51-60% loss of her enjoyment of life. The economist then calculated a final loss of enjoyment of life value of $685,493, through a formula that included the psychologist's estimate, the plaintiff's life expectancy, and the average value of $1.7 million.

The court ruled the testimony inadmissible under Rule 702 because the underlying studies that supported the loss-of-enjoyment-of-life value were not offered into evidence, so there was no explanation of their methodology. Furthermore, the court indicated that even if the witness had provided a satisfactory explanation of the reliability of the "willingness-to-pay" studies, the studies may not have been sufficiently relevant to support the witness's opinion concerning loss of enjoyment of life.

Worklife Expectancy

In an economist's calculation of worklife expectancy in *Marcel v. Placid Oil Co.*,[113] the court found no abuse of discretion in the trial court's exclusion of

---

[110] *Id.* 1994 WL 30084, at *8.

[111] No. 21708. (W. Va. Sup. Ct. App. Dec. 13, 1993) (1993 WL 517042).

[112] *Id.* at *8.

[113] 11 F.3d 563 (5th Cir. 1994).

testimony concerning the worklife expectancy of an oil field worker where
there was no evidence of worklife expectancies of other occupations, and no
evidence of a national average worklife expectancy, and therefore no basis for
comparing the plaintiff's worklife expectancy with others. The court
observed that the trial court could have excluded the evidence on several
grounds, including that it was not sufficiently reliable and was more
prejudicial than probative.

5. Hypnotically Refreshed Memory

In *Borawick v. Shay*[114] — a civil action brought by a woman against her
aunt and uncle based on alleged sexual assault, molestation, and exploitation
when the plaintiff was four and seven years old — the defendant filed a
motion in limine to exclude testimony regarding the plaintiff's post-hypnotic
memories of childhood sexual abuse. The district court ruled the evidence
inadmissible on the ground that the hypnotherapist was not appropriately
qualified. The court observed that the Second Circuit had not previously
considered the admissibility of post-hypnotic testimony under the Federal
Rules of Evidence and identified three approaches that courts have taken in
determining its admissibility. The first approach considers a witness who has
undergone hypnosis in order to refresh her recollection to be *per se*
incompetent to testify concerning any subject discussed while under hypnosis;
the second approach considers such a witness to be *per se* competent and
directs the question of the witness's credibility concerning the refreshed
recollection to the trier of fact; the third approach considers such a witness
competent to testify if the witness suffered a type of memory loss that
hypnosis may remedy, *and* if safeguards were undertaken to guard against
suggestion and confabulation.

The court adopted the third approach, reasoning that safeguards are
necessary in order both to bolster legitimate claims of childhood sexual abuse
and to protect innocent defendants against devastating charges. The purpose
of safeguards would be to minimize the possibility of suggestibility (i.e.,
trying to please the hypnotist with answers the subject thinks will be met with
approval), confabulation (i.e., filling in details from the imagination so that
an answer is more coherent and complete), and memory hardening (i.e.,
great confidence in both true and false memories, making effective cross-
examination more difficult). To meet these purposes, the court concluded
that minimum safeguards would include (1) an appropriately qualified
hypnotist, who (2) avoided adding new elements to the subject's descriptions
of memories, (3) a permanent record of the sessions, to ensure against
suggestive procedures, and (4) due to the heinousness of the allegations, other
evidence to corroborate the hypnotically enhanced testimony.[115]

---

[114] 842 F. Supp. 1501 (D. Conn. 1994).
[115] *Id.* at 1503-05.

Additional discovery under these criteria revealed that the hypnotist was 71 years old; had no formal education beyond high school; had apprenticed with a retired Swiss psychiatrist in a search for "faith healers" for five years when he was 15 to 20 years old; had worked as a stage hypnotist on tour boats and in night clubs and resorts as a young man; had been a hypnotherapist "on and off for 50 years" prior to his deposition, including employment for one year in "a rather eclectic clinic;" and currently maintained his own clinic, where he used hypnosis to help with problems such as obesity, tobacco addiction, stress, and pain.[116] The witness had attended and given numerous lectures on hypnosis; was a member of the American Association of Professional Hypnotherapists and the American Hypnotherapy Association; was not licensed as a clinical psychologist and was not a member of the American Society of Clinical Hypnosis; subscribed to only one "professional" publication — *Mind and Body*; had never testified in court as an expert in hypnotherapy and had been retained only once by a law enforcement agency dealing with misdemeanors; had developed a cranial electronic stimulation unit (CES) which he used in his procedure for hypnotizing subjects; and never taped his initial interview with patients but prepared notes for use in subsequent sessions.[117]

The plaintiff had been referred to the hypnotist while he was employed by the "eclectic clinic" and visited him 10 to 12 times over the course of a year. The hypnotist testified that he had prepared medical reports of his sessions with the plaintiff, but that the records were unavailable because they had been retained by the clinic, which had closed for financial reasons a few years prior to the deposition. He testified further that he had not made any suggestions to the plaintiff, but had simply used a "regression" approach which took her back to three to five years old, upon which she recounted numerous incidents of sexual abuse by the defendants and another relative. The plaintiff had no memory of the recollections when she came out of the hypnosis, and the hypnotist did not reveal them to her because they would be "absolutely devastating to her at the time." The hypnotist agreed that the plaintiff's subsequent recollections of the incidents, while not under hypnosis, were hypnotically refreshed recollections.[118]

Based on the foregoing, the court found no evidence that the hypnotist had added new elements to the plaintiff's hypnotically refreshed recollections but found his description of them to be inadmissible because there was no contemporaneous record of the sessions and, prior to his deposition, the witness had reviewed the plaintiff's deposition testimony concerning her subsequent memories. Furthermore, based on the witness's education and work history, the court concluded that he was not appropriately qualified as a hypnotherapist and may even have been in violation of a state statute which

[116] *Id.* at 1507.
[117] *Id.*
[118] *Id.* at 1508.

prohibits the practice of psychology without a license.[119] The defendant's motion in limine was granted.

6. Injury or Disability

Environmental Illness

The claimant in *Brown v. Shalala*[120] filed a Social Security disability claim based on an alleged "environmental illness." The administrative law judge (ALJ) denied the claim on the ground that the plaintiff's evidence of environmental illness was not based on medically acceptable diagnostic techniques. The district court granted summary judgment in favor of the government, and the Eighth Circuit affirmed.

The medical evidence consisted of testimony of four physicians —two of the claimant's treating physicians, one who evaluated the plaintiff at her employer's request, and one appointed by the ALJ. One of the plaintiff's experts testified that the diagnostic technique involved putting drops of various substances under the patient's tongue, or injecting them, and then recording reactions of the patient that are not observable by the physician but are reported by the patient. Such reactions might include dizziness, headache, or weakness in the limbs. The court found it significant that one of the plaintiff's witnesses — a specialist in adult allergies — acknowledged that there was a division of opinion in the medical community concerning the diagnosis of "environmental illness," and that the techniques used to make the diagnosis had not been validated by double-blind studies. In fact, the witness relied on an article from the *New England Journal of Medicine* that described a double-blind study of injected substances alleged to cause symptoms of environmental illness and concluded that reactions to the active and control (placebo) injections were indistinguishable.

"Reasonable Medical . . . Possibility"

Two paramedics who provided emergency treatment to a jail guard who was injured in an escape attempt testified in *State v. Barber*[121] that, in their opinions, the guard would have died if he had not received immediate medical attention. The defendant argued that these opinions were improperly admitted because they were not expressed in terms of medical certainty. One of the witnesses was qualified as an expert; the other was not.[122]

---

[119] *Id.*

[120] No. 93-1956, ____ F.3d ____ , 1994 WL 17033 (8th Cir. Jan. 25, 1994).

[121] No. 13340 (Ohio App. Feb. 16, 1994) (1994 WL 47681).

[122] The defendant also argued that the witnesses were not qualified as experts. See section V for a discussion of issues related to the qualifications of the witness who was qualified as an expert.

Concerning the testimony of the expert paramedic, the court acknowledged that expert opinions have traditionally been held competent only if
stated in terms of a reasonable degree of scientific certainty, but that the state
supreme court had recently revisited the issue, and held that the better
practice — at least in criminal cases — is to allow experts to testify in terms
of "possibility" under Evidence Rule 702.[123] Accordingly, the *Barber* court
held that "medical experts are no longer required to testify in terms of
probabilities or medical certainties . . . Testimony in terms of possibilities is
now sufficient for purposes of admissibility."[124] The expert paramedic's
testimony that "there was a very good possibility that [the guard] possibly
would have died" if he had not received immediate medical attention was,
therefore, properly admitted.[125]

The lay witness had testified that the guard suffered the most serious head
injuries he had ever seen in a patient who was still alive, and that the guard's
condition would have been fatal had he not received immediate medical
attention. The court considered these statements to be admissible as lay
opinion under Evidence Rule 701, because the statements were rationally
based on the perceptions of the witness and were helpful to a clear
understanding of his testimony concerning the extent of the guard's injuries.
The court found no authority that required a lay opinion to be stated in terms
of certainty, "medical or otherwise."[126]

7. Intoxication

Horizontal Gaze Nystagmus

Two recent cases[127] provide extensive reviews of case law governing the
admissibility of police testimony concerning the results of horizontal gaze
nystagmus (HGN) tests and come to different conclusions as to whether such
testimony is admissible without prior proof of the scientific basis of the
testimony.

In *City of Fargo v. McLaughlin*,[128] the North Dakota Supreme Court ruled
that it is not necessary to establish the scientific reliability of the HGN test
by expert testimony before allowing a police officer to testify as to the results

---

[123] *Id.* 1994 WL 47681, at *7 [citing State v. D'Ambrosio, 67 Ohio St. 3d 185, 191
(1993)].

[124] *Id.* 1994 WL 47681, at *7.

[125] *Id.*

[126] *Id.* 1994 WL 47681, at *6.

[127] City of Fargo v. McLaughlin, Crim. No. 930130 (N.D. Sup. Ct. Feb. 23, 1994)
(1994 WL 51963); State v. Cissne, 72 Wash. App. 677, 865 P.2d 564 (1994).

[128] Crim. No. 930130 (N.D. Sup. Ct. Feb. 23, 1994) (1994 WL 51963).

of the officer's administration of the test, where the HGN test was given withother field sobriety tests that, taken together, formed the basis of the officer's opinion as to the defendant's intoxication. The only foundation required for admissibility of the HGN test results is a showing of the officer's training and experience in administering the test, and a showing that the test was in fact properly administered.[129]

In reaching this conclusion, the *McLaughlin* court reviewed authority from several jurisdictions and identified three major approaches to HGN evidence. The first major approach identified in *McLaughlin* originated with *State v. Superior Court*,[130] in which the Arizona Supreme court found that the following propositions were generally accepted in the scientific community: (1) HGN occurs in conjunction with alcohol consumption; (2) its onset and distinctness are correlated to BAC (blood alcohol content); (3) BAC in excess of .10 percent can be estimated with reasonable accuracy from the combination of the eyes' tracking ability, the angle of onset of nystagmus and the degree of nystagmus at maximum deviation; and (4) officers can be trained to observe these phenomena sufficiently to estimate accurately whether BAC is above or below .10 percent.[131]

The Arizona court had emphasized that a specific BAC level cannot be established with HGN test results[132] and, in a later case,[133] explained that the results of HGN (and other field sobriety tests, such as the *one-leg stand* or the *walk and turn*) are admissible only for the purpose of allowing an officer to testify, based on the officer's training and experience, that the results of the tests indicate possible neurological dysfunction —one cause of which could be alcohol ingestion —and that a proper foundation for this testimony includes the officer's training, education, and experience in administering the particular field sobriety test, and a showing that the test was properly administered.[134] The court made it clear that the foundation could be laid in the presence of the jury, and that it could not include discussion of the correlation between BAC levels and HGN test results.[135] The *McLaughlin* court identified several cases which had relied on the Arizona rulings to hold that expert testimony is not necessary to establish the scientific reliability of the HGN test in every case, and in effect to hold HGN testing "scientifically reliable as a matter of law."[136]

---

[129] *Id.* 1994 WL 51963, at *8.

[130] 149 Ariz. 269, 718 P.2d 171 (1986).

[131] *Id.* at 181.

[132] *Id.* at 181-82.

[133] State *ex rel* Hamilton v City Court, 165 Ariz. 514, 799 P.2d 855 (1990).

[134] *Id.* at 859-60.

[135] *Id.*

[136] *See City of Fargo*, 1994 WL 51963, at *5.

The second major approach identified in *McLaughlin* considers the HGN test "no more scientific than other field sobriety tests, and does not require expert testimony as a foundation for admissibility."[137] The rationale for this approach is that field sobriety tests are not based on scientific expertise, but only on personal observations of the officer who administered the tests.[138]

The third major approach requires expert testimony to establish general acceptance in the scientific community before admitting HGN test results.[139] The rationale for this approach is that the HGN test, unlike other field sobriety tests, is based on scientific principles concerning a causal relationship between consumption of alcohol and the type of nystagmus measured by the HGN test.[140]

The defendant in *McLaughlin* had argued that a scientific foundation must be laid by expert testimony in each case because of the possibility of false positive results, other possible physiological causes for nystagmus, lack of a close correlation between degree of nystagmus and a specific blood alcohol content (BAC), bias of the testing officer, and threats to proper implementation of the HGN test in the field. The court was not persuaded by this argument and stated that "[n]one of these factors undercuts the scientific foundation of the test: intoxicated persons exhibit nystagmus, and a properly administered HGN test will identify that nystagmus."[141] The court considered these to be the only "scientific" components of the HGN test and reasoned that expert testimony is not necessary to interpret the testimony of an officer who has been trained to perform the test, and who is testifying as to her observations of "the subject's eyes following a moving object."[142] The factors identified by the defendant were directed to the weight of the evidence, not its admissibility, and could be addressed through cross-examination or expert testimony.[143]

Concerning the argument that expert scientific testimony is necessary because the effects of alcohol on nystagmus are not within the common knowledge of jurors, the court responded that the testimony is not offered as independent scientific evidence of intoxication, but only as observations of an officer who has specialized training in HGN — and other field sobriety tests — and can therefore "draw inferences and deductions from his observations of the accused that might elude laypersons."[144]

---

137 *Id.*
138 *Id.* at *6.
139 *Id.*
140 *Id.*
141 *Id.* at *7.
142 *Id.* at *7.
143 *Id.*
144 *Id.* at *8.

A different result was reached in *State v. Cissne*,[145] in which the court conducted a review of HGN cases in several jurisdictions and ruled HGN evidence inadmissible under a *Frye* analysis. The *Cissne* court found that several jurisdictions consider the HGN test "no more scientific than other field sobriety tests"[146] and therefore require no more than lay opinion evidence based on the personal observations of the officer who administered the test, and that several other jurisdictions had concluded that HGN testing was based on scientific principles that either met, or had not yet met, the *Frye* standard.[147] Observing that scientific challenges to HGN testing began appearing in the scientific literature after many states had ruled the evidence generally accepted under *Frye*,[148] the *Cissne* court concluded that the scientific basis of HGN testing is currently not generally accepted in the scientific community. The court ruled the evidence inadmissible "unless, on remand, the State is able to prove that it rests on scientific principles which are not 'novel' and are readily understandable by ordinary persons."[149]

Intoxilyzer

In *State v. Hofer*,[150] the South Dakota Supreme Court cited *Daubert*'s rejection of *Frye* for the proposition that "general acceptance in the scientific community is no longer required"[151] and adopted *Daubert*'s requirement that trial judges assure that expert testimony rests on a reliable foundation, is relevant to the case, and is based on scientifically valid principles.[152] Under this standard, the court found that the scientific principles underlying the intoxilyzer breath test are "beyond scientific dispute,"[153] and that the defendant's concerns over the assumptions and procedures for implementing the test go to the weight, not the admissibility, of intoxilyzer test results.

The defendant had pointed out that the manufacturers of the intoxilyzer machine assume that there is as much alcohol in 2100 parts of breath as in one part of blood, but that the state's expert had testified that scientific studies have found this ratio to vary among individuals, in a range from 1142:1 to 3478:1. Based on this variation, the defendant had argued that the 2100:1 ratio was not generally accepted in the scientific community.

---

[145] 72 Wash. App. 677, 865 P.2d 564 (1994).

[146] *Id.* at 567. This approach is similar to the second approach identified in *McLaughlin*.

[147] *Id.* at 568. This approach encompasses the first and third approaches identified in *McLaughlin*, both of which recognize the scientific basis of HGN testing, but only one of which considers the scientific basis to be sufficiently reliable, or generally accepted, so as to not require expert testimony to establish the scientific basis of the evidence at each trial.

[148] *Id.* at 568.

[149] *Id.* at 569.

[150] No. 18107-A-RAM (S.D. Sup. Ct. Feb. 23, 1994) (1994 WL 53756).

[151] *Id.* 1994 WL 53756, at *2.

[152] *Id.*

[153] *Id.*

Retrograde Extrapolation

Commonwealth v. Smith[154] involved a prosecution for negligent operation of a motor vehicle resulting in death to another and for leaving the scene of an accident. A breathalyser test on the defendant approximately two hours after the incident showed a blood alcohol level below the legal limit for driving, but the prosecutor mentioned in opening statement that "retrograde extrapolation" of the breathalyser reading would reveal a blood alcohol level at the time of the incident close to or at the legal limit. When the evidence was offered during the trial, the judge ruled it inadmissible. On appeal, the defendant claimed that allowing the reference to inadmissible evidence in opening statement was reversible error, but the court disagreed, noting that such evidence had been admitted in other Massachusetts cases and in other jurisdictions. The fact that the evidence was ultimately held inadmissible in the instant case did not render the prosecution's expectation of admissibility at the time of the opening statement improper.

The court cited *Daubert* for the proposition that evidence such as retrograde extrapolation should be based on "a scientifically acceptable or reliable method."[155] The court noted that *Daubert* had "enlarged on the 'generally accepted in the scientific community' standard for admissibility of scientific evidence which had initially been articulated in *Frye*"[156] and based its analysis on Fed. R. Evid. 702.

8. Photogrammetry

In *United States v. Quinn*,[157] the Ninth Circuit approved the admissibility of testimony based on "photogrammetry" to estimate the height of a person in surveillance photographs taken during a bank robbery. The witness was an FBI agent who analyzed two photographs and measured the change in the dimensions of objects in the photographs as their distance from the camera changed. Using objects with known dimensions, the witness prepared a formula by which he was able to estimate the height of the person in the photographs at between 5'3" and 5'6". The defendant was 5'5". The Ninth Circuit found no error in the trial court's admission of the testimony under Fed. R. Evid. 702 and *Daubert*, for the reason that the procedure used by the witness was simply a series of calculations that did not involve any novel or questionable scientific technique.[158]

---

[154] 35 Mass. App. Ct 655, 624 N.E.2d 604 (1993).

[155] *Id.* at 662, 624 NE2d at 609.

[156] *Id.* n.9.

[157] Nos. 92-10452, 92-10509 (9th Cir. Mar. 17, 1994) (1994 WL 82048).

[158] *Id.* 1994 WL 82048, at *3.

9. Product Liability

Design or Manufacturing Defect

In *Clement v. Griffin*,[159] a court of appeals in Louisiana invoked the state's *Daubert/Foret* standard[160] and ruled inadmissible the testimony of a tire failure analyst.[161] The witness had opined that a tire failure was caused by a "glass-like black object" approximately 50 thousandths of an inch across, which was embedded inside the tire as a result of a manufacturing defect, and which penetrated the inner liner of the tire and thereby allowed air to migrate between the cords, causing them to separate and the tire to blow. The court found that the witness's theory — that the object entered the tire during the manufacturing process — was "not testable" and had not been subjected to peer review or publication; there was nothing in the record to suggest a known or potential rate of error for the theory; and the witness's methodology consisted of a review of photographs taken of the object by another person.[162]

Product Safety Warnings

Testimony of a human factors expert was ruled admissible in *Hart-Albin Co. v. McLees Inc.*,[163] under *Daubert*'s "flexible inquiry" language, as scientific knowledge that would assist the jury in determining whether the defendant should have provided warnings or instructions with an electrical cord connector that the plaintiff's employee assembled improperly when connecting it to a holiday display in the plaintiff department store. Evidence established that the manner in which the connector was assembled caused it to overheat and start a fire.

10. Social Science Evidence

Deceptive Trade Practices

In *Davis v. Southern Bell Telephone & Telegraph Co.*,[164] a RICO action, the plaintiffs offered survey research evidence to show that purchasers of the defendant's services misunderstood the nature of those services, and that the defendant employed deceptive marketing and sales techniques. In ruling on a motion to strike affidavits of the plaintiffs' survey research evidence, the court ruled the survey evidence admissible under *Daubert*. An affidavit

---

[159] Nos. 91-CA-1664, 92-CA-1001, 93-CA-0591, 93-CA-0592, 93-CA-0593, 93-CA-0594, 93-CA-0595, 93-CA-0596, 93-CA-0597 (La. App. Mar. 3, 1994) (1994 WL 65134).

[160] See notes 46-51, *supra*, and accompanying text.

[161] See section V for a discussion of the witness's qualifications.

[162] 1994 WL 65134, at *10.

[163] No. 92-568 (Mont. Feb. 17, 1994) (1994 WL 47116).

[164] No. 89-2839-CIV (S.D. Fla. Feb. 1, 1994) (1994 WL 88981).

submitted by one of the witnesses involved in the survey research — a professor and an "expert in the psychology of influence and persuasion"[165] — identified the principles upon which the research was based. At an evidentiary hearing, the witness testified that each of the principles stated in the affidavit had been tested, discussed in the peer-reviewed literature in the field of social psychology, and had achieved general acceptance in the witness's field. Copies of pertinent literature were submitted to support the witness's testimony. The court observed that the defendant did not challenge the validity of the principles relied upon by the witness during the hearing but, instead, questioned the witness as to why he did not perform an independent scientific experiment to test whether the defendant's sales and marketing techniques were misleading. While acknowledging that this line of questioning may have some bearing on the reliability of the witness's conclusions, the court ruled that it was not relevant to a determination of the scientific validity of the witness's principles and methodology under Fed. R. Evid. 702.[166]

The court also admitted the testimony of another witness — a professor and an expert in the fields of consumer psychology and survey design[167] — on grounds that his methodology met Rule 702's requirement of scientific validity, and the facts or data on which the witness relied were of a type reasonably relied upon by experts in the field, under Fed. R. Evid. 703. The court indicated that, under Rule 703, a party offering expert testimony based on a consumer survey must demonstrate that the survey data is of a type reasonably relied upon by experts in the field, and that reliance on such data is reasonable. In determining the reasonableness of the reliance upon the survey, the court stated that it is necessary to assess the manner in which the witness gathered and analyzed the data, and that such an assessment must include an examination of:

1. Whether the universe for the survey was properly defined

2. Whether persons surveyed were a representative sample of the universe

3. Whether survey questions were clear, precise, and nonleading

4. Whether interview procedures were sound and were performed by competent interviewers who had no knowledge of the litigation or the purpose of the survey

5. Whether the data were accurately reported

6. Whether the data were properly analyzed, in accord with accepted statistical principles

7. Whether objectivity of the process was assured[168]

---

[165] 1994 WL 88981, at *3.

[166] *Id.* at *3-4.

[167] *Id.* at *4.

[168] *Id.* at *5.

The court found that the witness's testimony at the hearing established compliance with these requirements. The witness testified that he had designed the survey to measure the "awareness, beliefs, opinions and knowledge" of the service in question among residential telephone consumers who subscribed to the service; that the universe consisted of all households to which the defendant ran telephone lines; that each respondent was screened to assure that she was a residential customer whose household subscribed to the service, and that the respondent handled the purchase of telephone services for the household; that steps were taken to assure random selection of the respondents and a sample size sufficient to allow "extrapolation to the universe to within a five percent rate of error in either direction;"[169] that the questionnaire was designed to ensure substantial accuracy, objectivity, and nonleading questions, and to eliminate bias; and that he took steps to ensure sound interview procedures. The witness testified further that he employed an independent entity to call respondents who had submitted completed questionnaires, to assure that the respondents had in fact been interviewed and understood the nature of the interview; and that respondents who failed, in this follow-up, to identify properly the nature of the interview were excluded from the final data analysis. Finally, the witness testified that he coded the data from the questionnaires and employed an independent data processing company to perform a statistical analysis of the coded data with a computer package known as "Uncle."[170]

The witness presented the results of his analysis of the survey at the hearing. The defendant's cross-examination of the witness focused on his failure to supervise interviews personally or to train the interviewers, failure to produce his "coding frame" to the defendant on its request, failure to determine whether the interviewers were paid on a salary or on a quota basis, and failure to assure that respondents who participated actually received the sales or marketing materials at issue in the case. The court found none of these areas to affect the evidentiary reliability of the evidence, and only the latter to possibly affect the weight of the evidence, and therefore ruled the evidence admissible.[171]

Unconstitutionally Vague Jury Instructions

In *Free v. Peters*,[172] a death-row inmate in a habeas corpus action offered a study by Hans Zeisel to show that the jury instructions at his sentencing hearing were so confusing as to be constitutionally infirm. The district court accepted the Zeisel study and agreed with its conclusions, ordering the state to re-sentence the inmate. The Seventh Circuit reversed this portion of the

---

[169] *Id.* at *5.

[170] *Id.* at *6.

[171] *Id.*

[172] _____ F.3d _____, 1993 WL 526796 (7th Cir. Dec. 21, 1993).

district court's opinion, finding the Zeisel study to be fundamentally flawed in its methodology and therefore improperly considered. *Daubert* was not cited in the opinion.

Zeisel's study used a random group of people who had been summoned for jury duty but were not picked to serve. These people were given written summaries of the evidence presented at Free's trial and the judge's jury instructions. They were then administered a true-false test to illustrate the reasoning of the hypothetical jury. The results of the test demonstrated that many of the mock jurors had misunderstood the applicable law as described in the jury instructions, leading Zeisel to the conclusion that the instructions were unconstitutionally vague.

The Seventh Circuit found fault with the methodology of the study on several grounds, concluding that it measured more the subjects' ability to take written examinations rather than projecting a result of an actual jury's verdict. The court noted that an actual jury would sit through live testimony and argument, which would have a different impact on their memories and evaluation of the evidence than a written summary, making the comparison of the test-takers to an actual jury tenuous. In addition, the court found fault with the lack of any control in the study, in which another group would be given different, presumably clearer jury instructions. Without any means of determining whether other instructions would have resulted in a different verdict, the results of the study were not helpful in evaluating the constitutionality of the jury instructions.

Appreciation of Danger

In *Graves v. Atchison-Holt Electric Coop*,[173] a wrongful death and negligence action arising out the injury and death of operators of a grain auger that came into contact with an overhead power line, the defendant offered into evidence the results of a survey of farmers who were members of the electric cooperative that operated the power line. The survey asked questions concerning the farmers' knowledge of the hazards of electric power lines, the proper use of farm equipment near overhead electric lines, and whether the farmers believed they could be seriously injured or killed by contacting an overhead electric line. The results showed that 93.6% of those surveyed knew that death or serious injury could result from contact between equipment and power lines; 91% knew that contact between a power line and a grain auger could cause injury or death; 99.4% had seen, read, or heard warnings — via television, radio, newspapers, magazines, decals on farm equipment, or an operator's manual that came with farm equipment — about the dangers of contact between power lines and farm equipment; and "the overwhelming majority" of those surveyed had been aware of the dangers of power lines for four or more years.[174]

---

[173] No. WD 48015 (Mo. Ct. App. Feb. 15, 1994) (1994 WL 41819).
[174] *Id.* 1994 WL 41819, at *7.

The evidence was introduced through the testimony of an economist who had a Ph.D. in finance, and who had some training and experience in statistics and management. The witness testified as to how the survey was designed and performed, and as to the substance of the questions and responses, but did *not* provide an expert opinion based on the results of the survey. The court of appeals ruled that the testimony concerning the survey was inadmissible because it did not serve as a basis for an expert opinion but was offered as independent substantive evidence to rebut the plaintiffs' failure to warn claim, and to show that the plaintiffs were contributorily negligent. The court of appeals remanded for a new trial because the trial court's admission of the testimony was prejudicial to the plaintiffs, in that it

> had the effect of presenting inadmissible evidence from 350 farmers that went directly to the question of [the defendant's] failure to warn and the question of whether [the plaintiffs] appreciated the hazard to which they were exposed by showing that it was extremely rare for like persons, in what the jury could have inferred were similar circumstances, not to appreciate fully the danger of working with farm equipment around power lines. Furthermore, the survey adversely impacted the issue of [the plaintiffs'] contributory fault for lack of care in working around a power line. These were all questions for the jury . . . .[175]

IV. Assistance to Trier of Fact

A few cases have recently found expert or scientific evidence unnecessary and have therefore refused to reverse judgments for lack or insufficiency of expert or scientific evidence. In *United States v. Wright*,[176] for example, crack cocaine involved in several counts of an indictment was not available for scientific testing to determine whether it was, in fact, crack cocaine. The court held that the identity of the substance as the illegal drug was sufficiently established by circumstantial evidence in the testimony of several witnesses who would be familiar with crack cocaine, and that scientific analysis was not necessary to support the conviction.

Similarly, in a murder prosecution in *State v. Hodgson*[177] — in which the defendant's watch was splattered with blood and was missing a pin, and a pin that fit the defendant's watch was found at the scene — the state offered expert testimony to the effect that material scraped from the watch pin was consistent with material scraped from the part of the defendant's watch, in which the pin fit. The defendant challenged the foundation for this testimony. The court did not address the issue, because it considered the testimony unnecessary. The court found that "[t]he significant facts were that

---

175 *Id.* 1994 WL 41819, at *7-8.

176 No. 93-5103, _____ F.3d _____ , 1994 WL 38983 (6th Cir. Feb. 14, 1994).

177 No. C5-93-222 (Minn. Supr. Ct. Feb. 11, 1994) (1994 WL 37808).

a watch pin was found at the murder scene, the defendant's watch had blood on it and was missing a pin, and that the pin fit the defendant's watch. There is no reasonable likelihood that without [the expert's] testimony the jury would have concluded that these facts were all coincidental."[178] *See also* *Williams v. Poulos*[179] [district court acted within its discretion in excluding proffered expert witnesses on ground that fact finder was capable of understanding issues and determining facts without aid of experts].

V. Qualified Expert

Several courts have recently addressed the qualifications of various types of experts, including a tire failure analyst, a human factors engineer, a paramedic, numerous medical specialists whom a court found not qualified as teratologists, a physician/opthalmologist, and a geologist whom a court found not qualified to assess the commercial value of mineral deposits.

Tire Failure Analyst

In *Clement v. Griffin*[180] — a multiple-party action arising out of an automobile accident that occurred when an "original equipment" tire blew out on a full passenger van — a witness who had a Ph.D. in mechanical engineering, was the head of the engineering department at a private institute, had consulted with several automobile and tire manufacturers, and had experience in automotive engineering safety research that included the design of interstate highways and NASA's lunar roving vehicle was qualified as an expert in mechanical engineering and design, biomechanics engineering, accident reconstruction, tire failure analysis, and highway research design. The fact that the witness sent the tire to another expert to examine the inside of the tire through a microscope, and the fact that the witness admitted that he was not an expert in "tire chemistry," did not adversely affect the witness's qualifications as a tire failure analyst under La C Evid art 702. The evidence showed that the witness did not personally have the equipment necessary to examine the inside of the tire, and the party that challenged the witness's qualifications (the tire manufacturer) failed to provide any authority to establish that knowledge of tire chemistry is a necessary qualification for a tire failure analyst.

Human Factors Engineer

A witness who had a Ph.D. in industrial engineering and was "employed in the field of product safety warnings and instructions" was qualified as an

178 *Id.* 1994 WL 37808, at *3.

179 No. 93-1366, _____ F.3d _____ , 1993 WL 503326 (1st Cir. Dec. 14, 1993).

180 Nos. 91-CΛ-1664, 92-CΛ-1001, 93-CΛ-0591, 93-CΛ-0592, 93-CΛ-0593, 93-CΛ-0594, 93-CΛ-0595, 93-CΛ-0596, 93-CΛ-0597 (La. Λpp. Mar. 3, 1994) (1994 WL 65134).

expert in human factors in *Hart-Albin Co. v. McLees, Inc.*[181] The witness
defined *human factors* as "the field of studies that looks at human capabilities
and limitations and tries to design jobs, workplaces, and products so that
human beings can use them comfortably, efficiently, productively, and
safely."[182]

Paramedic

In *State v. Barber*,[183] a paramedic who provided emergency treatment to a
jail guard who was injured in an escape attempt was qualified to testify that
the guard would have died if he had not received immediate medical
attention. The fact that the witness was not a physician did not render her
unqualified to state an opinion related to the guard's medical condition,
because the guard's condition was within her field of expertise as a
state-certified paramedic who had received more than 500 hours of training
in her field.

Not a Teratologist

In *Wade-Greaux v. Whitehall Laboratories, Inc.*,[184] a product liability action
in which the court ruled that although the plaintiff's medial experts may have
been qualified in their particular fields of specialization — including
pediatric subacute critical care, internal medicine, clinical pharmacology,
pediatric pathology, cell biology, and physical chemistry — none were
qualified in human teratology and were therefore not permitted to testify
concerning causation.[185]

Physician/Opthalmologist

A physician was permitted to testify concerning a plaintiff's disability due
to secondary angle closure glaucoma, and concerning the relationship
between stress and intraocular pressure, in *Flores v. Puerto Rico Telephone
Co.*[186] over defense objections that the witness was not a specialist in
ophthalmology. The court found that the witness was recognized as an
opthalmologist in Puerto Rico, that he specialized in corneal and external
diseases of the eyes, and that in 15 years of practice he had treated hundreds
of glaucoma patients without referring them to a glaucoma specialist. The
court concluded that based on this experience, the witness possessed scientific
knowledge concerning glaucoma that met the requirements of *Daubert* and
Fed. R. Evid. 702, and that the means of attacking the witness's testimony
was through cross-examination and presentation of contrary evidence.

---

[181] No. 92-568 (Mont. Supr. Ct. Feb. 17, 1994) (1994 WL 47116).
[182] *Id.* 1994 WL 47116, at *5.
[183] No. 13340 (Ohio App. Feb. 16, 1994) (1994 WL 47681).
[184] Civ. No. 30/1988 (D. V.I. Mar. 3, 1994) (1994 WL 80840).
[185] 1994 WL 80840, at *35-42.
[186] Civ. No. 89-1697 (D. P.R. Jan. 19, 1994) (1994 WL 52570).

Geologist/Mineral Evaluator

McLendon v. Georgia Kaolin Co.[187] was an action premised on alleged fraudulent concealment of the value of real property by a purchaser under a duty to disclose, in which the purchaser filed a motion in limine to exclude the testimony of a geologist offered by the plaintiffs to show the quantity, quality, commercial uses, and value of a kaolin deposit on the property. The court granted the motion on the ground, *inter alia*, that the witness was not qualified to testify as an expert on the issue.[188] The witness testified that he was an economic geologist and an expert on industrial minerals — of which kaolin was one. He had Bachelors and Masters degrees from the University of Georgia, where he took standard courses in geology but did not study kaolin, or clay mineralogy, in any depth. On this basis, the court found that the witness was not qualified by training and education alone as an expert on kaolin. Furthermore, the court found that the witness had minimal work experience with kaolin evaluation, and that his testimony revealed limited knowledge of criteria used to evaluate the market value of a kaolin deposit, and virtually no knowledge of processes required to render a kaolin deposit commercially acceptable. The testimony was, therefore, excluded under Fed. R. Evid. 702.

VI. Bases of Opinion Testimony

In *McLendon v. Georgia Kaolin Co.*,[189] discussed in the preceding section, the geologist's opinion was challenged on the ground that it was not based on facts or data of a type reasonably relied upon by experts in the field.[190] The witness had relied exclusively on memoranda written by employees and consultants of the defendant that discussed the processes used to brighten kaolin, and the possibility of a large kaolin deposit on the plaintiffs' property. The court ruled that these were not the type of facts or data normally relied upon by scientific experts. See also *B. F. Goodrich Co. v. Murtha*,[191] a CERCLA remediation action in which the court excluded expert testimony on the ground that there was inadequate foundation for the witness's opinion concerning unspecified hazardous substances in the municipal solid waste of some municipal generators, where the witness based his opinion on "references to facts, without specification, in various documents relied on."[192]

---

[187] 841 F. Supp 415 (M.D. Ga. 1994).

[188] Another basis for excluding the testimony was that the witness relied on facts or data of a type not reasonably relied upon by experts in the field. See section VI for a discussion of this aspect of the case.

[189] 841 F. Supp 415 (M.D. Ga. 1994).

[190] Another basis for excluding the testimony was that the witness was not qualified as an expert in the pertinent field. See section V for a discussion of this aspect of the case.

[191] 840 F. Supp. 180 (D. Conn. 1993).

[192] *Id.* at 189.

The court in *Clement v. Griffin*[193] addressed both 702 and 703 to find the factual basis of an opinion inadequate. The court relied on La Code Evid art 702 to exclude testimony of an engineer on the ground, *inter alia*, that the expert's methodology was "suspect" since it relied wholly on photographs taken by another expert.[194] Following exclusion of the evidence under article 702, the court found it unnecessary to rule whether the testimony would be inadmissible under article 703 on the ground that it was improperly bolstered by the photographs and findings of another expert. Nonetheless, the court noted that "neither the Code of Evidence nor the jurisprudence limit an expert's ability to use the findings of other experts in reaching his conclusions."[195]

Part of the state's evidence in a murder prosecution in *State v. Demery*[196] involved blood profile evidence. The state's forensic serologist testified that the defendant's blood profile was the same as .2% of the population and the victim's blood profile was the same as 8.2% of the population. The defendant, a Lumbee Indian, argued that the foundation for the evidence was inadequate, because the expert had included Lumbee Indians in the Caucasian population rather than calculating the frequency with which defendant's blood profile would occur in the subpopulation of Lumbee Indians. The court concluded that calculating the incidence in the general population was appropriate. The defendant also argued that the serologist's testimony was inadmissible hearsay, since the data on the frequency of blood group factors or characteristics in the North Carolina population were compiled by other parties. The court rejected this argument and found that the statistics on which the expert relied were of a type relied upon by experts in the witness's field.

VII. Practice and Procedure

Focus of In Limine Motion May Waive Right to Challenge Evidence at Trial

In *State v. Bauer*,[197] the defendant filed a pre-trial motion to exclude statistical evidence of the probability of a DNA match, on the ground that the evidence was unreliable and potentially prejudicial; the trial court granted the motion. During trial —just prior to the state's proffered evidence from a forensic scientist involved in the DNA testing —the defendant requested a *Frye* hearing to determine whether the DNA testing methods conformed with

---

[193] Nos. 91-CA-1664, 92-CA-1001, 93-CA-0591, 93-CA-0592, 93-CA-0593, 93-CA-0594, 93-CA-0595, 93-CA-0596, 93-CA-0597 (La. App. Mar. 3, 1994) (1994 WL 65134).

[194] See section III.A.9 for a discussion of other reasons for excluding the testimony.

[195] 1994 WL 65134, at *10-11.

[196] 437 S.E.2d 704 (N.C. App. 1993).

[197] No. C8-93-1073 (Minn. App. Feb. 15, 1994) (1994 WL 42240).

pertinent laboratory standards. The trial court denied the request for a mid-trial *Frye* hearing; the court of appeals affirmed on the ground that the defendant had waived the right to challenge the testing procedures by not including this challenge of the evidence in the pre-trial proceeding.[198]

Preservation of Evidence for Future Scientific Testing

In a habeas corpus proceeding in *Holdren v. Legursky*[199] — six years after a trial in which a forensic biologist matched pubic hair found on a rape victim with pubic hair of the defendant — DNA testing revealed that the victim was the source of one of two pubic hairs found on the victim, and that either the victim or the defendant could be the source of the other hair. Other tests performed by a medical examiner for the original trial had rendered the defendant's semen samples useless for subsequent blood typing and DNA analysis, and unused samples had been discarded, so there was no other physical evidence available for DNA testing in the habeas corpus proceeding.

The defendant requested a new trial on the basis of the DNA hair analysis, and on the ground that the state violated his due process rights by destroying other exculpatory evidence. The court refused to grant a new trial, based on a conclusion that any error resulting from admission of the original trial testimony was harmless and not prejudicial, and the defendant had failed to show that the state acted in bad faith in failing to preserve potentially exculpatory evidence. The court stated that good faith does not require that the state preserve physical evidence for the possibility of performing every known scientific test.

Paternity Re-Testing of DNA Not Allowed

In *Wright v. Department of Health & Rehabilitative Services*,[200] the court held that the dismissal with prejudice of a paternity action following a Human Leukocyte Antigen (HLA) blood test precluded a second paternity action which sought DNA testing of the putative father. The court ruled that under Fla Stat section 742.12(1), the mother, child, and putative father in a paternity case are required to submit to an HLA test or other generally accepted scientific test, and that the action must be dismissed if the test shows that the putative father cannot be the biological father. The putative father had undergone an HLA test in 1986 that excluded him as the biological father, and the case was dismissed.

Effect of Failure to Object to Foundation at Trial

In *People v. Bynum*,[201] the defendant argued on appeal that the testimony of a police chemist concerning the identity of PCP — based on the use of a

---

[198] *Id.* 1994 WL 42240, at *3-4.

[199] No. 92-6258, _____ F.3d _____ , 1994 WL 32620 (4th Cir. Feb. 7, 1994).

[200] No. 93-2295, _____ So.2d _____ , 1993 WL 504433, 18 Fla L Week D2624 (Fla. App. 5 Dist. Dec. 10, 1993).

[201] No. 1-92-1176 (Ill. App. Feb. 4, 1994) (1994 WL 30178).

gas chromatograph/mass spectrometer (GCMS) testing device — should not have been admitted because the state had not laid a proper foundation for the testimony. The court acknowledged that a proper foundation under Rule 703 requires the proponent of the evidence to show that the facts or data relied upon by the expert are of a type reasonably relied upon by experts in the field, and that where expert testimony is based on the use of an electronic or mechanical device, such as the GCMS, the witness must lay a foundation that shows the method by which the device records information and that the device was functioning properly at the time it was used. Furthermore, the court found that the requisite foundation had not been laid in this case — in that the witness had *not* testified that the GCMS testing device is generally relied upon by experts in the witness's field, nor had the witness testified as to how the machine was calibrated or why she considered the results accurate — but that the defendant had not objected on these grounds at trial and therefore could not complain on appeal.[202]

Surprise Testimony

Williams v. General Motors Corporation[203] was a product liability action arising out of an accident caused by an alleged failure of a vehicle's steering mechanism, in which the plaintiff's pre-trial theory was that a torsion spring in the vehicle's rack and pinion unit broke as a result of a metallurgical or manufacturing error. Three days into the trial, the plaintiff's engineering expert testified —for the first time, and without notice — that the rack and pinion might have become temporarily disengaged, and thereby caused the accident. On appeal from a verdict in favor of the plaintiff, the majority opinion found no prejudice in the trial court's admission of this testimony, but the dissent argued that the testimony should have been excluded because it unfairly deprived the defendant of the opportunity to investigate and rebut the new theory of the alleged product defect. Furthermore, the dissent argued that admission of the testimony was clearly prejudicial to the defendant, since the jury was incapable of comprehending the "subtle but significant" effects of the change in the theory, and the lack of any tests or examinations in support of the new theory failed to accord with the state's *Daubert/Foret* requirement that the testimony have a reliable scientific basis.[204]

Spoliation of Evidence

The dissent in *Williams v. General Motors Corporation*[205] also would have ordered a new trial on the ground that the trial court failed to instruct the jury that the loss of the allegedly defective part by the plaintiff's mechanic would allow the jury to presume that the missing part would have been unfavorable to the plaintiff's case. The fact that the plaintiff was not in

---

[202] *Id.* 1994 WL 30178, at *9-10.

[203] No. 93-CA-0287 (La. App. Feb. 11, 1994) (1994 WL 42511).

[204] *Id.* 1994 WL 42511, at *14-15.

[205] No. 93-CA-0287 (La. App. Feb. 11, 1994) (1994 WL 42511).

possession of the part at the time it was discarded would have been immaterial to the dissent; the plaintiff had selected the mechanic and was negligent in allowing the mechanic to dispose of the allegedly defective part.

Table of Cases

First Circuit

Flores v. Puerto Rico Telephone Co., Civ. No. 89-1697 (D. P.R. Jan. 19, 1994) (1994 WL 52570)

In re Wells Fargo Securities Litigation, No. 92-15344, ___ F.3d ___, 1993 WL 535682, Fed. Sec. L. Rep. 98,007 (1st Cir. Dec. 29, 1993)

United States v. Sepulveda, ___ F.3d ___, 1993 WL 516354, No. 92-1362 (1st Cir. Dec. 20, 1993)

Williams v. Poulos, No. 93-1366, ___ F.3d ___, 1993 WL 503326 (1st Cir. Dec. 14, 1993)

Second Circuit

Tamarin v. Adam Caterers, ___ F.3d ___, 1993 WL 535877, No. 93-7634 (2d Cir. Dec. 27, 1993)

B. F. Goodrich Co. v. Murtha, 840 F. Supp. 180 (D. Conn. 1993)

Borawick v. Shay, 842 F. Supp. 1501 (D. Conn. 1994)

Third Circuit

Wade-Greaux v. Whitehall Laboratories, Inc., Civ. No. 30/1988 (D. V.I. Mar. 3, 1994) (1994 WL 80840)

Fourth Circuit

Holdren v. Legursky, No. 92-6258, ___ F.3d ___, 1994 WL 32620 (4th Cir. Feb. 7, 1994)

Fifth Circuit

Marcel v. Placid Oil Co., 11 F.3d 563 (5th Cir. 1994)

United States v. Ridlehuber, No. 92-8296, ___ F.3d ___, 1993 WL 536874 (5th Cir. Dec. 29, 1993)

Sixth Circuit

United States v. Wright, No. 93-5103, ___ F.3d ___, 1994 WL 38983 (6th Cir. Feb. 14, 1994)

Seventh Circuit

Free v. Peters, ___ F.3d ___, 1993 WL 526796 (7th Cir. Dec. 21, 1993)

O'Conner v. Commonwealth Edison Co., ___ F.3d ___, 1994 WL 3794 (7th Cir. Jan. 7, 1994)

Eighth Circuit

Brown v. Shalala, No. 93-1956, ___ F.3d ___, 1994 WL 17033 (8th Cir. Jan. 25, 1994)

Thomas v. FAG Bearings Corporation, No. 92-5070-CV-SW-8 (W.D. Mo. Feb. 10, 1994) (1994 WL 65307)

Ninth Circuit

United States v. Quinn, Nos. 92-10452, 92-10509 (9th Cir. Mar. 17, 1994) (1994 WL 82048)

Tenth Circuit

Wilson v. Merrell Dow Pharmaceuticals, Inc., No. 90-5257, ___ F.3d ___ (9th Cir. Mar. 10, 1994) (1994 WL 73253)

Dodd-Anderson v. Stevens, Nos. 92-1015-MLB, 92-1016-MLB (D. Kan. Jan. 5, 1994) (1994 WL 26922)

Eleventh Circuit

Davis v. Southern Bell Telephone & Telegraph Co., No. 89-2839-CIV (S.D. Fla. Feb. 1, 1994) (1994 WL 88981)

McLendon v. Georgia Kaolin Co., 841 F. Supp. 415 (M.D. Ga. 1994)

California

People v. Webb, 6 Cal. 4th 494, 862 P.2d 779, 24 Cal. Rptr. 2d 779 (1993)

In re Clara B., 20 Cal. App. 4th 988, 25 Cal. Rptr. 2d 56 (1993)

Colorado

Grogan v. Taylor, No. 92CA1298 (Colo. App. Feb. 10, 1994) (1993 WL 524131)

Delaware

State v. Cephas, 1994 WL 17029 (Del. Supr. Ct. Jan. 20, 1994)

Florida

Bass v. Florida Department of Law Enforcement, 1993 WL 513937, 18 Fla L Week D2639 (Fla. App. 3 Dist. Dec. 14, 1993)

Wright v. Department of Health & Rehabilitative Services, No. 93-2295, ___ So.2d ___ , 1993 WL 504433, 18 Fla L Week D2624 (Fla. App. 5 Dist. Dec. 10, 1993)

Illinois

People v. Bynum, No. 1-92-1176 (Ill. App. Feb. 4, 1994) (1994 WL 30178)

People v. Watson, No. 1-91-1351 (Ill. App. Jan. 28, 1994) (1994 WL 30084)

Louisiana

Clement v. Griffin, Nos. 91-CA-1664, 92-CA-1001, 93-CA-0591, 93-CA-0592, 93-CA-0593, 93-CA-0594, 93-CA-0595, 93-CA-0596, 93-CA-0597 (La. App. Mar. 3, 1994) (1994 WL 65134)

Williams v. General Motors Corporation, No. 93-CA-0287 (La. App. Feb. 11, 1994) (1994 WL 42511)

Massachusetts
Commonwealth v. Smith, 35 Mass. App. Ct 655, 624 N.E.2d 604 (1993)

Minnesota
State v. Bauer, No. C8-93-1073 (Minn. App. Feb. 15, 1994) (1994 WL 42240)

North Carolina
State v. Demery, 437 S.E.2d 704 (N.C. App. 1993)

North Dakota
City of Fargo v. McLaughlin, Crim. No. 930130 (N.D. Sup. Ct. Feb. 23, 1994) (1994 WL 51963)

Oklahoma
Paxton v. State, 867 P.2d 1309 (Okla. Crim. App. 1993)

South Dakota
State v. Hofer, No. 18107-A-RAM (S.D. Supr. Ct. Feb. 23, 1994) (1994 WL 53756)

Washington
State v. Riker, No. 58970-4 (Wash. Sup. Ct. Mar. 3, 1994) (1994 WL 61683)

State v. Cissne, 72 Wash. App. 677, 865 P.2d 564 (1994)

West Virginia
Wilt v. Buracker, No. 21708 (W. Va. Sup Ct. App. Dec. 13, 1993) (1993 WL 517042)

The Revolution in Practice and Procedure: "*Daubert* Hearings"

Marc S. Klein

Given the trial court's expanded function in evaluating the reliability of expert evidence, it is now more important than ever for the trial court to take an active role in the presentation of expert evidence. Daubert may require pretrial or in limine 'Daubert hearings' under Rule 104 of the Federal Rules of Evidence to determine whether, and under what conditions, expert testimony is admissible.[1]

I. INTRODUCTION

It has been almost one year since the U.S. Supreme Court decided *Daubert v. Merrell Dow Pharmaceuticals, Inc.*[2] The initial reactions — from the popular media *and* legal experts in this field — differed immensely.

One leading newspaper concluded that the decision ruled out active judicial scrutiny of scientific evidence, at least in personal injury actions.[3] By contrast, an equally prestigious newspaper characterized *Daubert* as a major *victory* for advocates of active judicial gatekeeping.[4]

---

[1] *In re* Joint Eastern & Southern Districts Asbestos Litigation, 151 F.R.D. 540, 545 (E. & S.D.N.Y. 1993) (Weinstein, J.).

[2] 113 S.Ct. 2786, 125 L. Ed.2d 469 (decided June 28, 1993).

[3] In an article entitled *Justices Rule Against Business in Evidence Case,* The Wall Street Journal reported that:

> The Supreme Court rejected a strict standard that has been widely used by federal judges to keep scientific evidence out of personal-injury lawsuits and other trials.
>
> The unanimous decision was a defeat for business and the medical profession, which have argued for years that they are subjected to countless consumer lawsuits based on dubious scientific evidence.

Wall St. J., June 29, 1993, at A3.

[4] In an article entitled *Justices Put Judges in Charge of Deciding Reliability of Scientific Testimony,* The New York Times reported:

> Ruling for the first time on the place of scientific evidence in Federal courtrooms, the Supreme Court today established Federal judges as active gatekeepers charged with insuring that "any and all scientific testimony or evidence admitted is not only relevant, but reliable."
>
> The 7-to-2 decision invited judges to be aggressive in screening out ill-founded

This split of opinion was not limited to the popular media. Legal scholars and leading practitioners basically divided along the same lines.[5] Indeed, both sides in *Daubert* claimed victory and worked hard on "spin control."[6]

With *Daubert* on the books, lower courts then began to apply it. We have already tracked well over 100 federal and state cases citing *Daubert* for some proposition or another. Many scholars have considered its application in a wide variety of contexts, from toxic tort litigations to criminal prosecutions. Most have naturally focused on the holding and not the *dictum* of *Daubert* — *i.e.*, the "death of *Frye*."[7]

In my view, the technical "holding" of *Daubert* is its least interesting aspect. For most purposes, particularly toxic torts, *Frye* was already dead on arrival at the Supreme Court. Thus, for the most part, *Daubert* simply represents the official death certificate.

What has replaced *Frye* — the Court's interpretation of the federal rules and their application — is far more important. The Court effectively empowered trial judges to *actively* screen out unreliable expert and scientific evidence. This aspect of *Daubert*, in my view, will *revolutionize* practice and procedure in this field, and the "death of *Frye*" will eventually be seen as a great episode of creative destructionism.

The evidence of this revolution in practice and procedure will come in the form of "*Daubert* hearings." Consequently, this article examines the nature and role of *Daubert* hearings in cases involving questionable expert or scientific evidence.[8]

---

or speculative scientific theories. The Court held that judges should focus on the reasoning or methodology behind the scientific testimony, rather than on whether the conclusions of an expert witness have won general acceptance.
N.Y. Times, June 29, 1993, at A13.

[5] In our first issue of SESEQ—published one month after the Supreme Court handed down its decision—prominent scholars in science and the law split on the meaning and likely effect, if any, of *Daubert*. *Compare* Michael D. Green, *Relief at the Frying of Frye: Reflections on Daubert v. Merrell Dow Pharmaceuticals*, 1 Shepard's Expert & Sci. Evid. Q. 43 (Summer 1993) (*Daubert* signals the death of *Frye* and a major defeat for those who claim to be anti-"junk science") *with* David E. Bernstein & Peter W. Huber, *Defense Perspective*, 1 Shepard's Expert & Sci. Evid. Q. 59 (Summer 1993) ("The Bendectin plaintiffs won a narrow technical battle in *Daubert*, but they plainly lost the war. . . . All in all, the *Daubert* opinion is highly favorable to litigants . . . who confront junk science claims by the other side").

[6] *See, e.g.*, Barry J. Nace, *Reaction to Daubert*, 1 Shepard's Expert & Sci. Evid. Q. 51 (Summer 1993) (spinning and counter-spinning).

[7] *See, e.g.*, Edward J. Imwinkelried, *The Daubert Decision: Frye Is Dead, Long Live the Federal Rules of Evidence*, Trial Mag., Sept. 1993, at 60. Indeed, Cardozo Law School recently hosted a lively conference on the "Death of *Frye*."

[8] In state courts, the precise nature of the hearing (and its nomenclature) may differ. Some jurisdictions continue to apply their own strain of the *Frye* rule (or at least purport

II. DEFINITION OF A "*DAUBERT* HEARING"

A "*Daubert* hearing" may be defined as any proceeding, conducted at any time in advance of trial, for purposes of determining whether (or to what extent) any specific expert or scientific evidence will be admissible at trial.

A *Daubert* hearing may resemble a motion for summary judgment more than a formal hearing. Thus, in an appropriate case, it could be conducted on a paper record (for example, with only affidavits, interrogatory answers, deposition testimony, and briefs). When direct testimony or cross-examination is necessary, however, a *Daubert* hearing could resemble a *mini-trial* involving live expert testimony in open court.[9] In fact, some courts may utilize innovative methods to resolve the central issues.[10]

The focus of the *Daubert* hearing is *not* the "ultimate issue" in the case. The trial judge does not sit as the trier of fact to determine which side has presented the more credible (or more persuasive) expert or scientific evidence. Rather, the judge sits only as the trier of *preliminary* facts — *i.e.*, those facts that must be found, under the governing rules of evidence, *before* a witness is permitted to express an opinion.[11]

Not every case involving expert or scientific testimony will warrant a *Daubert* hearing. To the contrary, most cases, particularly routine litigations, involve a classic "battle of the experts." In these cases, experts on both sides will clearly disagree with each other. But neither litigant could sincerely argue that the other's expert is (1) not qualified to render an opinion; (2) relying on a type of information not reasonably relied on by experts in the field; or (3) failing to utilize a recognized (or recognizable) methodology.

The party who seeks to have a *Daubert* hearing must fire the first shot. *Daubert* has not shifted any procedural burden in that regard. The opponent

---

to do so), while others have essentially embraced the logic of *Daubert* without formally adopting it. Some jurisdictions have already explicitly embraced *Daubert*, *see*, *e.g.*, State v. Hofer, 512 N.W.2d 482 (S.D. 1994); Wilt v. Buracker, _____ S.E.2d _____ , 1993 WL 517042 (W. Va. 1993); State v. Alberico, 861 P.2d 192 (N.M. 1993), while others will undoubtedly do so.

This article focuses not so much on the *substantive* standard that different courts may use to gauge the admissibility of expert testimony, but rather the practice and procedure of hearings *in limine* to determine admissibility. For the sake of simplicity, this article refers to this type of proceeding as a "*Daubert* hearing." In a New Jersey state court, by contrast, counsel might just as well ask for a "*Rubanick* hearing." *See* Rubanick v. Witco Chem. Co., 125 N.J. 421, 593 A.2d 733 (1991) (endorsing the extensive use of hearings *in limine* to determine the admissibility of expert and scientific evidence).

[9] Testimony may be necessary *not* so much to resolve "credibility issues" (based on tone and demeanor) but rather to facilitate the dynamic education of the judge (through dialectic or didactic methods available only through a "live" proceeding).

[10] For example, some judges may prefer to call the experts and counsel together for a "discussion" of the issues and exchange of views. The purpose, in part, would be to educate the judge and perhaps narrow the areas of disagreement. *See In re* Joint Eastern & Southern Districts Asbestos Litigation, 151 F.R.D. 540, 545-46 (E. & S.D.N.Y. 1993).

[11] *See Daubert*, 113 S.Ct. at 2797 (the reliability inquiry "focuses solely on principles and methodology, not the conclusion that they generate").

bears the burden of *coming forward* with credible evidence to challenge the other side's expert or scientific evidence. The challenge — on whatever ground — should be raised in a timely fashion.[12]

Once a suitable and timely challenge has issued, the burden of *persuasion* in the *Daubert* hearing rests squarely on the *proponent* of the expert's testimony. The party who wants to elicit expert testimony must show, among other things, that the witness is qualified to express an opinion and has a proper basis for the opinion.[13]

III. AUTHORITY FOR A *DAUBERT* HEARING

[U]nder the Rules the trial judge must ensure that any and all scientific testimony or evidence admitted is not only relevant, but reliable. The primary locus of this obligation is Rule 702, which clearly contemplates some degree of regulation of the subjects and theories about which an expert may testify.

*   *   *   *

Faced with a proffer of expert scientific testimony, then, the trial judge must determine at the outset, pursuant to Rule 104 (a), whether the expert is proposing to testify to (1) scientific knowledge that (2) will assist the trier of fact to understand or determine a fact in issue. This entails a preliminary assessment of whether the reasoning or methodology underlying the testimony is scientifically valid and of whether that reasoning or methodology properly can be applied to the facts in issue.[14]

With these "general observations" in *Daubert*, the Supreme Court created the necessity (and inevitability) of *Daubert* hearings. They will become a regular and essential part of practice and procedure in cases involving expert and scientific evidence. The reason is clear. Trial judges simply cannot fulfill their "gatekeeping" function without them.

From the moment the Court handed down its decision in *Daubert*, many commentators correctly foresaw this consequence. Many noted that *Daubert* would require trial judges to "role up their sleeves" and come to grips with

---

[12] *See* Fed. R. Civ. P. 16; Hockett v. United States, 730 F.2d 709, 715 (11th Cir. 1984) (in a swine-flu case, the government could not be permitted, on appeal, to first challenge the qualifications and testimony of the plaintiff's expert).

[13] *See Daubert*, 113 S.Ct. at 2796 n.10 ("These matters should be established by a preponderance of proof"); Gier v. Educational Service Unit No. 16, ___ F. Supp. ___ , 1994 WL 85420, at *7 (D. Neb. 1994) ("[P]laintiffs have not demonstrated by a preponderance of the evidence that the techniques employed [by their experts] are sufficiently reliable to satisfy Rule 702") (citing *Daubert*); *id.* at *10 ("[T]he methodologies have not been shown to be reliable enough to provide a sound basis for investigative conclusions and confident legal decision-making").

[14] *Daubert*, 113 S.Ct. at 2795.

the underlying science.[15] As some scholars recently noted: "Properly applied, the *Daubert* test should mean a *deeper and more detailed preliminary review of scientific claims* than most courts have heretofore undertaken."[16]

For this reason, the gatekeeping function contemplated by *Daubert* will require an *attitudinal* correction on the part of many judges and lawyers. They must change their *theoretical* and *methodological* points of view.[17] In truth, changes of this sort — the transformation of beliefs (theoretical and methodological) — lie at the core of any intellectual revolution.[18]

As some commentators have noted, the *Frye* test worked fairly well when trial judges were willing to scrutinize the evidence, and poorly when they were not.[19] Some have predicted that the effects of *Daubert* will depend more on each judge's "temperament" than anything else.[20] This may hold true in the short term, but sooner or later parties (and appellate courts) will insist that trial judges really exercise their gatekeeping function.[21]

Thus, *Daubert* will eventually revolutionize this field. The day will come when the "*Daubert* hearing" is as well known to the general litigator — as much a part of our lexicon — as the *Jencks* hearing is to the criminal bar.

---

[15] *See, e.g.*, Natalie Angier, *Ruling on Scientific Evidence: A Just Burden*, N.Y. Times, June 30, 1993, at A12 ("In making the first ruling ever on the proper use of scientific evidence in the courtroom, the United States Supreme Court has assured that a great many judges will be frantically playing catch-up on the basics of scientific method"); Jeffrey Kangie, *Subtle Changes Expected in Wake of Evidence Ruling*, 134 N.J.L.J. 913 (July 12, 1993) (quoting the author of this article for the proposition that "the trial judge sitting on the case will [have to] roll up his or her sleeves and dive into [the] science").

[16] Bert Black, Francisco J. Ayala, & Carol Saffran-Brinks, *Science and the Law in the Wake of Daubert: A New Search for Scientific Knowledge*, 72 Tex. L. Rev. ____ (1994).

[17] *See* Marc S. Klein, *After Daubert: Going Forward with Lessons from the Past*, 15 Cardozo L. Rev. 901 (1994) (discussing the philosophical implications and practical ramifications of *Daubert*).

[18] *See* T. Kuhn, *The Structure of Scientific Revolutions*, in 2 International Encyclopedia of Unified Science 16-17 (2d ed. 1970). In other words, a revolution entails a shift in "the particular *loci* of commitment" brought to the subject at hand. *Id.* at 43.

[19] *See, e.g.*, Bert Black, Francisco J. Ayala, & Carol Saffran-Brinks, *Science and the Law in the Wake of Daubert: A New Search for Scientific Knowledge*, 72 Tex. L. Rev. ____ (1994) ("The great Frye debate notwithstanding, the real difference in scientific evidence cases is not general acceptance versus relevance/reliability, but whether or not the court is willing to undertake a thorough and active review. Courts that want to dig into the details of an expert's reasoning and the validity of her testimony can do so with or without Frye.").

[20] *See, e.g.*, Jeffrey Kangie, *Subtle Changes Expected in Wake of Evidence Ruling*, 134 N.J.L.J. 913 (July 12, 1993) (quoting one commentator's view that the outcomes under *Daubert* will "vary greatly from judge to judge"); Honorable Marilyn Hall Patel, U.S.D.J., *Judicial Control of Scientific Evidence: The Implications of Daubert*, Transcript of ABA Program, New York City, August 9, 1993, at 102 (predicting that most trial judges will continue with their prior practice, and "for judges who are inclined to let everything in and let the jury sort it out, that they will continue to do that under *Daubert*").

[21] In a clear case, moreover, counsel might even apply to a circuit court for a writ of *mandamus* to compel a trial judge to do his or her job.

IV. PUBLIC POLICY CONSIDERATIONS FAVORING *DAUBERT* HEARINGS

> *The trial judge's function of determining the "reliability" of the evidence provides the mechanism for screening junk science.*[22]

In helping trial judges to screen out junk science, *Daubert* hearings will advance several important public policies. Litigants and judges should keep these policy considerations in mind in determining whether to seek or hold a *Daubert* hearing in any particular case.

A. Judicial Economy

Daubert hearings will take time, but, on balance, they will save time. In other words, they will promote judicial economy. In one landmark pre-*Daubert* toxic tort case, *In re Paoli Railroad Yard PCB Litigation*,[23] the Third Circuit heartily endorsed this view. The court, emphasizing the interests of judicial economy, observed that:

> [T]he most efficient procedure that the district court can use [in determining the admissibility of expert testimony] is an *in limine* hearing . . . We suggest that in complex litigation . . . where there are numerous experts presenting voluminous testimony on the cutting edge of scientific research, an *in limine* hearing may be a very useful tool in conducting both the inquiry and the fact-finding and balancing which are the hallmarks of Rule 703 and 403, respectively.[24]

The same is even true of the controversial decision of the Supreme Court of New Jersey in *Rubanick v. Witco Chemical Corp.*[25] The case was generally. perceived as a triumph for those who *oppose* active judicial gatekeeping.[26]

---

[22] *In re* Joint Eastern & Southern District Asbestos Litigation, 827 F. Supp. 1014, 1033 (S.D.N.Y. 1993).

[23] 916 F.2d 829 (3d Cir. 1990).

[24] *Paoli*, 916 F.2d at 859 (citations omitted). To be sure, like most other "intellectual revolutions," there were precursors to *Daubert*. Thus, some forward-looking judges really scrutinized the data and methods underlying an expert's testimony—even before *Daubert* directed them to do so. *See, e.g.*, Christophersen v. Allied-Signal Corp., 939 F.2d 1106 (5th Cir. 1991) (*en banc*), *cert. denied*, 112 S.Ct. 1280 (1992); *In re* "Agent Orange" Prod. Liab. Litig., 611 F. Supp. 1223 (E.D.N.Y. 1985) (Weinstein, J.). Some of these courts—like the Third Circuit in *Paoli*—clearly recognized the utility of hearings *in limine* to determine the admissibility of expert testimony, particularly in matters involving complex scientific issues.

[25] 125 N.J. 421, 593 A.2d 733 (1991).

[26] *See, e.g.*, Ronald L. Fleury, *The State Supreme Court Year in Review, 1991-92*, N.J.L.J., Sept. 7, 1992, at 3 (*Rubanick* "pulled out all the stops on admission of expert testimony"); Kathleen Bird, Jeffrey Kanige, and Ronald J. Fleury, *Reconstructing New Jersey*, N.J.L.J., Feb. 17, 1992, at 4 (*Rubanick* threatens to "unleash another wave of pro-plaintiff rulings" with a "no-holds-barred doctrine").

This initial reaction was not without some justification.[27] Indeed, the court rejected "general acceptance" and claimed to recognize a "broader standard" for the admissibility of expert testimony in toxic tort cases.[28]

In reality, however, the court did not embrace a "broader standard" and did not reject active judicial gatekeeping. It actually embraced the same *substantive* standard as *Daubert*.[29] Moreover, the Supreme Court of New Jersey stressed the utility and importance of hearings *in limine* — what we are now calling *Daubert* hearings — to resolve issues of this sort. The court wrote that trial judges "*should* use the [hearing *in limine*] to assess the soundness of the proffered methodology and the qualifications of the expert."[30] In fact, the court emphasized that trial judges should use this device liberally, even though "the process for determining the admissibility of such scientific evidence will be complicated and the ultimate decision difficult."[31]

Pre-trial hearings of this sort — to determine the admissibility of expert testimony — will eventually be common. The advantages are obvious. *Daubert* hearings "can save the litigants vast amounts of time and money by disposing of the need for trial if key evidence would ultimately be rejected."[32] Moreover, "they avoid wasting the jury's time that would otherwise be squandered in the jury room as counsel slug it out in the courtroom."[33]

---

[27] The court favorably cited the usual hit parade of cases in the "junk science" camp, including *Ferebee* and *Wells*. The court also seemed to criticize many leading cases espousing strict scrutiny, like Judge Weinstein's *Agent Orange* opinions. *See* 125 N.J. at 438-49, 593 A.2d at 742-47.

[28] *Id.* at 433, 593 A.2d at 739.

[29] *See* Editorial, *Weird Science*, N.J.L.J., Oct. 3, 1991, at 14 (noting the views of the author of this article "denying that [*Rubanick*] amounted to a 'broader standard,' and praising it as the opposite of 'junk science' "). The Supreme Court of New Jersey actually adopted a rather "stringent" standard:

> [W]e hold that in toxic-tort litigation, a scientific theory of causation that has not yet reached general acceptance may be found to be sufficiently reliable if it is *based on a sound, adequately-founded scientific methodology involving data and information of the type reasonably relied on by experts in the scientific field.* The evidence of such scientific knowledge must be proffered by an expert who is *sufficiently qualified* by education, knowledge, training, and experience in the *specific field* of science. The expert must possess *a demonstrated professional capability to assess the scientific significance of the underlying data and information, to apply the scientific methodology, and to explain the bases for the opinion reached.*

125 N.J. at 449, 593 A.2d at 747-48 (emphasis added).

[30] *Id.* at 454, 593 A.2d at 748 (emphasis added). Indeed, the court rejected the view of one intermediate appellate court judge who argued that hearings *in limine* "should address only the issue of the expert's qualifications; other issues concerning the expert's testimony go to its weight and therefore should be determined by the jury." *Id.* at 430-31, 593 A.2d at 738.

[31] *Id.* at 449, 593 A.2d at 748.

[32] Marc S. Klein, *Two-Year Review of Developments in the Law of Expert Testimony*, 1 Sci. Evid. Review—Monograph No. 1, 14-15 (ABA 1992).

[33] *Id.* at 15.

B. Correct Scientific Factual Findings

There is yet another major policy consideration — perhaps the most important — favoring *Daubert* hearings. They will unquestionably *improve* the fact-finding capability and precision of our judicial system. This is true for several reasons.

First, to the extent that judges have to rule on preliminary issues of admissibility at trial, hearings *in limine* are clearly superior. They "enable judges to actually focus on the issues in calmer moments (not in the midst of trial, when they may not have time to reflect on the issues)."[34]

Second, judges (on the average) are far better educated and more sophisticated about science and the scientific method than jurors. This proposition might not be "politically correct," but it is nonetheless true. Judges are simply less likely than juries to be misled by junk science or journeymen experts.[35]

Finally, "the *process of judicial decisionmaking*, including the methods by which information is received and decisions are reviewed, is better suited than is the rather awkward process of juror decisionmaking for evaluation of evidence that is beyond at least the usual ken of laypeople, judges, and jurors alike."[36] Stated another way, "judges are in a better position than juries to acquire and consider the kind of information that bears on the resolution of such disputes."[37]

Judges occupy this "better position" for a host of reasons. First, "[j]uries must depend mostly on listening to oral testimony, often mixed in with evidence about other issues. Judges, however, have the benefit of reviewing documents and briefs."[38] Indeed, the "Learned Treatise" exception to the hearsay rule effectively *prohibits* jurors from reviewing a treatise or study itself.[39] In effect, the jury can only *listen* to *selected portions* of the relevant literature.

In that regard, we must consider *how* we come to understand a new subject (scientific, legal, or otherwise). The process is typically an *iterative* one.[40] A

---

[34] *Id.* at 15.

[35] A majority of the general public is ignorant of basic scientific principles and methodology. *See* William Celis, *Many Americans Flunk Pop Science Quiz*, N.Y. Times, Apr. 21, 1994, at D23.

[36] Richard D. Friedman, *The Death and Transfiguration of Frye*, 34 Jurimetrics J. 133, 144 (Winter 1994) (emphasis added).

[37] Bert Black, Francisco J. Ayala, & Carol Saffran-Brinks, *Science and the Law in the Wake of Daubert: A New Search for Scientific Knowledge*, 72 Tex. L. Rev. ____ (1994).

[38] *Id.* at ____ .

[39] *See* Fed. R. Evid. 803(18) (statements from "published treatises, periodicals, or pamphlets . . . established as a reliable authority . . . may be read into evidence but may not be received as exhibits").

[40] When I get involved in a new line of litigation, I try to understand the scientific or medical issues through this type of process. I will typically first read some basic literature,

judge can read briefs and scientific literature, and then ask the lawyers or the experts some questions, and then re-read the briefs and the literature, and then ask some more questions. Moreover, a judge can pick up a general medical or scientific treatise and read it (over and over again, if necessary, while deriving new insights).

The jury, of course, only gets to hear the whole story at once. It simply cannot engage in this iterative learning process — or anything remotely like it.[41]

Lastly, judges, unlike jurors, may "consult advisers to help them understand scientific questions, or even use special masters or magistrates to investigate questions inadequately addressed by the parties' experts."[42] Juries, of course, cannot even ask questions in most jurisdictions, much less consult with independent advisers.[43]

Some scholars have suggested that the jury has some institutional advantages over a trial judge in determining scientific issues.[44] This may be true. But whatever theoretical advantages a jury may have, they certainly pale in comparison to those of a judge engaged in preliminary fact finding as part of his or her gatekeeping function.

V. THE POST-*DAUBERT* EXPERIENCE

Daubert has begun to take hold as more appellate and trial courts recognize the need for active judicial gatekeeping, including *Daubert* hearings.

---

then talk with an expert, then read some more, then talk with the expert some more, and so on, until I feel that I really understand the issues. Legal research often progresses in a similar iterative manner.

[41] *Compare In re* Joint Eastern & Southern Districts Asbestos Litigation, 151 F.R.D. 540, 545 (E. & S.D.N.Y. 1993) (Weinstein, J.) (noting that *in limine* "*Daubert* hearings," or "Rule 16 conferences, or summary judgment formal proceedings or informal consultations among experts, counsel and court may result in necessary education of the court and parties with respect to critical scientific issues. . . . Requiring that the Panel be questioned and cross-examined at a court-supervised pretrial hearing would allow all parties and the court to review the evidence simultaneously"); *see also* Bert Black, Francisco J. Ayala, & Carol Saffran-Brinks, *Science and the Law in the Wake of Daubert: A New Search for Scientific Knowledge*, 72 Tex. L. Rev. ____ (1994) (discussing the broad range of "dialectic" and "didactic" approaches available to educate judges about the scientific issues in a case).

[42] Bert Black, Francisco J. Ayala, & Carol Saffran-Brinks, *Science and the Law in the Wake of Daubert: A New Search for Scientific Knowledge*, 72 Tex. L. Rev. ____ (1994).

[43] In some jurisdictions, jurors cannot even take notes. Just imagine sitting through a short course on immunology or toxicology—with a test to follow—without the ability to take any notes.

[44] The jury, unlike the judge, is a collective body. Thus, "[b]y pooling the collective wisdom of six or twelve citizens in a group deliberation, the jury reduces the chance that factual misunderstandings will lead to faulty verdicts." Valerie P. Hans, *Is the Jury Competent? The Jury's Response to Business and Corporate Wrongdoing*, 52 Law & Contemp. Probs. 177, 219 (1989). Jurors are also skeptical of expert testimony. Jurors know that experts are chosen by a party precisely because they will support that party's position. *See* Neil J. Vidmar & Regina A. Schuller, *Juries and Expert Evidence: Social Framework Testimony*, 52 Law & Contemp. Probs. 133, 171 (1989).

Some Federal Circuits have held that *Daubert* hearings are appropriate even for types of expert testimony previously rejected as a matter of law. For example, in *United States v. Amador-Galvan*,[45] the trial judge, relying on long-standing Ninth Circuit precedent, prohibited the defendant from calling an expert to address the unreliability of eyewitness testimony. The Ninth Circuit held that the trial judge abused his discretion in rejecting this expert testimony without a *Daubert* hearing:

> Under the *Daubert* rule, the district court should decide whether such testimony is relevant, and if so, whether the theory propounded is trustworthy and scientifically valid. Testimony attacking the reliability of eyewitness testimony is clearly relevant to Amador-Galvan's defense; it is his main line of defense. Less clear is whether the theories on eyewitness identification are "sufficiently valid," helpful, and of sufficient "evidentiary reliability" and trustworthiness. The district court did not consider whether Amador-Galvin's proffered expert testimony met *Daubert*'s requirements. Thus, we remand to the district court for it to consider whether, under *Daubert*, the testimony should have been admitted.[46]

Even when an appellate court is ready to follow precedent, the court itself will carefully examine the scientific issues. In *United States v. Martinez*,[47] a defendant convicted of sexual abuse challenged the trial court's decision to admit DNA profiling evidence. The Eighth Circuit discussed the nature of this evidence in detail and concluded, as the Second Circuit had done earlier, that lower courts could judicially notice its reliability. But, in the course of so holding, the Eighth Circuit cautioned trial judges that, in the future, "[i]f new techniques are offered . . . the district court *must* hold an *in limine* hearing under the *Daubert* standard. . . ."[48]

Trial judges have likewise recognized that a *Daubert* hearing is the appropriate vehicle to resolve preliminary issues concerning the admissibility

---

[45] 9 F.3d 1414 (9th Cir. 1993).

[46] *Id.* at 1418 (citation omitted).

[47] 3 F.3d 1191, 1197 (8th Cir. 1993).

[48] *Id.* at 1197 (emphasis added). *See also* United States v. Rincon, 11 F.3d 922 (9th Cir. 1993) ("The case is remanded to the district court for the limited purpose of reexamining the admissibility of the expert testimony offered by the defendant in light of [*Daubert*]. In complying with this mandate, the district court may hold such hearings as it deems appropriate . . ."); Robinson v. Missouri Pacific RR Co., 16 F.3d 1083 (10th Cir. 1994) ("In the case before us, the expert has, in part, based his opinion on the science of physics. In cases presenting opinions grounded in science, as observed in *Daubert*, the trial judge assumes a most important function relating to expert testimony."); United States v. Bonds, 12 F.3d 540 (6th Cir. 1993) (evaluating the testimony from a "*Frye* hearing" to determine whether the government's DNA evidence satisfied the later-adopted requirements of *Daubert* as well; the district court's extensive *Frye* hearing approximated a *Daubert* hearing in all respects save the name).

of expert testimony. As a result, some of them have begun to grapple with scientific issues in ways rare before *Daubert*.

Consider, for example, *Gier v. Educational Service Unit No. 16.*[49] In that case, a U.S. Magistrate conducted an extensive *Daubert* hearing to determine whether a psychiatrist and two psychologists could testify that children had been sexually, physically, and emotionally abused. After a full-blown *Daubert* hearing, the court handed down a comprehensive opinion. It first properly noted that, "[t]o fully analyze the reliability of the techniques of the witnesses in this case, it is necessary to describe those techniques and the resulting bases for the witnesses' conclusions about the purported abuse suffered by the plaintiffs."[50]

Magistrate Piester found, among other things, that these experts did not employ any cognizable methodology. Thus:

> [T]he evaluations of the children deal almost exclusively in vague psychological profiles and symptoms, and unquantifiable evaluation results. There is much criticism [in the professional literature] attacking the attempts to compile a list of symptoms and behaviors to serve as an accurate indicator of whether a child has been sexually abused.[51]

The problem is compounded (and effectively renders the evidence "irrefutable") when the expert relies on some *unique combination* and interpretation of *several factors*.[52] You just cannot pin these witnesses down. As Magistrate Piester explained:

> The difficulty in refuting the evidence is borne out by the resulting inability to cross-examine the witness' opinion. As in most cases [of this

---

[49] ____ F. Supp. ____, 1994 WL 85420 (D. Neb. 1994).

[50] *Id.* at *2.

[51] *Id.* at *5. The *Gier* opinion relied extensively on the New Hampshire Supreme Court's reasoning in State v. Cressey, 628 A.2d 696 (NH 1993). For a discussion of the evidentiary issues in *Cressey*, see Stephen A. Brunette, *Significant Developments in Expert and Scientific Evidence*, 1 SESEQ 127, 136-39 (Fall 1993).

[52] We saw this phenomenon—a classic hallmark of junk science—in the Bendectin cases, particularly Oxendine v. Merrell Dow Pharmaceuticals, Inc., 506 A.2d 1100 (D.C. 1986). In *Oxendine*, Dr. Done, a notorious expert in the Bendectin cases, somehow combined four very weak strains of evidence—*structure-activity analysis* (raising a "clue"), *in vivo studies* (raising a "suspicion"), *in vitro studies* (indicating "the potential for teratogenicity"), and *unique epidemiological data* (an unpublished "reanalysis" of published data purporting to show a relatively small relative risk)—into a triable issue of fact. The Court was impressed by the fact that, '[a]lthough he was vigorously and exhaustively cross-examined by very able counsel, he did not waver from his opinion that Bendectin had caused appellant's birth defects." *Id.* at 1108. Of course not. Dr. Done undoubtedly *knew* that his amalgamation was impenetrable. Thus, Dr. Done "repeatedly stated that this opinion was based not on any single study or type of evidence, but on four different types of scientific data viewed in combination." *Id.* Of course, it was a practically unique view of the scientific data in combination—one that the rest of the scientific community just happened to miss. But that was no reason to "waver." Indeed, it was the very reason why he never had to waver.

sort], the witnesses' opinions are based on an interpretation of all of the factors before them as opposed to a single indicator or symptom. . . . "So even though the defendants may be able to discredit several of the indicators, symptoms or test results, the expert's overall opinion is likely to emerge unscathed. *An expert using this methodology may candidly acknowledge any inconsistencies or potential shortcomings in the individual pieces of evidence she presents, but can easily dismiss the critique by saying that her evaluation relies on no one symptom or indicator and that her conclusions still hold true in light of all the other available factors and her expertise in the field.* In such a case, the expert's conclusions are as impenetrable as they are unverifiable."[53]

VI. THE BREADTH OF *DAUBERT*

A *Daubert* hearing may not be necessary in all or even most cases, but neither is it necessarily limited to unusually complex or sophisticated cases, like mass torts. Indeed, *Daubert* should be and has been applied in appropriate "run of the mill" cases, including auto accident cases.[54]

It is true that, in *Daubert*, the Court technically addressed only a limited aspect — albeit a very important aspect — of the judicial gatekeeping function. The Court, in the context of "novel" scientific propositions (in a toxic tort case), focused on determinations of "whether the expert is proposing to testify to (1) scientific knowledge that (2) will assist the trier of fact."[55] In an interesting footnote, the Court expressly limited its opinion to the context of *scientific* testimony.[56]

Despite this caveat, *Daubert* hearings should eventually encompass *all* preliminary issues concerning the admissibility of any expert or scientific evidence. These include, among others, whether the issue even warrants expert testimony (Rule 702), whether the witness is really qualified to express an opinion in the relevant discipline (Rule 702), whether the witness has based his or her opinion on proper sources of information (Rule 703), and whether the probative value of the expert's testimony would outweigh any potential prejudice that it might cause (Rule 403).[57]

---

[53] *Id.* at *6, quoting State v. Cressey, 628 A.2d 696, 701 (NH 1993) (emphasis added). For these reasons, the court rejected the experts' *methodologies*, not their ultimate conclusions. *See Gier*, at *10 ("[T]he methodologies have not been shown to be reliable enough to provide a sound basis for investigative conclusions and confident legal decision-making").

[54] *See, e.g.*, Robinson v. Missouri Pacific R.R. Co., 16 F.3d 1083 (10th Cir. 1994) (auto accident).

[55] 113 S.Ct at 2796

[56] *See id.* at 2795 n.8 ("Rule 702 also applies to 'technical, or other specialized knowledge.' Our discussion is limited to the scientific context because that is the nature of the expertise offered here").

[57] Some might disagree. *Cf.* Honorable Marilyn Hall Patel, U.S.D.J., *Judicial Control of Scientific Evidence: The Implications of Daubert*, Transcript of ABA Program in New York

Likewise, *Daubert* hearings may be appropriate for a wide range of matters, not simply those involving "novel" scientific testimony. They may be warranted in cases involving other forms of expertise (like medicine, engineering, accounting, or plumbing).[58]

One court recently recognized that a *Daubert* hearing is the appropriate forum to resolve threshold questions involving "experts" who are not technically "scientists." In *Liu v. Korean Air Lines Co.*,[59] the defendant moved to exclude the testimony of a professional economist on the grounds that his economic projections were "speculative, conjectural, based on improper assumptions, and not helpful to the jury."[60] Judge Leval wrote:

> Under the authority of the Supreme Court's recent decision in [*Daubert*], the court conducted a hearing ... Although *Daubert* concerned the admissibility of expert testimony based on novel scientific theories, its holding that the trial judge should determine "whether the expert is proposing to testify to (1) scientific knowledge that (2) will assist the trier of fact," is equally applicable where, as here, an expert is called to testify to matters that the opponent contends are neither specialized knowledge, nor helpful to the jury, but are more likely to inflame and prejudice.[61]

After the *Daubert* hearing, Judge Leval wrote:

> Based on the submission of the parties and the testimony at the hearing, the court finds that in several respects the proffered opinions of [the economist] should be excluded. In other respects, I find that his testimony represents professional, scientific, or technical knowledge within the meaning of Rule 702 that would assist the jury, and in those respects I will permit him to testify.[62]

Finally, the principles of *Daubert* should not be limited to oral testimony *per se*. Rather, *Daubert*'s principles should govern *demonstrative* evidence,

---

on August 9, 1993, at 103 ("[I]t's clear that *Daubert* is about only one type of 702 evidence—scientific evidence. Footnote eight makes that clear. Now there is a definition in the opinion of 'knowledge' and what constitutes 'knowledge' and it may be that, not given solely in the context of science, it may be transportable to the other evidence that may be treated under 702 (technical or other specialized knowledge)").

[58] *See, e.g.*, J. Stratton Shartel, *Causation Leads List of Issues Shaping Strategy in EMF Litigation*, 7 No. 11 Inside Litig. 1 (Nov. 1993) ("Observers initially thought that the ruling in *Daubert* would be applied only to novel scientific evidence previously subject to the *Frye* test. However, federal court decisions .. . have shown that nearly all expert testimony ... might be evaluated according to criteria laid out by the court in *Daubert*") (citation omitted).

[59] 1993 WL 478343 (S.D.N.Y. 1993).

[60] *Id.* at *1.

[61] *Id.*

[62] *Id.*

particularly new and most potent media, like video animation. In *Robinson v. Missouri Pacific Railroad Co.,*[63] Judge Bright wrote:

> Video animation adds a new and powerful evidentiary tool to the trial scene. McCormick's work on evidence observes that with respect to one party's staged reproduction of facts "not only is the danger that the jury may be confuse art with reality particularly great, but the impressions generated by the evidence may prove particularly difficult to limit ." Because of its dramatic power, trial judges should carefully and meticulously examine proposed animation evidence for proper foundation, relevancy and the potential for undue prejudice.

>   *   *   *   *

> Concerning future similar issues under Rule 702, we suggest that as "gatekeeper" the district court carefully and meticulously make an early pretrial evaluation of issues of admissibility, particularly of scientific expert opinions and films or animations illustrative of such opinions.[64]

In sum, the *Daubert* criteria, and a *Daubert* hearing, should be applied in a wide variety of contexts. Of course, the nature of the inquiry in each case will depend on a host of case-specific factors. But the view espoused by some — that *Daubert* applies only to *scientists* who seek to rely on a *novel* scientific theory — is not tenable.

VII. COUNSEL'S CHALLENGES

The *Daubert* revolution is still unfolding, of course, and securing its advantages may not be easy. *Daubert* clearly presents litigators with some new challenges.

A. Getting a *Daubert* Hearing

Like many other cutting-edge developments in practice and procedure, *Daubert* has not yet fully taken hold. This is not at all surprising. Even after *formal* rules of procedure have been amended, in my experience, judges and lawyers often ignore the amendments, at least for some period of time, as they go about business as usual. Slowly but surely, however, the new regime becomes part of the routine. The revolution is forced by a few lawyers and judges (including appellate judges) who insist on exercising the new rules.

It may not be easy to get a *Daubert* hearing, at least initially. Several months ago, I was called to try a major pharmaceutical product liability case

---

[63] 16 F.3d 1083 (10th Cir. 1994) (Bright, J., sitting by designation).

[64] *Id.* at 1088-89 (emphasis added; citation omitted).

pending in a United States District Court. After reviewing the file, I concluded that we could knock out the plaintiffs' experts on several grounds (including, among others, their lack of qualifications, lack of reliable evidence, and lack of any semblance of a scientific methodology).

I moved orally in advance of trial for a *Daubert* hearing. I was optimistic that our application would be granted. The judge in the case has a well-deserved reputation as fair, bright, and diligent. Moreover, most trial judges, with huge case loads, leap at an opportunity to avoid a four- to six-week trial. To me, the prospects of a *Daubert* hearing looked good.

The colloquy — at the final pretrial conference two weeks before trial — went something like this:

THE COURT: What is your application, counsel?

DEFENSE COUNSEL: Your Honor, I would like to have a brief *Daubert* hearing in advance of trial.

THE COURT: A what? Please explain.

DEFENSE COUNSEL: Your Honor, in the Supreme Court's recent decision in *Daubert v. Merrell Dow Pharmaceuticals*, the Court indicated that trial judges, like yourself, must actively exercise a gatekeeping function to insure that only reliable scientific evidence is presented to the jury.

In this case, Your Honor, the plaintiffs' two experts simply cannot be permitted to testify. This is true for three reasons.

First, neither of these men is really an expert in any field relevant to this case. Their resumes may look impressive, at least at first blush, but they are over their heads. They do not understand the most rudimentary principles of epidemiology, for example, and yet both rely heavily on epidemiological data. So they simply cannot and should not qualify as experts in this case.

Second, neither has based his opinion on any credible scientific evidence. The only real scientific data that they have considered unequivocally supports our position, not theirs, but they don't understand that fact because they just don't understand what they are reading. The anecdotal reports that they have also cited are not the sort of information that real experts in the field actually or reasonably rely on in seeking to determine whether a drug causes this type of effect.

Finally, neither has utilized any semblance of a scientific methodology. Their reasoning is entirely *ad hoc* and internally inconsistent. Their opinions are based on nothing more than *post hoc ergo propter hoc* reasoning, which is not a valid scientific methodology.

THE COURT: Well, why aren't these points that you could make with the jury? I am sure that, if what you say is true, you should have no problem getting a verdict in your favor.

DEFENSE COUNSEL: I would hope so, Your Honor. But what I am saying is this: If you would just give me a one or two day hearing in advance of trial, I am sure that, acting as a gatekeeper, Your Honor would find the plaintiffs' expert evidence totally inadmissible. Your finding to that effect would end this case. We would not need to have a four- to six-week trial. We could all go home early.

THE COURT: But for me to do what you ask, wouldn't I have to read the scientific studies presented by both sides? How am I supposed to decide this scientific dispute between the two sets of experts. After all, I am not a scientist.

DEFENSE COUNSEL: This is true, Your Honor, but that is part of your job as a trial judge. You must exercise a gatekeeping function. Someone has to first decide, in a case like this, whether the witnesses are really experts and, if so, whether their opinions are really scientific. After all, not everyone who claims to be a scientist really is one, and not everything that a scientist says is necessarily scientific. The rules, in effect, only allow a party to call a qualified expert to present valid scientific evidence.

In this case, we contend that the plaintiffs do not have a qualified expert to present any valid scientific evidence in their favor. Under the teaching of *Daubert*, Your Honor, you have to resolve these issues first. It may not be easy, but you have to make the call.

If these witnesses are not real experts, or their opinions are not scientific — as I am prepared to show you — then you should not allow them to present their views to the jury.

THE COURT: I understand what you are saying. Let me hear from your adversary.

PLAINTIFFS' COUNSEL: Your Honor hit the nail on the head. You are not a scientist, and you cannot become one overnight.

What defense counsel really wants Your Honor to do is to decide the merits of this case. He really thinks that his client has a better chance of winning if you make the decision, rather than the jury. Our system, of course, does not work that way. So for this reason alone, Your Honor should deny his application.

Moreover, defense counsel's proposal creates all kinds of logistical nightmares. I would have to bring my experts here twice, in effect, once for this so-called "*Daubert* hearing" and then again to testify at trial. They are very busy men, and I am not sure that I could arrange for two appearances. It would also double my expert witness expenses.

And why should any of us have to go through all of this twice? Your Honor, the proposal just makes no sense.

THE COURT: Well, I will reserve my formal decision on the application. But I must say that I have no intention of trying this case twice. So I think counsel should be prepared to pick a jury and try this case when we return.[65]

You can be sure that this colloquy — or some version of it — will be repeated in a number of federal and state courts over the next few years. Yet,

---

[65] The court never formally ruled on my motion for a *Daubert* hearing because the parties settled the case immediately following the pre-trial conference.

as we have seen, other courts have already embraced the teachings of *Daubert*. The job is now largely in the hands of judges and lawyers who really want to take advantage of *Daubert*'s revolution in practice and procedure.

B. Attorney Education

Many lawyers (like me) chose law over science because we are more comfortable with words than numbers. The same is true, of course, of many judges (who began their careers as lawyers). It no longer matters. Under the new regime, the bench and bar are just going to have to comprehend and apply basic principles of modern science.[66]

The utility and efficacy of *Daubert* depends not only on the courts, but on counsel as well. Unfortunately, "the data . . . suggest that many lawyers are ill-prepared to evaluate critically and challenge expert testimony."[67] Indeed, we have already seen too many cases in which counsel have failed to even challenge the admissibility of poor scientific or expert testimony.[68]

In the years to come, we are going to see more "short courses" for lawyers on different aspects of science and medicine. These should include lessons in scientific reasoning and methodology. In college, I took "Physics for Poets." Now watch for courses entitled, "Science for Lawyers."

C. Strategic Decisions

While a *Daubert* hearing offers many advantages to the opponent of some expert or scientific evidence, it may have one significant *disadvantage*. Counsel should consider this factor *before* seeking a *Daubert* hearing.

Suppose the court entertains a *Daubert* hearing and decides in favor of admissibility. An adverse decision in the context of a *Daubert* hearing should then preclude the opponent from *voir dire*, in the jury's presence, on the threshold issues at trial. To be sure, the opponent can still attack the expert's credibility (on cross-examination), but there should be no opportunity to do so *before* the expert testifies.

It is a bittersweet strategic position for the party challenging the expert. The party will forfeit the opportunity to "rough up" the expert — in the presence of the jury — *before* that expert is allowed to give the jury his or her

---

[66] *See* Marc S. Klein, *A Review of Science and Technology in Judicial Decision Making: Creating Opportunities and Meeting Challenges, Carnegie Commission on Science, Technology, and Government (Mar. 1993)*, 1 Shepard's Expert & Scientific Evid. Q. 273, 274-75 (Fall 1993) (discussing proposals for "judicial education" about science and technology).

[67] Daniel W. Shuman, Elizabeth Whitaker, & Anthony Champagne, *An Empirical Examination of the Use of Expert Witnesses in the Courts—Part II: A Three City Study*, 34 Jurimetrics J. 193, 206 (Winter 1994)

[68] *See generally* Barry M. Epstein & Marc S. Klein, *The Use and Abuse of Expert Testimony in Product Liability Actions*, 17 Seton Hall L. Rev. 656, 674 (1987) ("On some occasions when these screening devices fail, the untoward results may simply reflect bad advocacy").

opinion. Sometimes an expert's credibility can be greatly damaged in a *voir dire,* even if the judge ultimately allows the expert to testify. By undertaking a pre-trial *Daubert* hearing, then, the opponent forfeits this strategic opportunity.[69]

VIII. CONCLUSION

It is vitally important for the bench and bar to consolidate the *Daubert* revolution as rapidly as possible. Our society does not need unreliable expert or scientific evidence to resolve disputes. Indeed, bad science is terribly destructive. Aside from yielding unjust results, it can compromise the integrity of our judicial system, undermine the public's perception of it, and drive vital products from the marketplace.[70]

The *Daubert* issue should not be considered in *pro-plaintiff* or *pro-defendant* terms. A defendant could use junk science to defeat a plaintiff's legitimate claim for compensation every bit as well as a plaintiff could use junk science to prevail on an unjust claim. The issue concerns precision — not politics — and we should let the chips fall where they may.

The *Daubert* hearing represents a powerful tool to screen out unreliable expert and scientific evidence. We can use it to avoid the terrible consequences of potentially serious errors. We must now simply have the wisdom and the will to use this tool effectively.

---

[69] This may be a particularly pertinent consideration when the case for preclusion is marginal.

[70] *See* Barry M. Epstein & Marc S. Klein, *The Use and Abuse of Expert Testimony in Product Liability Actions,* 17 Seton Hall L. Rev. 656, 661 (1987) ("Society can no longer afford factual findings based on shockingly bad science. The legal system today relies on scientists to provide facts about important and diverse matters of concern including the safety and efficacy of drugs, the dangers presented by chemicals in the work place, and the safety requirements of nuclear power plants. . . . [C]ourts now deal with scientific issues of profound significance").

Preclusion of Scientific Evidence after *Daubert**

*Clifton T. Hutchinson**
*Julie E. Blend***

I. Introduction

The Supreme Court's test for the admissibility of scientific evidence in *Daubert v. Merrell Dow Pharmaceuticals, Inc*[1] sets forth guidelines for trial courts to follow in ruling on the admissibility of expert testimony under the Federal Rules of Evidence. The Court gives a nonexhaustive list of factors for the trial court to consider in its determination of whether an expert proposes "to testify to (1) scientific knowledge that (2) will assist the trier of fact to understand or determine a fact in issue."[2] In addition to the factors cited in the text of the opinion,[3] the Supreme Court lists in a footnote several other sources for factors that may aid in a reliability analysis of expert testimony under Rule 702.[4] One such factor is the opinion or finding of other courts on the scientific evidence at issue.[5]

---

* Copyright 1994. Used with permission.

** Mr. Hutchinson is a partner in Hughes & Luce, L.L.P., Dallas, Texas, and practices in the areas of products liability and toxic tort defense. Mr. Hutchinson was one of the defense counsel in *Christophersen v. Allied Signal*.

*** Ms. Blend is an associate with Hughes & Luce, L.L.P. and practices in the area of commercial litigation.

[1] ____ U.S. ____ , 113 S.Ct. 2786 (1993).

[2] 113 S.Ct. at 2796.

[3] 113 S.Ct. 2786, 2796-97 (1993) (falsifiability, peer review, error rate, and general or "widespread" acceptance).

[4] 113 S.Ct. at 2797 n. 12, citing United States v. Downing, 753 F.2d 1224, 1238-39 (3d Cir. 1985); 3 J. Weinstein & M. Berger, Weinstein's Evidence ("Weinstein & Berger") ¶ 702[03], at 702-41 to 702-42 (1988); Mark McCormick, *Scientific Evidence: Defining a New Approach to Admissibility*, 67 Iowa L. Rev. 879, 911-12 (1982); and *Symposium on Science and the Rules of Evidence*, 99 F.R.D. 187, 231 (1983) (statement by Margaret Berger).

[5] *Downing*, 753 F.2d at 1239, 1241:

> Finally, the district [court] may take judicial notice of expert testimony that has been offered in earlier cases to support or dispute the merits of a particular scientific procedure.   . . . .
>
> In addition, the court may properly consider the testimony presented to other courts that have addressed the same evidentiary issue, and the opinions of those courts on the subject. If a technique has found favor with a significant number of other courts, a district court may exercise its discretion to admit the evidence through judicial notice.

Of the other sources for factors listed in *Daubert* at footnote 12, Weinstein and Berger do not list prior decisions among their factors but suggest that their analysis applies when

In the Third Circuit Court of Appeals' *Downing* decision,[6] cited with approval in *Daubert*,[7] Judge Becker suggested that a court may admit scientific evidence by judicial notice if it had "found favor with a significant number of other courts."[8] Such an approach makes sense using the *Daubert* test. If other courts have conducted the full, rigorous scrutiny of scientific evidence required by *Daubert*, and no new, significant scientific findings modify the calculus, a court should not be required to conduct, and indeed in some instances should be precluded from conducting, another evidentiary review before considering admissibility.[9]

With courts across the country considering multiple cases that involve similar issues of the admissibility of the same scientific evidence (*e.g.*, drug or chemical exposure causation issues), limiting unnecessary duplication of judicial analysis would further the interests of judicial economy.[10] This article discusses the possible application of the preclusion doctrines of collateral estoppel, *stare decisis*, or judicial notice,[11] in cases in which a prior court has already conducted a *Daubert* analysis of the scientific evidence at issue.

---

prior judicial precedent has *not* addressed the scientific evidence, implying that other court decisions may alleviate the need for additional Rule 702 scrutiny. *See* 3 Weinstein & Berger, ¶ 702[03], at 702-41 to 702-42 (1988). In the symposium cited in *Daubert* at footnote 12, Professor Moenssens seems to be making the same distinction: "If novel scientific evidence is to be proffered *in the absence of satisfactory legal precedent*, we think the judge has an obligation to screen it prior to trial." *Symposium on Science and the Rules of Evidence*, 99 F.R.D. 187, 231 (1983)(statement by Andre Moenssens)(emphasis added). Judge McCormick recognizes the potential effect of *appellate* determinations:

> The necessary showing must appear in the trial court record unless the general admissibility issue has been answered by an appellate court decision. For example, when the appellate court has recognized the accuracy and reliability of radar speed detection devices, the trial court has no reason to reconsider that question. In addition, certain principles and theories may become so well accepted that they are subject to judicial notice.

McCormick, *supra* note 4, at 904.

[6] United States v. Downing, 753 F.2d 1224 (3d Cir. 1985).

[7] *See* 113 S.Ct. at 2795-97.

[8] 753 F.2d at 1241. The result is to give preclusive effect to properly conducted *Daubert* reviews of scientific evidence.

[9] This is an approach acknowledged by some commentators before *Daubert*. *See, e.g.*, Paul C. Giannelli, *The Admissibility of Novel Scientific Evidence: Frye v. United States, a Half-Century Later*, 80 Colum. L. Rev. 1197, 1218 (1980) (noting that "[s]ome courts have considered prior judicial decisions in deciding whether general acceptance has been achieved" in conducting the pre-*Daubert Frye* analysis).

[10] A thorough scientific evidence review can be exhausting to the parties and the court as illustrated by United States v. Porter, 618 A.2d 629 (D.C. App. 1992), which upheld the admissibility of DNA typing evidence after testimony from eight expert witnesses during a 20-day *Frye* hearing and the receipt of over 1,300 pages of briefs. *Id.* at 630. The trial court's opinion ran 93 pages. *Id.*

[11] The *Daubert* Court observed that "well-established" propositions of science are properly subject to judicial notice under Fed. Rule Evid. 201. 113 S.Ct. at 2796 n.11.

II. Collateral Estoppel as a Tool of Judicial Economy

Collateral estoppel, or issue preclusion, prevents a party from relitigating an issue that was actually and necessarily determined by a judgment in a prior proceeding.[12] The doctrine was traditionally limited by the requirement of mutuality; preclusion could only be applied to parties, or those in privity to parties, in the prior litigation.[13] Erosion of the mutuality requirement began in *Blonder-Tongue Laboratories, Inc. v. University of Illinois Foundation*,[14] when the Supreme Court allowed a defendant not a party to the prior proceeding to use collateral estoppel defensively, to preclude the plaintiff in the prior proceeding from relitigating an issue decided adversely to the plaintiff.[15] In *Parklane Hosiery Co. v. Shore*,[16] the Supreme Court completed the demise of mutuality and allowed plaintiffs who were not parties to the prior proceeding to use collateral estoppel offensively to preclude defendants in a prior proceeding from relitigating an issue decided adversely to the defendants. Now the traditional mutuality requirements have been abandoned in federal courts and in a majority of state courts.[17] As described below, however, *Parklane* maintained constraints on collateral estoppel that create unfairness and could limit its applicability in *Daubert* scientific evidence issues.

A.   Offensive Use Creates Unfair Advantage

In *Parklane*, the Supreme Court stated the dual purpose of collateral estoppel: (1) to protect litigants from the burden of relitigating issues; and (2) to promote judicial economy.[18] But the Court restricted the application of the doctrine to offensive use and retained the requirement of privity.[19] Thus, in

---

[12] Parklane Hosiery Co. v. Shore, 439 U.S. 332, 326 n.5 (1979).

[13] 18 Charles Wright, Arthur Miller & Edward Cooper, Federal Practice and Procedure ("Wright, Miller & Cooper") § 4463 (1982).

[14] 402 U.S. 313 (1971).

[15] *Id.* at 327, 329-30.

[16] 439 U.S. 322 (1979).

[17] 18 Wright, Miller & Cooper, § 4464 at 570.

[18] 439 U.S. 322 at 326.

[19] *Id.* at 330-31. The Court established a four-factor test for testing the fairness of applying the doctrine. The first factor is whether the plaintiff seeking to use collateral estoppel offensively is a "wait and see" plaintiff. Could the plaintiff have easily joined in the first action? The remaining factors focus on unfairness to the defendant:

1. Whether the defendant had little incentive to defend the first action vigorously due to nominal damages, particularly if future suits are not foreseeable

2. Whether the judgment relied upon to invoke collateral estoppel is inconsistent with a previous judgment in favor of the defendant

3. Whether "the second action affords the defendant procedural opportunities unavailable in the first action that could readily cause a different result"

repetitive litigation, such as mass torts, the result does not protect litigants (usually defendants) who must face repeated trials on the same issue, or the courts who must conduct these trials.[20]

Offensive use of collateral estoppel after *Parklane* creates an "option effect" for plaintiffs that is not available to defendants.[21] A plaintiff has the option of using a prior favorable finding, or ignoring a prior unfavorable finding.[22] In defensive collateral estoppel, a defendant can only assert collateral estoppel as to a plaintiff who already had a full and fair opportunity to litigate the issue.[23] Otherwise, that plaintiff's due process rights to a day in court are violated.[24]

The "option effect" would be particularly unfair in the context of evaluating scientific evidence. Issues of the admissibility of scientific evidence often arise in the context of mass tort claims, in which hundreds or thousands of claimants may assert injury from a drug or chemical. A defendant, with no collateral estoppel "option," could thus face numerous trials, repetitively dealing with the scientific *ratio decidendi*, and be unable to staunch the defense cost hemorrhage absent a mass settlement. Conversely plaintiffs' counsel could retry the scientific issue until he or she obtained a favorable verdict, then assert *Parklane* estoppel effectively to eviscerate any further defense.

Professor Vestal and other commentators have argued that privity is not necessary for due process if the point of view of the precluded party has been

---

[20] *See* Michael Weinberger, *Collateral Estoppel and the Mass Produced Product: A Proposal*, 15 N. Eng. L. Rev. 1 (1979) (noting problems for defendants caused by privity requirement).

[21] *See* Jack Ratliff, *Offensive Collateral Estoppel and the Option Effect*, 67 Tex. L. Rev. 63 (1988). Because the Supreme Court recognized only offensive use the resulting law fits Professor Currie's famous train wreck paradigm in which successive plaintiffs can lose repeated verdicts without an estoppel effect, but a subsequent plaintiff can bind a common defendant after one favorable verdict. *See* Brainerd Currie, *Mutuality of Collateral Estoppel: Limits of the Bernhard Doctrine*, 9 Stan. L. Rev. 281, 284 (1957). The "wait and see" plaintiff, who opts out of the initial claim for strategic reasons, cannot be bound by the doctrine as a nonparty. *See* Lynch v. Merrell-National Laboratories, 830 F.2d 1190, 1992 (1st Cir. 1987) (plaintiffs not estopped though "they had ample opportunity to join the [prior] multi-district litigation and chose not to do so").

[22] *Id.* at 65.

[23] Parties have had a "full and fair opportunity" to litigate if they:
[A]ssume control over litigation in which they have a direct financial or proprietary interest and then seek to redetermine issues previously resolved, . . . [T]he persons for whose benefit and at whose direction a cause of action is litigated cannot be said to be "strangers to the cause." . . . [O]ne who prosecutes or defends a suit in the name of another to establish and protect his own right, or who assists in the prosecution or defense of an action in aid of some interest of his own . . . is as much bound . . . as he would be if he had been as party to the record.
Montana v. United States, 440 U.S. 147, 154 (1979) (quoting Schnell v. Peter Ekrich & Sons, Inc., 365 U.S. 260, 262 n.4 (1961)).

[24] *Id.* (citing *Blonder-Tongue Labs., Inc.*, 402 U.S. at 329).

adequately represented in the first trial.[25] This would seem particularly appropriate in mass tort cases where there is usually extensive coordination among claimants' and defendants' counsel and thus a greater likelihood that an issue of scientific evidence would be fully and fairly litigated.[26] But the trend of cases since *Parklane* has been to apply collateral estoppel with such careful attention to the formula of that case that its application has not been unfair but instead ineffectual. The doctrine seems better suited for the single incident mass tort, like Professor Currie's train wreck, than the drug or chemical exposure cases that might benefit from a *Daubert* scientific evidence review.[27]

B.   Collateral Estoppel Applied Pre-*Daubert*

1. Offensive Use.   Prior to *Daubert*, few courts approved the use of collateral estoppel in evaluating scientific issues, even in mass tort cases. Because of the widespread litigation, and repetitive nature of the claims, many of the collateral estoppel questions arose in asbestos cases.[28] Plaintiffs sought to preclude further litigation of medical causation, whether asbestos caused various diseases, and broader tort issues such as whether a defendant's asbestos product was defective or unreasonably dangerous. After a plaintiff verdict was affirmed by the Fifth Circuit in *Borel v. Fibreboard Paper Products Corp.*,[29] several cases applied collateral estoppel to asbestos

---

[25] *See* Allan D. Vestal, *Res Judicata/Preclusion: Expansion*, 47 S. Cal. L. Rev. 357, 360 (1974) (to apply doctrine to nonparties initially seems questionable but precedents do exist that have barred litigation by a nonparty, which reflects "the application of a sound body of developing law"); Lawrence C. George, *Sweet Uses of Adversity; Parklane Hosiery and the Collateral Class Action*, 32 Stan. L. Rev. 655, 657 (1980) (court should rid itself of constraint of privity and recognize class of "other plaintiffs" who must share in an earlier plaintiff's loss to a common defendant). *But see* Elinor R. Schroeder, *Relitigation of Common Issues: The Failure of Nonparty Preclusion and an Alternative Proposal*, 67 Iowa L. Rev. 917 (1982) (proposals for expanding doctrine underestimate the importance to parties of control and participation in their own presentation).

[26] Note, *Collateral Estoppel of Nonparties*, 87 Harv. L. Rev. 1485, 1504 (1974) (mass tort cases in which potential plaintiffs have had effective coordination illustrate that a majority's interest in relitigation is not always of paramount importance). *See* coordination of plaintiffs' counsel in mass tort litigation described in Paul Rheingold, *The MER/29 Story—An Instance of Successful Mass Disaster Litigation*, 56 Cal. L. Rev. 116 (1968). In the MER/29 litigation, over 1,500 lawsuits were filed claiming injuries from side effects of a cholesterol reducing drug. A plaintiffs' attorney group, ultimately with 288 members, was formed as a clearinghouse for information, which included an "MER/29 School" for trial preparations. *Id.* at 122-23, 131.

[27] Michael D. Green, *The Inability of Offensive Collateral Estoppel to Fulfill its Promise: An Examination of Estoppel in Asbestos Litigation*, 70 Iowa L. Rev. 141, 227 (1984).

[28] *See* Green, *supra*, note 27; *Products Liability: Inhalation of Asbestos*, 39 A.L.R. 4th 399 (1985).

[29] 493 F.2d 1076 (5th Cir.), *cert. denied*, 419 U.S. 869 (1974).

issues.[30] Al though "nonparty" plaintiffs were successful in urging collateral estoppel principles on certain asbestos issues, this effort at judicial efficiency ultimately failed, signalled by the Fifth Circuit's reversal of a preclusion ruling in *Hardy v. Johns Manville Sales Corp.*[31] The trial court had granted a partial summary judgment, *inter alia*, that asbestos insulation products were "unavoidably unsafe" and that asbestos is a competent producing cause of mesothelioma and asbestosis.[32] Applying federal law,[33] the circuit court reversed, primarily on the ground that the *Borel* verdict was ambiguous and was not necessarily decided on the issues being submitted for estoppel.[34]

Hardy reflects the major problem with applying offensive collateral estoppel in mass tort and other product liability claims: the difficulty of determining whether identical issues exist.[35] Product liability claims may be highly individualized and dependent upon specific facts concerning the claimant's background, medical history, employment history, and work with or exposure to the product.[36] Because of the mix of variables that may be present and form the bases of the prior judgment, a court consid-ering estoppel may have difficulty reading between the lines of a judicial opinion or extrapolating from a general jury verdict to find the dispositive

---

[30] *See, e.g.*, Amader v. Johns-Manville Corp., 541 F. Supp. 1384 (E.D. Pa. 1982) (partial summary judgment that defendant's asbestos product was defective) (Pennsylvania law); Hardy v. Johns-Manville Sales Corp., 509 F. Supp. 1353 (E.D. Tex. 1981), *rev'd in part*, 681 F.2d 334 (5th Cir. 1982) (applying federal collateral estoppel law to medical and defensive issues); Flatt v. Johns-Manville Sales Corp., 488 F. Supp. 836 (E.D. Tex. 1980) (partial summary judgment, based on collateral estoppel, that asbestos products of defendants were defective and unreasonably dangerous and caused lung diseases); Mooney v. Fibreboard Corp., 485 F. Supp. 242 (E.D. Tex. 1980) (summary judgment, based on collateral estoppel, that defendants' asbestos products were defective and unreasonably dangerous).

[31] 681 F.2d 334 (5th Cir. 1982).

[32] *Id.* at 336.

[33] An initial issue is whether to apply the state or federal law of preclusion. Given the constitutional due process issues at stake, particularly in questions of nonparty preclusion, the Supreme Court's guidelines in *Parklane* and *Blonder-Tongue* should be considered in any forum. One commentator has suggested that a uniform federal law should govern preclusion analysis. *See* Stephen B. Burbank, *Interjurisdictional Preclusion, Full Faith and Credit and Federal Common Law: A General Approach*, 71 Cornell L. Rev. 733 (1986).

[34] 681 F.2d at 345. The Court also held that collateral estoppel was inappropriate because of the presence of inconsistent verdicts and because, due to the small amount of the *Borel* claim, the defendants could not have foreseen the estoppel effect. *Id.* at 345-47.

[35] Green, *supra*, note 27 at 188-90 (problem exacerbated when preclusion attempted between states because product liability law will vary).

[36] Victor E. Schwartz & Liberty Mahshigian, *Offensive Collateral Estoppel: It Will not Work in Product Liability*, 31 N.Y.L. Sch. L. Rev. 583, 584 (1986); *See* Richard C. Ausness, *Cigarette Company Liability: Preemption; Public Policy and Alternative Compensa-tion Systems*, 39 Syracuse L. Rev. 897, 968 (1988) (use of offensive collateral estoppel not likely to facilitate management of cigarette litigation on issue of adequacy of warning because question may depend on unique circumstances of a plaintiff's knowledge).

issue.[37] Courts faced with other mass tort repetitive litigation have rejected estoppel because of the difficulty of finding identical issues.[38]

Underlying these decisions is the consideration of judicial economy. Collateral estoppel deprives the litigant of the opportunity of a trial and can be justified only if it decreases the burden on the parties and the court. Offensive collateral estoppel, however, because it frequently deals with preliminary issues (*e.g.*, asbestos may cause lung disease), does not resolve cases or even preclude expert testimony.[39] Asbestos plaintiffs, for example, still must elicit expert testimony about their medical history and condition, and the nature and effect of their exposure to specific asbestos products. In most cases involving the admissibility of expert scientific evidence, offensive preclusion would present little efficiency. In toxic tort cases, where the admissibility issue appears most frequently, a plaintiff who obtained preclusion on the admissibility of expert testimony on medical causation would still face trial, and the need for expert testimony from both sides, on exposure and specific causation for the plaintiff.[40]

2. Defensive Use. Defensive collateral estoppel encourages efficiency because it may preclude the need for repetitive trials if a defendant

---

[37] Kurt Erlenbach, *Offensive Collateral Estoppel and Products Liability: Reasoning with the Unreasonable*, 14 St. Mary's L.J. 19, 27-28 (1982) (finding an identity of issues is probably the most vexatious requirement of collateral estoppel in products liability cases).

[38] *See Quadrigen* — Ezagui v. Dow Chemical Corp., 598 F.2d 727 (2d Cir. 1979) (no collateral estoppel as to chemical defect of drug, but estoppel as to inadequacy of warning); Vincent v. Thompson, 50 A.D.2d 211, 377 N.Y.S.2d 118, 126 (2d Dept. 1975) (ultimate issue in prior decision "vastly different" from instant case). The Quadrigen cases involving a childhood vaccine are discussed in Erlenbach, *supra* note 37.
Swine Flu Vaccine — Erbeck v. United States, 533 F.Supp. 444 (S.D. Ohio 1982) (no collateral estoppel when prior case did not directly address questions currently at issue).
DES — Wetherill v. University of Chicago, 548 F.Supp. 66, 68-69 (N.D. Ill. 1982) (no collateral estoppel when plaintiffs cannot establish identity of issues supposedly determined in prior case); Kortenhaus v. Eli Lilly & Co., 228 N.J. Super. 162, 549 A.2d 437, 440-41 (1988) (prior opinion not reliable support for collateral estoppel).
But see Fraley v. American Cynamid Co., 570 F.Supp. 497, 502 (D. Colo. 1983) (collateral estoppel in Orimune polio vaccine case; court found sufficient identity of issues and distinguished inconsistent prior verdicts).

[39] *See* Green, *supra* note 27, at 151 ("while defensive issue preclusion frequently disposes of the entire case, offensive preclusion typically only eliminates one of the elements that plaintiff must establish").

[40] In the Bendectin cases, the initial issue was whether expert testimony was sufficient to establish a causal link generally between Bendectin and birth defects in humans. *See, e.g., Daubert*, 113 S.Ct. at 2791-92. In the few cases in which expert testimony on this issue was held sufficient, the plaintiffs still had to proceed through trial and an extensive appellate review. *See* Oxendine v. Merrell Dow Pharmaceuticals, 506 A.2d 1100 (D.C. App. 1986) (verdict of $750,000 for plaintiff, judgment n.o.v. for defendant reversed on appeal).

caneliminate an essential element of a plaintiff's claim.[41] But restraints on the doctrine after *Parklane* have prevented effective defensive preclusion as illustrated by the Bendectin cases.[42] Although prior cases had thoroughly examined the specific scientific evidence issues (and refuted plaintiffs' claims of medical causation), federal appellate courts felt constrained under established collateral estoppel doctrine to deny its binding effect on nonparties to prior litigation.[43] These cases illustrate how a thorough *Daubert* analysis should be used to foreclose reconsideration of a scientific evidence issue, and the waste of judicial (and party) resources when preclusion is rejected.

Probably no specific issue of scientific causation has been more litigated than the purported link between Bendectin and birth defects.[44] Plaintiffs filed almost 2,000 such claims and won some initial cases, but by the late 1980s courts were uniformly rejecting their scientific theory, often by summary judgment.[45] In Cincinnati, Ohio, in February and March 1985, more than 800 consolidated cases were tried in what was termed "the MDL

---

[41] See generally Richard D. Freer, *Avoiding Duplicative Litigation: Rethinking Plaintiff Autonomy and the Court's Role in Defining the Litigative Unit*, 50 U. Pitt. L. Rev. 809 (1989) (defensive use of nonmutual issue preclusion probably promotes packaging). Defendants have also had difficulty, however, with identity of issues. *See* Monahan v. Eagle Picher Industries, Inc., 21 Ohio App. 3d 179, 486 N.E.2d 1165 (1984), in which state asbestos defendants moved to estop collaterally a plaintiff following a finding of no liability in a companion federal case against three other asbestos suppliers. The court rejected estoppel on the ground that the first jury verdict addressed only specific causation as to the federal defendants and thus did not reach the liability issues as to the state defendants. 486 N.E.2d at 1167-69.

[42] Plaintiffs have also attempted unsuccessfully to use offensive collateral estoppel in the Bendectin cases based on the early plaintiff verdict in Oxendine. *See* Raynor v. Richardson-Merrell, Inc., 643 F. Supp. 238, 246 (D.D.C. 1986) (offensive collateral estoppel on medical causation rejected as unfair to defendant because of inconsistent prior decisions).

[43] *See, e.g.,* DeLuca v. Merrell Dow Pharmaceuticals Inc., 911 F.2d 941, 952 (3d Cir. 1990) (reversing and remanding summary judgment to consider admissibility and sufficiency of expert testimony regarding Bendectin causation and birth defects when district court relied upon prior cases that found same evidence inadmissible or insufficient to grant summary judgment); Lynch v. Merrell-National Labs., 830 F.2d 1190 (1st Cir. 1987) (summary judgment not proper on collateral estoppel grounds when plaintiffs did not have a full and fair opportunity to litigate Bendectin causation of birth defects in prior proceeding).

[44] *See* Joseph Sanders, *The Bendectin Litigation: A Case Study in the Life Cycle of Mass Torts*, 43 Hastings L. J. 301, 359 (1992); DeLuca v. Merrell Dow Pharmaceuticals, Inc., 911 F.2d 941, 952 (3d Cir. 1990) (citing Lynch v. Merrell-National Labs., 830 F.2d 1190, 1192-93 (1st Cir. 1987) and *In re* Bendectin Prod. Liab. Litig., 732 F. Supp. 744, 746-48 (E.D. Mich. 1990)).

[45] *See* DeLuca v. Merrell Dow Pharmaceuticals, 131 F.R.D. 71, 73 (D.N.J. 1989), *rev'd*, 911 F.2d 941 (3d Cir. 1990) (citing Richardson v. Richardson-Merrell, Inc., 649 F. Supp. 799, 802 (D.D.C. 1986), *aff'd*, 857 F.2d 823, 832 (D.C. Cir. 1988) (j.n.o.v. in favor of Merrell Dow); Lynch v. Merrell Nat'l Labs., 646 F. Supp. 856, 866-67 (D. Mass. 1986), *aff'd*, 830 F.2d 1190, 1194 (1st Cir. 1987) (summary judgment in favor of Merrell Dow); Hull v. Merrell Dow Pharmaceuticals, 700 F. Supp. 28 (S.D. Fla. 1988) (summary judgment in favor of Merrell Dow); Bernhardt v. Richardson-Merrell, Inc., 723 F. Supp. 1188 (N.D. Miss. 1989) (summary judgment in favor of Merrell Dow);

Common Issues Trial," resulting in a jury verdict that Bendectin did not cause birth defects. That trial involved 22 trial days on the sole issue of causation and the testimony of 19 experts.[46] Following the MDL Common Issues Trial, several courts sought to apply claim preclusion principles to avoid relitigating this complex issue. In October 1986, a Massachusetts district court expressly applied collateral estoppel in granting summary judgment to Merrell Dow in *Lynch v. Merrell-National Laboratories*.[47] The court recognized the difficulty after *Parklane* of applying collateral estoppel to persons not parties or privies to a prior suit.[48] But the court observed that collateral estoppel could be appropriate if the plaintiffs had an opportunity to participate in the prior litigation and had elected as a matter of litigation strategy not to intervene.[49] The *Lynch* plaintiffs had actually participated in the discovery phase of the MDL Common Issues trial, so they were not outsiders and were aware of the progress of the prior litigation.[50] As the central issue of causation had been fully litigated in the consolidated trial, and the Lynches offered no new medical or scientific evidence, the doctrine of collateral estoppel applied to bar their claims.[51] The district court also found support for summary judgment in the lack of scientific evidentiary support for the plaintiffs' claims.[52] The First Circuit affirmed that ground but rejected the application of collateral estoppel.[53] The circuit court recognized the benefit for judicial economy, particularly where "the plaintiffs had ample opportunity to join the multi-district litigation and chose not to do so," but

---

Monahan v. Merrell-Nat'l Labs., Civ. 83-3108-WD (D. Mass. Dec. 18, 1987) (summary judgment in favor of Merrell Dow)).

[46] *In re* Bendectin Litig., 857 F.2d 290, 294 (6th Cir. 1988), *cert. denied*, 488 U.S. 1006 (1989); *Lynch v. Merrell Nat'l Labs.*, 646 F. Supp. at 858.

[47] 646 F. Supp. 856, 859-62 (D. Mass. 1986), *aff'd*, 830 F.2d 1190 (1st Cir. 1987).

[48] 646 F. Supp. at 859.

[49] *Id.* at 860.

[50] *Id.*, quoting National Wildlife Fed'n v. Gorsuch, 744 F.2d 963, 971-72 (3d Cir. 1983). The court also mentioned the possible applicability of the doctrine of "virtual representation," "where there has been adequate litigation" in the prior case. 646 F. Supp. at 861, citing 18 Wright, Miller & Cooper, § 4457 at 502 (1981). That principle, under the federal law of *res judicata*, holds that a nonparty may be bound by a judgment if a party is so closely aligned with its interest as to be its virtual representative. *See* Aerojet-General Corp. v. Askew, 511 F.2d 710, 719 (5th Cir.), *cert. denied*, 423 U.S. 908 (1975). That theory was proffered by the *Hardy* plaintiffs in support of offensive preclusion but was rejected by the Fifth Circuit. 681 F.2d at 340 (collateral estoppel may not be based on similar legal positions). Cases that have accepted the "virtual representation" theory have weighed such factors as a close relationship with a party, participation, acquiescence in the prior litigation, or tactical maneuvering to avoid the effects of the first action. *See* 18 Wright, Miller & Cooper, § 4457 (1981 & 1993 Supp).

[51] 646 F. Supp. at 862. The Court was apparently troubled by the Lynch plaintiffs' election to opt out of the MDL litigation, with the inference that they sought the "option effect" of accepting the MDL verdict if favorable or rejecting it if unfavorable. "This would be the type of tactical or procedural maneuvering that should be discouraged and not rewarded." *Id.*

[52] 646 F. Supp. at 862-67.

[53] Lynch v. Merrell-National Labs., 830 F.2d 1190 (1st Cir. 1987).

rejected estoppel because of unfairness arising from the "opt out" procedure of the consolidated litigation.[54] Both the Sixth Circuit and the trial court had recognized that the MDL litigation would not be binding on nonparties.[55] Thus the *Lynch* plaintiffs were not to be penalized if they thought they could opt out without prejudice.[56] The circuit court did not reject the idea that the causation issue had been determined in the prior litigation, and sustained the summary judgment after a review of the underlying evidence. The effect was estoppel, although the appellate court was hesitant to adopt the principle.

This pattern was repeated in the Third Circuit, but with a more wasteful outcome for judicial economy. In *DeLuca v. Merrell Dow Pharmaceuticals, Inc.*,[57] the trial court granted summary judgment for defendant Merrell Dow in an opinion focused primarily on the numerous prior decisions that uniformly found insufficient evidence of a causal link between Bendectin and limb reduction birth defects.[58] The district court did not base summary judgment solely on prior decisions, however,[59] but also briefly noted that plaintiffs' expert had no scientific support for his opinion and was not qualified as an epidemiologist to provide such support.[60] The Third Circuit reversed, after a lengthy discussion of evidentiary issues and only a brief reference to issue preclusion.[61] Although expressing "concern" over "the wastefulness of continued reconsideration of an identical scientific issue in the court," the court felt bound by the formal precedents of collateral estoppel to reject preclusion for plaintiffs not parties to prior litigation.[62] The court cited

---

[54] *Id.* at 1192.

[55] In rejecting class certification for the MDL plaintiffs, the Sixth Circuit noted that nonparty plaintiffs could not invoke a benefit from a favorable result. *In re* Bendectin Prods. Liab. Litig., 749 F.2d 300, 305 (6th Cir. 1984) (citing *Parklane* for rule that offensive collateral estoppel not available in mass torts). The trial judge had also refused to give the estoppel effect to defendants in subsequent cases. 830 F.2d at 1193. In *Parklane*, the Supreme Court mentions Professor Currie's railroad wreck paradigm as an example of the potential unfairness of applying offensive collateral estoppel when a defendant had won in other, inconsistent cases. 439 U.S. at 330 n.14. But the court did not say estoppel could not be applied in multiple plaintiff or mass tort situations.

[56] 830 F.2d at 1193.

[57] 131 F.R.D. 71 (D.N.J. 1989).

[58] *Id.* at 73.

[59] "Of course, the Court may not grant summary judgment in this matter solely on the basis of other courts' conclusions of law in similar cases." *Id.* at 74.

[60] *Id.* at 74.

[61] DeLuca v. Merrell Dow Pharmaceuticals, Inc., 911 F.2d 941 (3d Cir. 1990).

[62] "Principles of issue preclusion have not developed to the point where we may bind plaintiffs by the finding of previous proceedings in which they were not parties, even by a proceeding as thorough as the multi-district common issues trial." 911 F.2d at 952. Although the Third Circuit discussed the prior Bendectin opinion in *Brock* at length, it refused to adopt the *Brock* court's suggestion that appellate courts should resolve trial court splits in scientific evidence issues. *Id.* at 951-52. *See* Brock v. Merrell Dow Pharmaceuticals, Inc., 874 F.2d 307, 310, *modified*, 884 F.2d 166 (5th Cir. 1989), *cert. denied*, 494 U.S. 1046 (1990):

> Moreover, in mass torts the same issue is often presented over and over to juries in different cases, and the juries often split both ways on the issue. The effect of this

the First Circuit decision in *Lynch* as well as the Michigan district court decision by Judge Rubin, who presided over the MDL litigation, to reject preclusion based on the results of the MDL Common Issues Trial.[63] The Third Circuit ruled that with no issue preclusion support, the summary judgment could not stand; the trial court had not adequately stated the grounds for evidentiary exclusion.[64] The result is that on remand Merrell refiled its motion for summary judgment, and the trial court engaged in an exhaustive review and discussion of the causation evidence.[65] The outcome was the same —summary judgment for the defendant, later affirmed by the Third Circuit[66] —but adherence to formalism caused needless delay and expense to the courts and the parties.

The lesson of *Lynch* and *DeLuca* is that scientific issue preclusion, at least under the rubric of collateral estoppel, may be a difficult matter even when the scientific issues have been fully analyzed and their resolution is clear. Admissibility of expert testimony after *Daubert*, however, presents a rifleshot issue, and one that under the *Daubert* guidelines must be analyzed thoroughly with close adherence to scientific principles. The trustworthiness of a *Daubert* determination thus should be accorded significance in a preclusion analysis even as to nonparties to the initial case.

III. The Precedent Alternatives to Preclusion

The privity requirement, founded on Due Process principles, arises from the absolutely preclusive nature of collateral estoppel and res judicata. A more flexible approach[67] that may avoid the strictures of estoppel is to treat determinations of the admissibility of scientific evidence as precedents that

---

is to create a state of uncertainty among manufacturers contemplating the research and development of new, and potentially life-saving drugs. Appellate courts, if they take the lead in resolving those questions upon which juries will go both ways, can reduce some of the uncertainty . . . .
The Third Circuit apparently felt that *Brock* had been limited by the panel opinion in Christophersen v. Allied-Signal Corp., 902 F.2d 362 (5th Cir. 1990), *see DeLuca*, 911 F.2d 941, 951 n.11; but that opinion was rejected by the Fifth Circuit *en banc*. Christophersen v. Allied-Signal Corp., 939 F.2d 1106 (5th Cir. 1991)(*en banc*), *cert. denied*, ____ U.S. ____ , 112 S.Ct. 1280 (1992).

[63] 911 F.2d at 951-52. In *In re* Bendectin Products Liab. Litig., 732 F. Supp. 744 (E.D. Mich. 1990), Merrell Dow moved for summary judgment on the theory that plaintiffs should be collaterally estopped from litigating the issue of whether Bendectin causes birth defects. *Id.* at 745. Judge Rubin denied the motion, based on the principles of Montana v. United States, 440 U.S. 147 (1979), because the Michigan plaintiffs had no direct financial interest in or control over the MDL Common Issues trial.

[64] 911 F.2d at 952-59.

[65] DeLuca v. Merrell Dow Pharmaceuticals, Inc., 791 F. Supp. 1042 (D.N.J. 1992), *aff'd*, 6 F.3d 778 (3d Cir. 1993).

[66] 6 F.3d 778 (3d Cir. 1993).

[67] *See* Restatement (Second) of Judgments §28 cmt. b (1982) ("if the issue is one of the formulation or scope of the applicable legal rule, and if the claims are substantially unrelated, the more flexible principle of stare decisis is sufficient to protect the parties and

may be adopted or followed by subsequent courts under principles of judicial notice or stare decisis.[68] These interrelated doctrines offer the reviewing court the opportunity, but not the necessity, to accept the prior ruling and avoid redoing the perhaps elaborate scientific inquiry.

A.   Stare Decisis[69]

Stare decisis requires adherence to judicial precedent[70] and dictates that when a court decides an issue as a matter of law, that decision is binding on subsequent cases involving the same issue. A court's determination of an issue of law "is binding and conclusive in all subsequent suits involving the same subject matter, whether the parties and the property are the same or not."[71] If a case has similar facts to a prior decision of the court, the court should render a similar decision.[72]

Stare decisis has much broader application than the doctrine of collateral estoppel[73] because it has no fairness requirements regarding which parties are subject to the doctrine. Unlike collateral estoppel, *stare decisis* "is not narrowly confined to parties and their privies" and reaches "strangers to

---

the court from unnecessary burdens") and §29 cmt. i ("When the issue involved is one of law, stability of decision can be regulated by the rule of issue preclusion or by the more flexible rule of stare decisis").

[68] Precedent is a term usually discussed within the doctrine of stare decisis. *See* Ruggero J. Aldisert, *Precedent: What it Is and What It Isn't; When Do We Kiss It and When Do We Kill It?*, 17 Pepperdine L. Rev. 605 (1990). The two doctrines of notice and stare decisis interrelate, however; a court's adoption of prior "legislative" as opposed to "adjudicative" facts may be interpreted as more akin to stare decisis than notice. *See* Judge Becker's discussion in *In re* Asbestos Litigation, 829 F.2d 1233, 1245-52 (3d Cir. 1987), *cert. denied sub nom.* Owens-Illinois, Inc. v. Danfield, 485 US 1029 (1988); Robert E. Keeton, *Legislative Facts and Similar Things: Deciding Disputed Premise Facts*, 73 Minn. L. Rev. 1, 26 (1988) ("a premise-fact decision has force analogous to that of the decision of law"); Harold L. Korn, *Law, Fact and Science in the Courts*, 66 Col. L. Rev. 1080, 1105-07 (the distinction between announcing a rule of law and judicially noticing a proposition of fact may be "tenuous indeed"). At least one court has referred to judicial notice of a scientific fact as "a type of *stare decisis*." *See* United States v. Bell, 335 F.Supp. 797, 800-01 & n.2 (E.D.N.Y. 1971), *aff'd*, 464 F.2d 667 (2d Cir.), *cert. denied*, 409 U.S. 991 (1972) (judicial notice of prior court's finding that government "profile" did rely on characteristics related to the pre-flight apprehension of air pirates: "This type of *stare decisis* development is an application of black-letter law").

[69] *Stare decisis* is the Latin term that means, "to abide by, or adhere to, decided cases." Black's Law Dictionary 1261 (5th ed. 1979).

[70] United States v. O'Leary, 833 F.2d 663, 667 (7th Cir. 1987).

[71] Meadows v. Chevron, U.S.A., Inc., 782 F. Supp. 1189, 1192 (E.D. Tex. 1991) (citing Pomeroy Oil Corp. v. Pure Oil Co., 279 S.W.2d 886, 888 (Tex. Civ. App. — Waco 1955, writ ref'd)).

[72] Flowers v. United States, 764 F.2d 759, 761 (11th Cir. 1985).

[73] Peregoy v. Amoco Prod. Co., 742 F. Supp. 372, 374 (E.D. Tex. 1990), *aff'd*, 939 F.2d 196 (5th Cir. 1991).

earlier litigation."[74] The doctrine is usually invoked, however, on general principles of law[75] and seems unsuited for application to a fact-based determination such as the admissibility of scientific evidence in a given case. But there is no theoretical basis why a court could not use the doctrine to address specific evidentiary rulings.

The problem of stare decisis is the identification of the basis of the prior decision, the *ratio decidendi*, which becomes a precedent.[76] A case is important only for *what* it decides, not the *why* or *how*.[77] Nevertheless the material facts that form the basis of a court's decision are part of the ratio decidendi and ultimately the precedent. The principle of the case is found by determining the facts treated by the court as material and the decision based upon them.[78]

When the decision in the case is founded on the exclusion of scientific evidence, the ratio decidendi clearly includes the material facts that led to the exclusion. The doctrine thus will be most applicable when used defensively. For example, when a judge determines that an expert's theory that a substance caused a medical condition is unsupported by good science, resulting in exclusion and summary judgment, that ruling and the related material facts form a precedent.[79] The nature of the ruling thus will affect the scope but not the availability of stare decisis.[80]

---

[74] Meadows v. Chevron, U.S.A., Inc., 782 F. Supp. 1189, 1192 (E.D. Tex. 1991) (citing EEOC v. Trabucco, 791 F.2d 1, 2 (1st Cir. 1986)).

[75] 1B Moore's Federal Practice ¶ 0.402[2]. *See* State v. Phillips, 400 A.2d 299, 308 (Del. Ch. 1979):

> The prerequisite for stare decisis is a judicial opinion by the court, on a point of law, expressed in a final opinion . . . . [S]tare decisis is applicable only to questions of law, unlike res judicata, which is applicable to questions of both law and fact.

> . . . .

> It therefore follows that a case which merely settled factual questions and articulated or decided no question of law cannot be stare decisis as to a subsequent case.

[76] 1B Moore's Federal Practice ¶ 0.402[2], at I-26.

[77] Aldisert, *supra*, note 68, at 607.

[78] Arthur L. Goodhart, *The Ratio Decidendi of a Case*, 22 Mod. L. Rev. 117, 119 (1959).

[79] The defensive exclusion of scientific evidence will frequently be dispositive. *See* Christophersen v. Allied Signal Corp., 939 F.2d 1106 (5th Cir. 1991) (en banc), *cert. denied*, 112 S.Ct. 1280 (1992) (summary judgment after plaintiffs' sole expert on medical causation excluded). *Daubert* cited with approval cases decided solely on the insufficiency of expert evidence. 113 S.Ct. at 2798, citing Turpin v. Merrell Dow Pharmaceuticals, Inc., 959 F.2d 1349 (6th Cir.), *cert. denied*, 113 S.Ct. 84 (1992); Brock v. Merrell Dow Pharmaceuticals, Inc., 874 F.2d 307 (5th Cir.), *modified*, 884 F.2d 166 (5th Cir. 1989), *cert. denied*, 494 U.S. 1046 (1990).

[80] The holding may have broad precedential value if the judge determines that science does not show any link between a drug or chemical and a class of illnesses or injury, as in the Bendectin cases. *See Brock*, 874 F.2d at 315 ("We expect that our decision here will have a precedential effect on other cases pending in this circuit which allege Bendectin as the cause of birth defects"). The much narrower determination that the scientific evidence is insufficient to show causation in the facts of the particular plaintiff's exposure and illness

The difficulty for offensive use is not in the doctrine but in determining which issue was decided in the prior lawsuit. This was the specific problem with the offensive application of stare decisis in the Fifth Circuit asbestos cases. The trial court wished to use offensive preclusion to improve the efficiency of managing the massive number of asbestos cases in the Eastern District of Texas. Collateral estoppel was not a complete solution for defendants who had not participated in the initial plaintiffs' verdict in *Borel*, so the judge concluded his rulings in terms of stare decisis.[81] The judge ruled that the jury verdict in *Borel* established as a matter of law that defendants' products were unreasonably dangerous.[82] The Fifth Circuit reversed because *Borel* did not contain the broad conclusion found by the trial court.[83]

By contrast, the Third Circuit in addressing a similar asbestos issue in *In re Asbestos Litigation*[84] upheld preclusion based upon the precedents of a series of New Jersey Supreme Court rulings.[85] A New Jersey federal district court had certified to the Third Circuit the question whether the decisions of the New Jersey Supreme Court abolishing the state-of-the-art defense for all defendants in the asbestos personal injury cases violated the Equal Protection Clause.[86] The opinion by Judge Weiss answered in the negative, but the most detailed analysis of the precedential effect of the underlying decisions is in the concurrence by Judge Becker[87] and the dissent by Judge Hunter.[88]

---

would, of course, present limited stare decisis value. *See* Arthur L. Goodhart, *Determining the Ratio Decidendi of a Case*, 40 Yale L. J. 161, 181 (1930) ("It may be said that a doctrine which finds the principle of a case in its material facts leaves us hardly any general legal principles, for facts are infinitely various").

[81] *See* Migues v. Nicolet Indus., 493 F.Supp. 61 (E.D. Tex. 1980), *rev'd sub nom* Migues v. Fibreboard Corp., 662 F.2d 1182 (5th Cir. 1981); Flatt v. Johns-Manville Sales Corp., 488 F.Supp. 836 (E.D. Tex. 1980). Professor Green points out that the trial court overlooked the problem that stare decisis could not be based on the jury verdict in *Borel* because jury findings are not awarded the weight of law. Green, *supra* note 27, at 174-75 n. 199. Although the opinion dealt primarily with collateral estoppel, the district court in Mooney v. Fibreboard Corp., 485 F. Supp. 242 (E.D. Tex. 1980), also cited the *stare decisis* effect of *Borel* as an alternate ground for preclusion. *Id.* at 249. But if the issue was not fully and specifically determined in the first lawsuit, it should not be held conclusive thereafter under either principle. The *Mooney* "court's wellfounded doubt that due process would permit issue preclusion should apply equally to the *stare decisis* theory." 18 Wright, Miller and Cooper § 4457, at 499-500 n.17.

[82] *Flatt*, 488 F.Supp. at 841.

[83] 662 F.2d 1182, 1187-89 (1988) ("we must conclude that there is no such *decisis* in *Borel* to *stare*").

[84] 829 F.2d 1233 (3d Cir. 1987), *cert. denied sub nom.* Owens-Illinois, Inc. v. Danfield, 485 U.S. 1029 (1988).

[85] Beshada v. Johns-Manville Products Corp., 90 N.J. 191, 447 A.2d 539 (1982); Feldman v. Lederle Laboratories, 97 N.J. 429, 479 A.2d 374 (1984); Fischer v. Johns-Manville Corp., 103 N.J. 643, 572 A.2d 466 (1986) (manufacturers deemed to know of hazards of asbestos at relevant times).

[86] 829 F.2d at 1235.

[87] *Id.* at 1245-52.

[88] *Id.* at 1252-62.

Judge Becker justifies the ruling using the language of judicial notice describing the rulings of the New Jersey courts as based on findings of "legislative facts,"[89] but he effectively recognizes that the New Jersey rulings have stare decisis effect on the specific issue[90] and hence do not create constitutional problems like preclusion under collateral estoppel or res judicata.[91] The result is to recognize that offensive use of stare decisis is appropriate when based on material issues clearly determined by the prior court.

In the *Daubert* context, it would not be appropriate to assert that one court's determination that certain expert testimony is admissible in one case should have stare decisis effect on all subsequent similar litigation, regardless of the nature of the product or other matter at issue, the alleged injury or damages, and the variables surrounding causation. Stare decisis effect must be limited to the specific finding of the prior court as defined by the facts of that case. But if the prior issues are substantially similar to the case under consideration and the prior decision is unambiguous on a point of scientific evidence, then the doctrine of stare decisis may be applicable to avoid the necessity of relegating the evidentiary issue.

B. Judicial Notice

Judicial notice is a procedure that allows trial courts to accept facts without formal evidentiary proof in the pending case.[92] The procedure is

---

[89] Facts subject to judicial notice have been distinguished as "adjudicative" facts or "legislative" facts. See discussion at part III.B *infra*. Legislative facts are those relevant to legal reasoning in the formulation of a legal principal by a judge or court. Advisory Committee's Note to Federal Rule of Evidence 201.

[90] The ruling in *Beshada* was that the hazard of asbestos was knowable to all industry members, so they would be precluded in all cases from proffering state-of-the-art evidence to prove they did not or could not have known of such danger. 447 A.2d at 542, 546-47. *Beshada* describes the resolution of the question as a *principle* (derived from Freund v. Cellofilm Properties, Inc., 87 N.J. 229, 432 A.2d 925 (1981)) or *rule, id.* at 546-47, thus signalling its effect as precedent. *Feldman* later limited *Beshada* to the "circumstances giving rise to its holding," 479 A.2d at 388, which one federal judge interpreted to reflect that *Beshada* was decided on broad "circumstances," not facts: "[T]here were no facts which were decided in *Beshada* or the cases that were joined with it." *In re* Asbestos Venued in Middlesex County, 99 N.J. 201, 491 A.2d 200 (1984), transcript of proceedings of September 9, 1984, at 94-95 (quoted in *In re* Asbestos Litigation, 628 F.Supp. 774, 777-78 (D.N.J. 1986) (*Beshada* created common law rules; rule shall be "law of the case" for all asbestos litigation in District of New Jersey)).

[91] The argument made by Judge Hunter in dissent is that Judge Becker's invocation of the term "legislative facts" was an attempt to avoid the problems of collateral estoppel for asbestos manufacturers not parties in the New Jersey state cases. 829 F.2d at 1256.

[92] *See* 1 Weinstein & Berger ¶ 200[01] (1993). See the illustration of the precedential effect of judicial notice in United States v. Jakobetz, 955 F.2d 786, 799 (2d Cir. 1992), *cert. denied*, 113 S.Ct. 104 (1993) (given findings of district court and after careful review, "it appears that in future cases with a similar evidentiary issue, a court could properly take judicial notice of the general acceptability of the general theory and the use of these specific [DNA typing] techniques").

ingrained in common law — indeed, it simply reflects the thinking process of judicial decision marking[93] — and is now codified in Federal Rule of Evidence 201, which restricts notice to instances when a fact is "not subject to reasonable dispute in that it is either (1) generally known within the territorial jurisdiction of the trial court or (2) capable of accurate and ready determination by resort to sources whose accuracy cannot reasonably be questioned."[94] The procedure of Rule 201 is limited to *adjudicative* facts rather than *legislative* facts, reflecting an artificial distinction that may cause more confusion than clarity in dealing with scientific evidence. The distinction between classes of notice facts was coined by Professor Kenneth Davis.[95] *Adjudicative facts* are the facts related to the parties in a case,[96] while *legislative facts* are those that relate to general reasoning and the lawmaking process. But the identification of when a question of scientific evidence passes from merely party-related adjudication to a policy or "legislative" fact is difficult.[97] If a court determines that scientific research is insufficient to support the admission of expert testimony that a chemical could cause a plaintiff's illness or injury, is that an adjudicative fact about the "event which gave rise to the lawsuit" or a legislative fact addressing a general policy?[98]

One effect of the distinction is on the scope of discretion allowed the judge. Rule 201 is phrased narrowly: notice is not appropriate unless the accuracy of the noticed fact "cannot reasonably be questioned." An example of the

---

[93] "In conducting a process of judicial reasoning, as of other reasoning, not a step can be taken without assuming something which has not been proved." Thayer, A Preliminary Treatise on Evidence 279 (1898) (*quoted* in Kenneth Culp Davis, *Judicial Notice*, 55 Col. L. Rev. 945, 949 (1955)).

[94] Fed. R. Evid. 201.

[95] Kenneth C. Davis, *An Approach to Problems of Evidence in the Administrative Process*, 55 Harv. L. Rev. 364, 404-07 (1942). *See* discussion of the distinction in Advisory Committee's Note on Rule 201(a).

[96] Adjudicative facts are facts about a particular event giving rise to the lawsuit that help explain "who did what, when, where, how, and with what motive and intent." 2 McCormick on Evidence §328, at 385 (4th ed. 1992).

[97] *See* 2 McCormick on Evidence 388 (judicial notice of fact phenomenon has characteristics of universal solvent: it cannot be totally contained in any known vessel); 1 Stephen A. Saltzburg & Michael M. Martin, Federal Rules of Evidence Manuel 70-71 (5th ed. 1990) (labels may be difficult to apply in many cases); Kenneth J. O'Connell, *Patterns of Decision-Making: A Device for Teaching Appellate Judges et al*, 70 Or. L. Rev. 57, 156 (1991) ("Adjudicative facts may, however, also be legislative facts, as when the court uses the facts at hand as a premise for reshaping the rule of law").

[98] Judicial notice of nonadjudicative facts was not precluded by the enactment of Rule 201. *See* Keeton, *supra* note 68, at 38 ("The advisors were merely saying that no rule stated in the Federal Rules of Evidence applies to legislative fact determinations"). Instead certain subjects of notice were excluded as inappropriate for "formalized treatment." 1 Weinstein & Berger ¶ 200[05], 201[01], at 201-16 (excluded from formal requirements of Rule 201 is "extra-record information a judge utilizes in formulating evidential hypotheses by which he determines the admissibility and sufficiency of evidence"). Weinstein and Berger argue that a judge's legislative fact-finding function is outside the province of the law of evidence. *Id.* ¶ 200[03], at 200-17 n.13.

problem is the Fifth Circuit opinion in *Hardy*.[99] The district judge had held the defendants collaterally estopped on the issue that asbestos is a competent producing cause of asbestosis and mesothelioma.[100] In the alternative, the court held that the determination could be made by judicial notice: "Relying upon the wealth of authority on this issue which is not subject to question, judicial notice may be taken of the disease-relation as an alternative to collateral estoppel."[101]

The Fifth Circuit, citing the parameters of Rule 201, rejected the application of judicial notice. While notice is appropriate under Rule 201 for medical facts not in dispute, the doctrine applies only to "self-evident truths that no reasonably person·could question, truisms that approach platitudes or banalities."[102] If notice is to be limited to "truisms that approach platitudes," its application to scientific evidence disputes, which will by definition include disagreements about the scientific support for proposed expert testimony, will be limited or nonexistent.

Faced with a different set of asbestos fact precedents, dealing with whether the danger of asbestos exposure was "knowable" in the industry, Judge Becker identified prior New Jersey Supreme Court findings as legislative facts, citing Professor Davis for the view that judges may take into account, by notice, facts that they believe but which are not indisputable.[103] Once the New Jersey state court had made a factual assessment of the knowledge of the asbestos industry, "the court was also justified in precluding the relitigation of the factual basis of the state-of-the-art defense."[104] Judge Becker seems to be distinguishing legislative facts as those that have broad application, *e.g.*, an industry-wide question such as whether all asbestos suppliers should be held to have had knowledge of the health hazards of asbestos.[105] The issue of "knowability" of asbestos harm concerned not just one litigant but an entire industry, so knowability must be a legislative fact.[106] Of direct relevance, Judge Becker in his rationale expressly includes expert scientific issues in the category of legislative facts that merit precedential effect. "Thus, for example, the decision to admit into evidence novel scientific testimony is first tested by individual adjudications before judicial

---

[99] 681 F.2d 334 (5th Cir. 1982).

[100] *Hardy v. Johns Manville Sales Corp.*, 509 F.Supp. at 1360-62; *Flatt v. Johns Manville Sales Corp.*, 488 F.Supp. at 838-39.

[101] 509 F.Supp. at 1362-63 (footnote omitted). By citing Rule 201(b)(2) and (c), the judge seemed to determine that the ruling, although quite general in phrasing and effect, is one of adjudicative fact.

[102] 681 F.2d at 347.

[103] 829 F.2d at 1247 (quoting Kenneth Davis, A System of Judicial Notice Based on Fairness and Convenience, in Perspectives of Law 69, 82 (1964)).

[104] 829 F.2d at 1248.

[105] *Id.* at 1248-49 (quoting 3 Kenneth Davis, Administrative Law Treatise §15:5, at 152-53 (2d ed. 1980)).

[106] 829 F.2d at 1248.

recognition eliminates the need for a preliminary foundation."[107] Judge
Hunter in dissent criticized the decision as "a de facto exercise of collateral
estoppel without benefit of the procedural niceties."[108] Judge Hunter viewed
legislative facts more as broad concepts that "inform judicial policy-marking"
and rejected notice of legislative facts as a way to address the resolution of an
"ultimate fact."[109]

Professor Davis in considering the case, and the judicial notice controversy, seems to side with Judge Becker that the New Jersey courts could
make a legislative fact-finding that should be subject to notice.[110] Davis's
greatest criticism is reserved for the constraints of notice under Rule 201,
which he states should not have been restricted to adjudicative facts and have
resulted in faulty reasoning.[111]

Perhaps a better construct for judicial notice is provided by Judge Keeton
in his use of the descriptive term *premise facts* as a replacement for legislative
facts.[112] "Premise facts include all facts that serve as premises for a decision
of law — even when one or more of these facts is genuinely in dispute." Judge
Keeton believes that the distinction should not be based on the *nature* of the
question, but on whether the court used the facts as premises for deciding
issues of law.[113] Under this approach, a determination of whether good
science supported expert evidence would qualify as a premise fact subject to

---

[107] *Id.* at 1250 (citing *Downing*, 753 F.2d at 1234).

[108] *Id.* at 1255.

[109] *Id.* at 1256-57. Ultimate facts are those decisive to the outcome of a case because
their proof is absolutely necessary to establish the elements of a claim or defense. *Id.* at
1258-59 n.4. Of course, defensive use of judicial notice to preclude scientific expert
testimony will often result in the resolution of an ultimate fact.

[110] Kenneth Culp Davis, Administrative Law of the Eighties §15:1-1, at 365-67
(1989).

[111] *Id.* at 369-71. Professor Davis points out that almost 100% of courts' applications
of Rule 201 involve legislative facts. *Id.* at 369; *see, e.g.*, United States v. Perez, 769 F.2d
1336, 1340 (9th Cir. 1985) (judicial notice of "adjudicative" fact that travel between Rota
and Guam crossed international waters; finding is actually of legislative fact).

[112] Keeton, *supra* note 68.

[113] *Id.* at 14-17. Later in his discussion, Judge Keeton suggests, however, that the
"generality" of a fact finding may distinguish it. "Adjudicative facts are material
specifically to the case at hand (case facts or discrete facts) and, in contrast, premise facts
bear on the determination of what legal rule courts should apply to a specific case and other
like cases generally (general facts)." *Id.* at 19 n.50. Judge Keeton applied the notice fact
distinction in two subsequent copyright cases. *See* Lotus Dev. Co. v. Borland International,
Inc., 788 F.Supp. 78, 95 (D. Mass. 1992) (question of whether program contained
copyrightable elements should be considered a premise fact); Lotus Dev. Corp. v.
Paperback Software International, 740 F.Supp. 37, 73-74 (D. Mass. 1990) (proffered
expert opinion on policy arguments against restrictive copyright ruling admitted into the
record as evidence to be used in deciding legislative fact).

notice outside the constraints of Rule 201. The court would be determining facts forming the basis of a decision of law to admit or exclude evidence.[114]

The potential problem of judicial notice of legislative facts is procedural. Should a party have an opportunity to be heard on the propriety of judicial notice of a legislative or premise fact? A court conducting a judicial notice determination, outside the reach of Rule 201 or analogous state rules, is not bound to conduct further hearing or debate, but can merely adopt the premise fact-finding of prior decisions.[115] But, although formal rules of judicial notice do not apply to legislative or premise facts, courts should give litigants notice and an opportunity for a hearing when the facts are reasonably disputable.[116] Such a notice procedure as prescribed by Rule 201 is better suited for decisions based on science that must reflect advances in research; the parties must be allowed at least some opportunity to advise the court of new evidence or flaws in prior decisions that require a more complete reconsideration of the issue.

Courts have long applied judicial notice to receive well-known scientific and medical facts although seldom describing their rationale in terms of legislative or adjudicative fact finding.[117] Courts have specifically used judicial notice of prior judicial opinions in addressing the issue of general acceptance under *Frye*.[118] The Third Circuit in *United States v. Downing*

---

[114] Judge Keeton cites the admissibility of expert evidence as an illustration of the use of premise facts. "Premise facts also influence other decisions such as the admissibility of expert opinion testimony bearing on adjudicative-fact disputes." 73 Minn. L. Rev. at 11. *See also* discussion at 67-68 & 67 n.183. But if the fact-finding resolves admissibility only as to the case at hand, it may be more like an adjudicative decision and is not a precedent. *Id.* at 68.

[115] *See In re Asbestos Litigation*, 829 F.2d at 1249 (no further need for opportunity to comment when earlier decisions were conducted "with the full panoply of procedural protections"); O'Connell, *supra* note 97, at 157 ("whereas in the treatment of adjudicative facts courts are constrained by the principle of judicial notice and by the formal rules of evidence, no such constraint impedes the court's authority to rely on facts deemed suitable in shaping the policy underlying the rule of law under consideration"); 2 McCormick on Evidence § 333, at 408 ("there are cases where the legislative facts which form the bases of an appellate opinion first appear in the decision itself and counsel never have the opportunity to respond to them").

[116] Keeton, *supra* note 68, at 29-32.

[117] *See, e.g.*, Hines *ex rel.* Sevier v. Department of Health & Human Servs., 940 F.2d 1518, 1526 (Fed. Cir. 1991) (judicial notice of incubation period of measles, derived from medical textbook, appropriate under Federal Rules or "informal rules"); Franklin Life Ins. Co. v. William J. Champion & Co., 350 F.2d 115, 130 (6th Cir. 1965), *cert. denied*, 384 U.S. 928 (1966) ("common knowledge" that cancer slow to manifest itself); Bey v. Bolger, 540 F. Supp. 910, 916 (E.D. Pa. 1982) ("The Court can take judicial notice that a person suffering hypertension is susceptible to stroke, heart attack or other physical ailments").

[118] *See, e.g.*, Jones v. United States, 548 A.2d 35, 42, 44 (D.C. App. 1988) (EMIT drug test "generally accepted" based in part on "numerous cases from other jurisdictions"); Lahey v. Kelly, 71 N.Y.2d 135, 518 N.E.2d 924, 929 (1987) (court may find

discussed the binding effect of prior determinations of admissibility in terms of judicial notice.[119]

In *Jones v. United States*,[120] the appellate court noted that prior judicial opinions may be better support for judicial notice of general acceptance of scientific evidence than an extra-record review of scientific research, which may be problematic for the court.[121] *Jones* cites several cases that dispensed with expert testimony at trial based on prior decisions that were "sufficiently complete and persuasive,"[122] but cautioned against the use of notice of other opinions not based on expert testimony.[123] Otherwise, there is a danger of effectively delegating the decision making to another court "which itself ruled

---

scientific test reliable based on general acceptance as shown through legal writings and judicial opinions). *Compare* People v. Kelly, 129 Cal. Rptr. 144, 549 P.2d 1240 (1976) (review of cases establishes lack of general acceptance of voiceprint testimony) *with* Commonwealth v. Lykus, 367 Mass. 191, 327 N.E.2d 671, 678 (1975) (citing McCormick, Evidence § 203, at 491 (2d ed. 1972) for rule that general acceptance is proper condition for judicial notice, and acceptance of voiceprints established in part by other judicial opinions). Lykus is illustrative of the danger of giving too much credence to prior court analyses that may have failed to evaluate scientific evidence properly. Voiceprint testimony has been shown to be insufficiently accurate to be admissible. *See* Andre Moensens, *The Admissibility of Scientific Evidence: An Alternative to the Frye Rule*, 25 Wm. & Mary L. Rev. 545, 550-51 (1984).

[119] 753 F.2d 1224, 1237, 1239, 1241 (3d Cir. 1985); *see supra* note 5. *Downing* suggested that the trial court conduct a "preliminary inquiry focusing on, [*inter alia*,] the soundness and reliability of the process or technique used in generating the evidence." *Id.* at 1237. In determining such reliability, the court stated one factor to consider is that "the district [court] may take judicial notice of expert testimony that has been offered in earlier cases to support or dispute the merits of a particular scientific procedure." *Id.* at 1239. The court then suggested that the most efficient procedure for the court in making the reliability determination is an *in limine* hearing. *Id.* at 1241. At the hearing, the court may consider, *inter alia*, "the testimony presented to other courts that have addressed the same evidentiary issue, and the opinions of those courts on the subject. If a technique has found favor with a significant number of other courts, a district court may exercise its discretion to admit the evidence through judicial notice." *Id.*

[120] 548 A.2d 35, 44 (D.C. App. 1988).

[121] The court may fail to find relevant articles on the scientific issue. *Id.*

[122] *Id.* citing Spence v. Farrier, 807 F.2d 753, 756 (8th Cir. 1986) (reliance on other decisions to establish acceptance of double EMIT test); Lahey v. Kelly, 71 N.Y.2d 135, 524 N.Y.S.2d 30, 34, 518 N.E.2d 924, 929 (1987) (judicial opinions show acceptance of EMIT); Vasquez v. Coughlin, 118 A.D.2d 897, 898, 499 N.Y.S.2d 461, 462 (1986) (judicial decisions show acceptance of EMIT); People v. Walker, 164 Ill.App.3d 133, 135-37, 517 N.E.2d 679, 680-81 (1987) (acceptance of double EMIT test).

[123] *Id.*, citing Paul C. Giannelli, *The Admissibility of Novel Scientific Evidence: Frye v. United States, a Half-Century Later*, 80 Col. L. Rev. 1197, 1218-19 (1980). Professor Giannelli referred to expert opinion offered through scholarly writing or actual courtroom testimony. 80 Col. L. Rev. at 1218. The concern is that a decision based solely on other court rulings might accept a finding not adequately based on experts; thus the ruling would be based on a judge's view of science, not that of experts qualified in the field at issue. *See id.* at 1218-19. *See also* United States v. Porter, 618 A.2d 629, 634 (D.C. App. 1992) (consensus that will satisfy *Frye* is that of scientists not courts, for courtroom is not a research laboratory) (*quoting* People v. Reilly, 196 Cal. App. 3d 1127, 1135, 242 Cal. Rptr. 896, 500 (1987); United States v. Brown, 557 F.2d 541, 556 (6th Cir. 1977)). *Porter* upheld the admissibility of DNA typing evidence based on scientific testimony as

on the basis of an inadequate record."[124] The *Jones* court carefully reviewed prior expert testimony and prior scientific evidence submissions before concluding that EMIT drug tests were reliable and admissible.[125]

As with the application of *stare decisis*, courts should be circumspect in defining the exact issue of which they take judicial notice.[126] Judicial notice must not overstep the bounds of a prior holding. And judicial notice in the context of scientific evidence must effectuate the purpose of precedent; it should add efficiency and relieve the court of the need for adjudication of a material fact. In *Wooden v. Missouri Pacific Railroad*,[127] the Fifth Circuit acknowledged that judicial notice must mirror the issue previously decided as well as aid in the disposition of a relevant issue. In *Wooden*, the plaintiff requested the court to take judicial notice that "it was common knowledge in the 1950's that working in silicon dust subjected one to a substantial risk of contracting silicosis," based upon a New York state court opinion that held that "[i]t is a matter of common knowledge that it is injurious to the lungs and dangerous to health to work in silica dust, a fact which defendant was bound to know."[128] The problem was that the plaintiff sought judicial notice of a general truism that might not apply to the specifics of his case. Even if it was common knowledge that inhaling silica dust could lead to lung disease, that did not resolve whether "the particular concentration of dust to which Wooden was exposed entailed a specific risk of silicosis."[129] Judicial noticethus would only confuse the jury's consideration of the factual issue before them.[130]

The rationale of *Wooden* and *Laster* suggests that offensive use of judicial notice is of little utility when individual questions of causation (such as

---

well as prior cases. "The case law overwhelmingly supports the trial judge's conclusion that the 'match' technology is generally accepted." 618 A.2d at 636. *Compare* State v. Bible, 175 Ariz. 549, 858 P.2d 1152, 1188 (1993) (rejecting DNA evidence after review of recent decisions and scientific literature).

[124] 548 A.2d at 44.

[125] *Id.* at 45-46.

[126] Courts should be careful in taking notice of scientific "facts" that are derived from sources that can be misleading in the context of tort litigation. For example, lists of "harmful" or "toxic" substances maintained for "hazard" identification, such as the classifications established in the National Toxicology Program or maintained by the International Agency for Research on Cancer, do not reflect regulatory "findings" or standards for toxic tort litigation. *See* Anthony J. Thompson & Traci J. Stegemann, *Current Hazard Identification Programs: Potential Societal and Regulatory Consequences*, 8 Toxics L. Rep. 417 (BNA) (Sept. 8, 1993).

[127] 862 F.2d 560 (5th Cir. 1989).

[128] 862 F.2d at 563 (citing Sadowski v. Long Island R.R., 292 N.Y. 448, 55 N.E.2d 497, 500 (1944)). In declining to take judicial notice, the court observed that the defect in Wooden's request was that the fact to be noticed was "closely joined" to a controverted issue.

[129] 862 F.2d at 563.

[130] *Id.* citing Laster v. Celotex Corp., 587 F. Supp. 542, 543-44 (S.D. Ohio 1984) (taking "judicial notice that the inhalation of asbestos *may* cause asbestosis under certain conditions would have no appreciable impact on the length of expert testimony").

exposure) are present, as in a typical toxic tort case. Proof of toxic tort injury always requires a showing of exposure to the alleged toxin at a level known scientifically to be harmful.[131] From a defense perspective, however, a claim may be resolved, as in the Bendectin cases, by whether the substance at issue can be scientifically linked at any reasonable level of exposure with the claimed injury. If uncontroverted scientific evidence establishes no such link, the procedure of judicial notice *will* preclude the need for expert testimony or further factual determination.

IV. Judicial Economy and the *Daubert* Analysis

In determining the admissibility of scientific expert testimony under *Daubert*, the trial court considers both the qualifications of the expert witness to give the testimony and the scientific validity of the testimony. Doctrines of judicial economy may come into play in both determinations. An expert who has been found qualified in a particular substantive scientific area in repeated litigation may not need close scrutiny to pass muster under Rule 702. But qualifications are interrelated with the subject matter of the scientific testimony, and the court must be careful not to "rubber stamp" a witness with scientific credentials who may proffer testimony outside of his or her area of training or expertise. Judicial economy also dictates that a court give consideration to prior judicial investigations on a scientific issue, if such investigations were conducted with proper consideration of the scientific principles of *Daubert*. The reviewing court must also be mindful of new evidence that may obviate any binding effect, but the "new" evidence must itself be valid and relevant to mandate a reconsideration.

A. Qualifying the Expert

The threshold issue in the consideration of scientific expert testimony under Rule 702 is the qualification of the witness "by knowledge, skill, experience, training, or education" to provide assistance to the trier of fact. In cases turning on scientific evidence, such qualifications most often come in the form of educational credentials. Indeed, prior to *Daubert*, such credentials were sometimes taken as shorthand for the entire evidentiary review process: once the credentialed expert was found qualified, he or she could testify so long as the testimony was marginally relevant.[132] The credentials of an

---

131 *See* Casarett & Doull's Toxicology 13-15 (3d ed. 1986).

132 *See, e.g.*, Compagnie des Bauxites de Guinee v. Insurance Co. of N. Am., 721 F.2d 109, 116-17 (3d Cir. 1983) (once expert's qualifications established, opinion as to cause of loss held admissible under Rule 702). This approach was criticized in Bert Black, *A Unified Theory of Scientific Evidence*, 56 Fordham L. Rev. 595, 662-65 (1988) ("merely looking at an expert's qualifications, therefore, proves a poor surrogate for reviewing his or her reasoning").

expert may present no controversy, and courts should be able to review and accept prior judicial determinations on this issue.[133]

The court must assure, however, that the witness has actual qualifications rather than merely a title.[134] And in this analysis, if the court looks at prior determinations it faces two concerns: First, do prior court appearances show the witness is a "hired gun" rather than a credible expert; secondly, has the witness's prior testimony (and expertise) been directed at the specific issue before the court.

Prior court appearances by an expert witness may show professional stature,[135] but too often will be a signal that the witness is more a professional testifier than a scientist or physician. At the least, such a long judicial track record may demonstrate that the witness is an advocate for a particular position or litigious cause, and hence his or her testimony should be given little or no weight in a scientific evidence analysis.[136]

A court examining an expert's prior judicial qualifications should also consider whether such qualifications address the topic *sub judice*.[137] Courts may properly deny qualification when the witness, though having specialized training, does not have credentials or experience directed at subject matter germane to the facts of the case.[138] This qualification inquiry is intertwined

---

[133] *See* United States v. Foster, 939 F.2d 445, 451 (7th Cir. 1991) (witness had been qualified as an expert on approximately 50 prior occasions); Chrysler Credit Corp. v. Whitney Nat'l Bank, 824 F. Supp. 587, 601 (E.D. La. 1993) (witness had qualified as an expert on commercial banking "in a number of courts").

[134] "Rule 702 recognizes that it is the actual qualifications of the witness that count, rather than his title. . . ." 3 Weinstein & Berger ¶ 702[04], at 702-51 (1993).

[135] The qualifications and professional stature of the testifying expert is a separate factor in the *Daubert* calculus pursuant to the sources in footnote 12. *See Downing*, 753 F.2d at 1239; 3 Weinstein & Berger ¶ 702[02], at 702-19 nn.10-11 (1990); *Symposium on Science and the Rules of Evidence*, 99 F.R.D. 187, 231 (1983) (statement by Margaret Berger).

[136] *In re* Air Crash Disaster, 795 F.2d 1230, 1234 (5th Cir. 1986) (those "whose opinions are available to the highest bidder have no place testifying in a court of law, before a jury, and with the imprimatur of the trial judge's decision that he is an 'expert' "); Johnston v. United States, 597 F. Supp. 374, 411 (D. Kan. 1984) (rejecting testimony of expert witnesses who had "departed from the ranks of objective expert witnesses" and become "advocates for a cause"). While not dispositive, the background of claimant's expert was certainly an important issue in the decision for defendant on a DPT vaccine claim in Haim v. Department of Health & Human Services., No. 90-1031V, 1993 WL 346392, at *15 (Ct. Cl. Aug. 27, 1993) ("Dr. Geier has made a career of testifying in cases involving long-onset encephalopathy following DPT vaccine. . . . His testimony is merely subjective belief and unsupported speculation").

[137] For example, in *Wilkinson v. Rosenthal & Co.*, the court held that the expert witness, who had served as an expert in excessive trading cases involving investment portfolios substantially comprised of securities that were not commodity futures, was not necessarily qualified to give expert testimony about excessive trading involving commodity futures contracts. 712 F. Supp. 474, 478 (E.D. Pa. 1989).

[138] *See* Marc S. Klein, *After Daubert: Going Forward With Lessons From the Past*, ____ Cardozo L. Rev. ____ (1994) ("In cases at the frontiers of science, expert witnesses

with the factual predicate, because to be admissible the expert testimony must "fit" these facts.[139]

An illustration of this principle comes from the *eyewitness expert* cases. In recent years, criminal defendants have proffered psychological expert testimony to demonstrate the fallibility of eyewitness identification at the scene of the crime.[140] Such testimony initially met with resistance[141] but gradually gained judicial acceptance.[142] The pattern of the testimony generally is that several factors — including stress, presence of a weapon, photograph bias, and other memory problems — create such psychological difficulties that identification by an eyewitness present during the course of the crime should be accorded little credence.[143] The credentials of the "eyewitness" psychologists to address the arcana of their field are now generally accepted, but that does not satisfy the Rule 702 inquiry. If the stress factors in a particular case do not match the psychological paradigm that the psychologists have the training and experience to address, they should be excluded.[144] If an expert's

---

should possess *real* expertise in the *specific* areas of their anticipated testimony"); 3 Weinstein & Berger ¶ 702[04], at 702-51 to 702-52 n.16 (1988); McCullock v. H. B. Fuller Co., 981 F.2d 656, 657 (2d Cir. 1992) (witness without training or experience in adequacy of warning labels not qualified as expert in products liability suit); Thomas J. Kline, Inc. v. Lorilland, Inc., 878 F.2d 791, 800 (4th Cir. 1989), *cert. denied*, 493 U.S. 1073 (1990) (judgment reversed in part because testimony allowed from expert not qualified to testify about credit decisions in credit discrimination suit due to lack of experience, training, and education in credit practices); Union Carbide Corp. v. Tarancon Corp., 682 F. Supp. 535, 538 (N.D. Ga. 1988) (affidavit of chemistry professor excluded in patent infringement action); *In re* Lipetzky, 66 B.R. 648, 650 (D. Mont. 1986) (appraiser with no education in real estate appraisal and no experience in commercial appraisals not qualified to testify in favor of debtor's challenge to county tax valuation); Will v. Richardson-Merrell, Inc., 647 F. Supp. 544, 548 (S.D. Ga. 1986) (plastic surgeon not an expert regarding Bendectin teratogenicity and not familiar with studies of drug).

[139] 3 Weinstein & Berger ¶ 704[04], at 702-51 to 702-52 (1988). The court in *Downing* stated that the trial court must consider "whether expert testimony proffered in the case is sufficiently tied to the facts of the case that it will aid the jury in resolving a factual dispute." 753 F.2d at 1242. The *Downing* court referred to this as the "fit" question.

[140] *See, e.g.*, United States v. Dowling, 855 F.2d 114, 118-19 (3d Cir. 1988), *aff'd*, 493 U.S. 342 (1990).

[141] *See* discussion in State v. Chapple, 135 Ariz. 281, 660 P.2d 1208, 1218-24 (1983).

[142] *See* People v. McDonald, 37 Cal.3d 351, 690 P.2d 709, 208 Cal. Rptr. 236 (1984).

[143] *See, e.g.*, *State v. Chapple*, 660 P.2d at 1220-24.

[144] *See* United States v. Nguyen, 793 F. Supp. 497, 508 (D.N.J. 1992) (citing *Downing*, 753 F.2d at 1242) (expert eyewitness testimony inadmissible when proffered testimony regarding stress factor and presence of weapon did not fit facts of case); Pierce v. State, 777 S.W.2d 399, 416 (Tex. Crim. App. 1989), *cert. denied*, 496 U.S. 912 (1990); (exclusion of eyewitness expert who had "no specific knowledge of the testimony of witnesses," hence testimony did not "fit" the case); United States v. Dowling, 855 F.2d 114, 118-19 (3d Cir. 1988), *aff'd*, 493 U.S. 342 (1990) (exclusion of eyewitness expert proper when proffered testimony regarding factors of stress, weapon focus, and photo identification did not fit facts of case); United States v. Poole, 794 F.2d 462, 468 (9th Cir. 1986) (exclusion of eyewitness expert proper when expert did not propose to testify regarding actual witness testimony in case).

qualifications, no matter how valid or extensive, do not address the facts of the case, or a subject relevant to the facts of the case, the evidence is inadmissible.[145]

B. Preclusion of the Scientific Validity Issue

The key inquiry for the admissibility of scientific evidence under *Daubert* is scientific validity.[146] The criteria of validity, while flexible, provide a solid framework to assure that the evidence is based on good science. The analysis mandated by the Supreme Court is stringent and, according to the *Daubert* factors discussed or referenced, may well be guided by objective information such as peer-reviewed scientific literature and published data on error rates. For some scientific evidence questions this background information is stable; a court should have little reason to repeat a thorough review of the data or do its own "meta-analysis" on a point of scientific evidence that is properly established. Thus a point of scientific evidence reviewed under *Daubert* is one of the more appropriate issues for preclusion.

The question will often arise as in the context of the Bendectin controversy: whether a chemical, drug, or toxin can be causally linked to a plaintiff's medical condition. Evidence of human medical causation can be a difficult and complex area of judicial investigation. Accordingly, when a court has made a determination on such an issue after a rigorous examination of supporting research and science, claim preclusion is particularly appropriate in the interest of avoiding costly repetition. Expert scientific evidence of causation is precisely the type of evidence that requires doctrines of judicial economy to relieve courts from repeating a *Daubert* analysis. At least one post-*Daubert* case has already recognized the benefits of judicial economy in determining the admissibility of scientific evidence of causation.[147]

In *Elkins v. Richardson-Merrell, Incorporated*,[148] the lower court granted summary judgment in favor of the defendant based upon two recent Bendectin cases that had granted summary judgment for the defendant on the basis of the weakness of the causal link between Bendectin and birth defects.[149] The plaintiff appealed on the basis that under *Daubert*, the

---

[145] *See* United States v. Cozminski, 821 F.2d 1186, 1188, 1199 (6th Cir. 1987) (expert on "captivity syndrome" excluded because no evidence that persons held captive).

[146] 113 S.Ct. at 2795 & n.9 ("In a case involving scientific evidence, *evidentiary reliability* will be based upon scientific validity").

[147] Elkins v. Richardson-Merrell, Inc., 8 F.3d 1068 (6th Cir. 1993), *petition for cert. filed*, 62 U.S.L.W. 3511 (U.S. Jan. 18, 1994) (No. 93-1172).

[148] 8 F.3d at 1068.

[149] *Id.* 1069-70 (citing Lee v. Richardson-Merrell, Inc., 772 F. Supp. 1027 (W.D. Tenn. 1991), *aff'd*, 961 F.2d 1577 (6th Cir.), and *cert. denied*, ____ U.S. ____, 113 S.Ct. 197 (1992) and Turpin v. Merrell Dow Pharmaceuticals, Inc., 736 F. Supp. 737 (E.D. Ky. 1990), *aff'd*, 959 F.2d 1349 (6th Cir.), and *cert. denied*, ____ U.S. ____, 113 S.Ct. 84 (1992)). The court pointed out that in *Turpin,* the court found additional authority in Wilson v. Merrell Dow Pharmaceuticals, Inc., 893 F.2d 1149, 1154 (10th Cir. 1990)

defendant's expert scientific opinions were inadmissible and, therefore, the defendant had failed to show the absence of a material issue of fact,[150] and that the trial court improperly took a "hard look" at plaintiff's scientific evidence.[151]

The Sixth Circuit Court of Appeals agreed with the lower court that the two recent Bendectin cases relied upon in granting summary judgment controlled in the case at bar, and further held that *Daubert* did not require a remand.[152] The court pointed out:

> The proof in this case is identical to the proof offered in the two other recent Bendectin cases in this circuit — *Turpin* and *Lee*. [footnote omitted] In all three cases, as in myriad Bendectin cases in other circuits, the plaintiffs rely on *in vitro* (in the test tube) studies, *in vivo* (animal) studies, and reanalyses of human epidemiological studies. The defendants, on the other hand, rely on more than 30 human epidemiological studies, all of which concluded that there was no identifiable link between Bendectin and birth defects. [footnote omitted] Relying almost exclusively on *Turpin*, the magistrate recommended that summary judgment be issued in Merrell's favor. The district court found "no material differences" between *Elkins* and *Lee*, and relying also on *Turpin*, accepted the magistrate's recommendation.[153]

Because the court found the facts in *Elkins* to be indistinguishable from *Turpin* and *Lee*, "both factually, and regarding the scientific evidence presented," the summary judgment was affirmed.[154]

C. Scrutiny Required

The ability of a court to rely on a prior *Daubert* analysis does not discharge the court's responsibility to scrutinize the bases and accuracy of the earlier

---

(finding "particularly significant" the "absence of epidemiological evidence showing a causal relationship between Bendectin and birth defects"); Brock v. Merrell Dow Pharmaceuticals, Inc., 874 F.2d 307, 315 (5th Cir. 1989), *cert. denied*, 494 U.S. 1046 (1990) (verdict for plaintiff set aside by j.n.o.v. — "we are convinced that the Brocks did not present sufficient evidence regarding causation to allow a trier of fact to make a reasonable inference that Bendectin caused [a] limb reduction defect"), and considered Daubert v. Merrell Dow Pharmaceuticals, Inc., 951 F.2d 1128 (9th Cir. 1981), *vacated*, ____ U.S. ____ , 113 S.Ct. 2786 (1993), and DeLuca v. Merrell Dow Pharmaceuticals, Inc., 911 F.2d 941 (3d Cir. 1990).

[150] 8 F.3d at 1070.

[151] *Id.*

[152] *Id.* at 1073.

[153] 8 F.3d at 1070. The court pointed out that in *Turpin* and *Lee*, seven different judges sitting on the court adhered substantially to the view of Judge Merritt, who authored the *Turpin* opinion. Further, the court noted that it did not count in that number "the three different additional judges on this court who considered and affirmed the class action jury verdict for the defendant on the issue of causation of human birth defects by ingestion of Bendectin." *Id.* n.3 (citing *In re* Bendectin Litig., 857 F.2d 290 (6th Cir. 1988), *cert. denied*, 488 U.S. 1006 (1989)).

[154] 8 F.3d at 1071.

determination.[155] Prior to *Daubert*, courts recognized the utility of examining decisions from other courts in determining the reliability of scientific evidence.[156] To be reliable under *Daubert*, a prior expert evidence determination must be based on scientific principles establishing that the scientific reasoning is well founded. If the determination is based on the glibness and demeanor of the expert witness or a theory not supported in scientific literature, it must not be replicated through the courts under principles of preclusion.

Blind adherence to a prior ill-founded admission of scientific evidence can have disastrous results. A prime example is the testimony of purported expert Dr. Louise Robbins whose unsupported anthropological musings were accepted in criminal cases for over 10 years.[157] Dr. Robbins was a qualified anthropologist, but her opinions about footprints and footprint identification were supported by no special education, no research, peer-reviewed or otherwise, and were shared by no other scientist. Yet she claimed to have testified in two dozen criminal trials with good results for the prosecution: . . . "There were convictions in all the cases I know of ."[158] Robbins explained that her studies had not been published in scientific journals because her work was primarily in law enforcement.[159] Although defense counsel challenged Robbins, based properly on the assertion that there was no such area of expertise as footprint identification,[160] her testimony was never excluded.[161] Although her claims have now been thoroughly debunked in the

---

[155] *See* discussion of caution to be used in applying prior decisions on scientific evidence in Giannelli, *supra* note 123, at 1218-19.

[156] Cherico v. National R.R. Passenger Corp., 758 F. Supp. 258, 261 (E.D. Pa. 1991) (considering conclusions of other courts regarding the admissibility of thermographic tests) (citing *Downing*, 753 F.2d at 1238-39); Windmere, Inc. v. International Ins. Co., 105 N.J. 373, 522 A.2d 405, 408 (1987) (considering judicial decisions that show lack of general acceptance of voiceprint analysis). Some courts and commentators have cautioned, however, that the appropriate inquiry is not one of the acceptance of prior judicial opinion, but of the acceptance of scientific opinion. *See, e.g.*, People v. Reilly, 196 Cal. App. 3d 1127, 242 Cal. Rptr. 496, 500 (1987); *see also* Edward R. Becker & Aviva Orenstein, *The Federal Rules of Evidence After Sixteen Years —The Effect of "Plain Meaning" Jurisprudence, the Need for an Advisory Committee on the Rules of Evidence, and Suggestions for Selective Revision of the Rules*, 114 F.R.D. 519 (1992); *reprinted from* 60 Geo. Wash. L. Rev. 857 (1992).

[157] Mark Hansen, *Believe it or Not*, 79 ABA J. 64 (June 1993).

[158] Vicki Quade, *If the Shoe Fits*, 71 ABA J. 34 (July 1985).

[159] *Id.*

[160] *See, e.g.*, State v. Bullard, 312 N.C. 129, 322 S.E.2d 370, 374 (1984). The appellate court observed that Robbins' "forensic experience included analyzing and testifying in at least four other states." 322 S.E.2d at 275 n.3.

[161] 79 ABA J. at 65; *but see* People v. Ferguson, 172 Ill.App.3d 1, 526 N.E.2d 525 (1988) (Robbins' identification of defendant by "wear pattern" of shoes rejected on appeal; theory not generally accepted in scientific community or by *"any other manner"* of field) (emphasis in original).

scientific community, courts allowed her testimony in significant criminal cases based in part on deference to prior judicial evaluation.[162]

A court reviewing a question of the admissibility of scientific evidence must be sure that the prior court's analysis followed the *Daubert* guidelines in determining the scientific validity of the proffered evidence. If the prior court failed to analyze the scientific bases of the evidence, and instead focussed on trivialities such as the expert's demeanor on the witness stand, then preclusive effect is not appropriate.

An example of an admissibility determination that should not be given preclusive effect is the trial court's evaluation in *Wells v. Ortho Pharmaceutical Corp.*[163] In *Wells*, the court allowed expert testimony that spermicidal jelly caused birth defects to support a $4.7 million judgment in the face of a widely held scientific view that spermicides do not cause birth defects. The district judge ignored the lack of qualifications of the plaintiffs' expert as well as scientific literature that negated plaintiffs' hypothesis of causation.[164] The decision was instead based largely on the "tone and demeanor" and "possible biases" of the expert witnesses.[165]

The Eleventh Circuit upheld the judgment despite the fact that the lower court "found [the expert testimony] to be inconclusive on the ultimate issue of whether the product caused [the plaintiff's] birth defects."[166] The trial court, therefore, was "forced to make credibility determinations" of the competing experts.[167] Instead of analyzing the scientific bases of the plaintiffs' expert testimony, the court of appeals merely listed the expert

---

[162] *See, e.g.*, United States v. Ferri, 778 F.2d 985, 988-89 (3d Cir. 1985), *cert. denied*, 476 U.S. 1172, and *cert. denied*, 479 U.S. 831 (1986) (upholding admission of Dr. Robbins' testimony based on *Downing* and taking judicial notice of three prior opinions allowing her testimony) (citing People v. Knights, 166 Cal. App. 3d 46, 212 Cal. Rptr. 307, 312 (1985), State v. Bullard, 312 N.C. 129, 322 S.E.2d 370 (1984); and State v. Maccia, 311 N.C. 222, 316 S.E.2d 241 (1984) (Robbins testified criminal defendant made imprints *inside* shoes)). In People v. Barker, 170 Cal. Rptr. 69 (Ct. App. 1980), the court of appeals noted that Dr. Robbins was the chief proponent of the "unique shoeprint" concept, "in that she was the only person presently working on this subject," but allowed her testimony on the basis that jurors could follow her comparisons of photographs and castings, unlike other forms of scientific tests. *Id.* at 71-72. *Barker* also emphasizes that Robbins had consulted "on a number of other cases." *Id.* at 72.

[163] 615 F. Supp. 262 (N.D. Ga. 1985).

[164] See the thorough discussion of *Wells* in Barry L. Shapiro and Marc S. Klein, *Epidemiology in the Courtroom: Anatomy of an Intellectual Embarrassment*, I Pharmacoepidemiology 87 (1989).

[165] 615 F. Supp. at 269-91 (plaintiffs' experts: "demeanor excellent," answered questions "fairly and openly in a balanced manner," manner "suggested objectivity and openness"); Shapiro & Klein, *supra* note 164, at 108-09.

[166] 788 F.2d 741, 745 (11th Cir.), *cert. denied*, 479 U.S. 950 (1986); *see* Bert Black, *A Unified Theory of Scientific Evidence*, 56 Fordham L. Rev. 595 (1988) (criticizing *Wells* for its passive acceptance of medical testimony).

[167] 788 F.2d at 745.

witnesses and studies relied upon by the plaintiffs, and stated that it was "satisfied that the district court's extensive credibility determinations are not clearly erroneous."[168]

D. New Evidence May Allow Reanalysis

Once a court conducts a proper *Daubert* analysis, the ability to relitigate that issue should not be completely foreclosed. If new scientific developments appear that did not exist at the time the analysis was conducted, then a reanalysis should be allowed to consider the new evidence. Courts have declined to apply collateral estoppel in the face of new evidence.[169] The new evidence, however, must rise to the level of scientific validity and not constitute a mere regurgitation of old arguments or a rehash of earlier studies that had supported the original determination.

The Bendectin cases contain some illustrations of the type of allegedly "new evidence" that does not merit re-evaluation. Plaintiffs offered Dr. Alan K. Done as an expert witness on the issue of Bendectin causation and birth defects.[170] One of the bases of Dr. Done's causation opinion was that according to his methodology, a grouping of data from all epidemiologic studies of Bendectin conclusively established an association with birth defects.[171] Although none of the underlying epidemiologic studies from which Dr. Done conducted his methodology concluded that a causal association with birth defects exists, Dr. Done determined that a reanalysis of these same studies showed such a causal link.[172] The *DeLuca* court's

---

[168] In contrast to the superficial analysis conducted by the district court judge in *Wells,* compare the review of scientific evidence by Judge Ward, also of the Northern District of Georgia, in Smith v. Ortho Pharmaceutical Corp., 770 F. Supp. 1561 (N.D. Ga. 1991). *Smith* involved the exact same issues as *Wells* —birth defects allegedly caused by Ortho Pharmaceutical Corp.'s spermicide. Whereas Judge Shoob in *Wells* focused on the credibility of the expert witnesses, *e.g.,* "[the plaintiff's expert] answered all questions fairly and openly in a balanced manner, translating technical terms and findings into common, understandable language, and he gave no hint of bias or prejudice," Judge Ward conducted an in-depth analysis of the epidemiological and genetic studies relied upon by the plaintiffs' experts and concluded that the evidence was not admissible. *See* Wells v. Ortho Pharmaceutical Corp., 615 F. Supp. 262, 273 (N.D. Ga. 1985), *aff'd in part, modified in part & remanded,* 795 F.2d 89 (11th Cir.), *cert. denied,* 479 U.S. 950 (1988); *Smith,* 770 F. Supp. at 1572-81. Although *Smith* expressly states that it is not in conflict with *Wells,* two of the three causation experts relied upon by the plaintiffs in *Wells* were the same witnesses used in *Smith.*

[169] Zweig v. E.R. Squibb & Sons, Inc., 222 N.J. Super. 306, 536 A.2d 1280 (1988); *see also* M. Stuart Madden, *Issue Preclusion in Products Liability,* 11 Pace L. Rev. 87 (1987).

[170] *See, e.g.,* Richardson v. Richardson-Merrell, Inc., 857 F.2d 823, 826 (D.C. Cir. 1988); DeLuca v. Merrell Dow Pharmaceuticals, Inc., 791 F. Supp. 1042, 1043 (D.N.J. 1992), *aff'd,* 6 F.3d 778 (3d Cir. 1993), *cert. denied,* 114 S.Ct. 691 (1994).

[171] *DeLuca,* 791 F. Supp. at 1046-47.

[172] *Id.* Dr. Done's methodology is a type of *meta-analysis,* a technique which analyzes the results of multiple studies. Michael D. Green, *Expert Witnesses and Sufficiency of Evidence in Toxic Substances Litigation: The Legacy of Agent Orange and Bendectin Litigation,* 86 Nw. U. L. Rev. 643, 685 n.184 (1992). Meta-analysis combines the results of the

examination of Dr. Done's methodology, however, uncovered blatant flaws and errors, and the court held that his testimony was inadmissible.[173] When a body of scientific research supports a given conclusion under a *Daubert* analysis, a court should rightfully be skeptical of "new evidence" that consists solely of a re-analysis of prior research, which reaches different conclusions than the original researchers.

"New evidence," if it is to rise to such a level of significance as to mandate reconsideration of an accepted rule of scientific evidence, must also be of a type that is directly pertinent to the issue. For example, in addressing the issue of human medical causation, new evidence that does not deal with human medical research should be accorded little weight. Animal studies that purport to contradict the results of human epidemiologic research should not alter the *Daubert* calculus.[174] Courts have recognized the limited usefulness of animal studies in cases of human injury and have held such studies to be inadmissible,[175] and at least one post-*Daubert* case has held that animal studies fail the *Daubert* criteria.[176]

If new evidence is grounded in scientific validity, however, it should be considered. In *Zweig v. E.R. Squibb & Sons, Inc.*,[177] the plaintiff in a New Jersey state court suit sought to invoke offensive collateral estoppel against a defendant on the basis that a Utah judgment found that the drug Delalutin caused limb reduction and other birth defects.[178] The court did not invoke collateral estoppel because new biological studies showed Delalutin did not cause limb reduction.[179] The court held: "Later scientific discoveries that cast

---

studies to provide a best estimate from the multiple studies. *Id.* The technique is subject to misuse and, in fact, has been misused. *Id.*

[173] 791 F. Supp. at 1047-54, 1056-59.

[174] *See In re* "Agent Orange" Product Liab. Litig., 611 F. Supp. 1223, 1231 (E.D.N.Y. 1985), *aff'd on other grounds*, 818 F.2d 187 (2d Cir. 1987), *cert. denied*, 487 U.S. 1234 (1988); *Haim*, 1993 WL 346392, at *15 (reliance on animal studies insufficient for medical causation); G. B. Gori, *The Regulation of Carcinogenic Hazards*, 208 Sci. 257 (1980) (questioning whether results of animal tests have any validity in predicting human effects). *But see* Villari v. Terminix International, Inc., 692 F. Supp. 568, 570-72 (E.D. Pa. 1988) (animal studies routinely relied upon in assessing carcinogenic effects of chemicals on humans).

[175] *See, e.g.*, Brock v. Merrell Dow Pharmaceuticals, Inc., 874 F.2d 307, 313-15 (5th Cir. 1989), *cert. denied*, 494 U.S. 1046 (1990). Although *Brock* held the plaintiff's expert evidence inadmissible, it expressly stated that its opinion should not bar "new and conclusive studies" that might emerge in the future. *Id.* at 315.

[176] Haim v. Department of Health & Human Servs., No. 90-1031V, 1993 WL 346392, at *15 (Ct. Cl. Aug. 27, 1993).

[177] 222 N.J. Super. 306, 536 A.2d 1280 (1988).

[178] *Id.* at 1282 (citing Barson v. E.R. Squibb & Sons, Inc., 682 P.2d 832 (Utah 1984)).

[179] *Id.*

doubt on prior findings of scientific facts deprive those earlier findings of collateral estoppel effect."[180] Courts have acknowledged this concept under the old *Frye* test:

> Once this court has made a determination that the *Frye* test is met as to a specific novel scientific theory or principle, trial courts can generally rely upon that determination as settling such theory's admissibility in future cases. However, trial courts must still undertake the *Frye* analysis if one party produces new evidence which seriously questions the continued general acceptance or lack of acceptance as to that theory within the relevant scientific community.[181]

V. Conclusion

Issue preclusion, under any theoretical label, is appropriate in dealing with the admissibility of scientific expert testimony. The opinions, as well as supporting testimony, affidavits, and scientific documentation, of prior cases may be helpful or even dispositive in a *Daubert* analysis. Although science is constantly evolving, many scientific questions may have been addressed by such substantial research that they need not be repeatedly re-evaluated in court.[182] If a thorough analysis of expert scientific testimony has been done by one or more courts in a manner fully calculated to test the bases of expert reasoning, and no new substantive, relevant evidence on the issue is available, courts dealing with the issue in subsequent proceedings should be able to rely, and base their rulings, upon that analysis. The trial judge must be circumspect in this reliance, however, ensuring that the prior investigations were conducted with an eye to the scientific principles of the *Daubert* test and not on the demeanor of an expert or his willingness to "say it is so."[183] Such scientifically based reliance promotes judicial economy and serves the goal cited by the Supreme Court of "quick, final and binding legal judgments."[184]

---

[180] *Id.* at 1283 (citing Ezagui v. Dow Chem. Corp., 598 F.2d 727, 731-32 (2d Cir. 1979)).

[181] State v. Cauthron, 120 Wash. 2d 879, 846 P.2d 502, 506 (1993).

[182] For example, the Bendectin/birth defect link had been researched in some 39 published epidemiologic studies before the *Daubert* ruling. *See* Sanders, *The Bendectin Litigation: A Case Study in the Life Cycle of Mass Torts*, 43 Hastings L. J. 301, 395 (1992). None of the studies showed a statistically significant link between Bendectin ingestion and birth defects. *Id.* at 348.

[183] *See* Viterbo v. Dow Chem. Co., 826 F.2d 420, 424 (5th Cir. 1987) ("without more than credentials and a subjective opinion, an expert's testimony that 'it is so' is not admissible.").

[184] *Daubert*, 113 S.Ct. at 2798.

Expert Hearsay: Will Somebody Please Object?

*Ronald L. Carlson**

If the expert were held to be entitled to detail every statement made to him that contributed to his conclusion, then the expert could be effectively used to present an infinite amount of evidentiary matters to the jury.[1]

I. Introduction

Modern trial lawyers are well familiar with the rule that an expert can factor into his or her courtroom opinion all manner of unintroduced data. However, the expert witness must do it as sort of a gestalt. Without detailing what others have told him or her, the witness simply identifies how he or she came to certain conclusions. In the case of a medical doctor, for example, it might be that he will describe his own tests performed on a patient, as well the fact that he reviewed medical and lab reports provided by other specialists. At that point, an examining attorney may solicit a diagnoses from the doctor, who then provides it. He gives his opinion.

So far so good. In an increasingly mobile society, patients may receive examination and treatment in a number of places. The courtroom doctor needs to be able to state that he was careful in reaching his opinions (both in and out of court), that he reviewed all of the relevant documents in the case, and for these reasons his conclusions are not incomplete or slipshod.

Suppose he does so, then states his conclusions. At this nexus, a critical problem arises. With increasing frequency, the proponent of the witness now moves the court to receive into evidence the background documents. "Since Dr. X has given his opinion, we now offer the background reports of Dr. Y and Dr. Z, the lab results, etc." What happens next? Again, with alarming frequency, the opponent may make no objection. Judges from around the country have reported this "no objection" phenomenon to this writer at various legal conferences. Many jurists offered the suspicion that lack of objection in these circumstances is usually not a tactical move but generally springs from another source: Absence of accurate knowledge by counsel respecting the procedural outlines of Federal Evidence Rule 703 and its state counterparts.

---

* John Byrd Martin Professor of Law, University of Georgia. B.A. 1956, Augustana College; J.D. 1959, Northwestern University (Clarion De Witt Hardy Scholar); L.L.M. 1961, Georgetown University (E. Barrett Prettyman Fellow in Trial Advocacy).

[1] First Southwest Lloyds Insurance Co. v. MacDowell, 769 S.W.2d 954 (Tex. Ct. App. 1989).

It is the thesis of this Article that the described objection should be made, subject to occasional exceptions dictated by a particular case's trial strategy. Further, it is also submitted that when made, the objection should be resoundingly sustained.

II. Rule 703

Any uncertainty as to the validity of a hearsay objection seems dispelled by current developments. Decisions from Virginia, Texas, and Florida will illustrate. First, in *Todd v. Williams*[2] a plaintiff urged the failure of the defendant doctor to perform a particular test. Medical malpractice was alleged. On the stand, a doctor called by the defense explained his reasoning for feeling that the omitted test, a platelet count, was not critical. He testified: "I have also posed that question to some other national authorities in this particular field [naming two doctors]. Their feeling is much like mine, that normal platelets are different from the platelets in the myeloproliferative disorders. . . ." An important and timely objection was lodged in this case, which objection had ramifications later. The trial court overruled the plaintiff's objection, remarking that the witness "was offered as an expert." Neither of the two physicians to whom the courtroom expert referred was present at the trial. There was a defense verdict.

The Supreme Court of Virginia reversed. While Virginia law authorized the admission into evidence of an expert's opinion which is based in whole or in part on inadmissible hearsay, the statute did not authorize the admission of the various hearsay conclusions which may have been reported by others to the courtroom expert. Citing an earlier case, the state Supreme Court observed: "No litigant in our judicial system is required to contend with the opinions of absent 'experts' whose qualifications have not been established to the satisfaction of the court, whose demeanor cannot be observed by the trier of fact, and whose pronouncements are immune from cross-examination."[3]

Justice Russell authored the *Todd* opinion, just as he had an earlier opinion which took a similar approach.[4] But Virginia is not alone in placing

---

[2] 242 Va. 178, 409 S.E.2d 450 (1991).

[3] 409 S.E.2d at 452.

[4] *Mc Munn v. Tatum*, 237 Va. 558, 379 S. E. 2d 908 (1989). The Virginia statute follows the language of Federal Evidence Rule 703 in civil cases, like Todd. Around the time of its decision this perceptive comment appeared in C. Friend, The Law of Evidence in Virginia 163 (Supp. 1991) (footnotes omitted):

> [A]nalysis and research suggests strongly that the statute was intended only to make the *expert's opinion* admissible, *not* to permit the admission on direct examination of *the hearsay source information* itself. This is the position of the majority of the courts which have construed the federal rules upon which §8.01-401.1 is based; it is also consistent with the apparent intent of the Virginia legislature in enacting §8.01-401.1.

> It is therefore suggested that the witness should be permitted on direct examination to state *what the source of the information was* (*e.g.*, "hospital records").

controls on open recitation of the hearsay underlying a courtroom expert's conclusions. Texas law was enhanced by the decision in *First Southwest Lloyds Insurance Co v. MacDowell*.[5] The plaintiffs sued on a fire insurance policy and the insurance company refused to pay, alleging arson. A fire marshal testified to his opinions that the fire was set and that the plaintiffs had done it. The trial court excluded the fire marshal's testimony concerning a spectator's specific statements made to the marshal that served as a partial basis for the marshal's conclusions. While the trial court allowed the marshal to state that an account of the fire by the witness contributed to his conclusion that the cause of the fire was incendiary, it refused to allow him to state before the jury the specifics of what the witness had told him, "namely that [the witness] had seen the fire begin from a nightclub across the street from the beauty supply and that a white male ran from the front of the beauty supply and sped away in a vehicle."[6]

The reviewing court approved exclusion of the hearsay report supplied by the out-of-court witness:

> [W]hile an expert in an arson case could properly state that he based his conclusion that a fire was incendiary upon many years of fire investigation training and experience, the physical findings at the fire scene, and reports made to him during the course of the investigation, he would not necessarily be entitled to express all the details of each of the bases of his opinion.[7]

The nature of the out-of-court hearsay sought to be introduced by the proponent of the expert varies. It may be a courtroom witness seeking to

---

However, it is submitted that the witness should be permitted on direct examination to disclose only the *nature* of the source, *not* the actual *content or language* of the source.

By contrast, since §8.01-401.1 expressly authorizes inquiry on cross-examination into the basis of the opinion, it appears that the *opponent* should be permitted *on cross-examination* to question the witness regarding the content or language of the source *if the opponent so chooses*. In that event, such information would be admissible, any evidentiary objection thereto having been waived by the opponent's act of inquiring about it. This information, even when elicited on cross-examination, is admissible only for the purpose of determining what weight should be given to the expert's conclusion. (Emphasis in original.)

[5] 769 S.W.2d 954 (Tex. Ct. App. 1989). This case and additional authorities are described in Carlson, *In Defense of a Constitutional Theory of Experts*, 87 Northwestern L. Rev. 1182 (1992).

[6] *Id.* at 957.

[7] *Id.* at 958. Texas courts have also addressed the issue of whether a party waives his objection to underlying data when he does not object to the expert's statement of his or her opinion but rather objects for the first time when an underlying report is offered in evidence. Holding against waiver is Beavers v. Northrop Worldwide Aircraft Servs., Inc., 821 S.W.2d 669, 674 (Tex. Ct. App. 1991) ("The better judicial position is not to allow the affirmative admission of otherwise inadmissible matters merely because such matters happen to be underlying data upon which an expert relies").

repeat conclusions stated by absent hearsay declarants, like third party lay witnesses or other experts; letters written by other specialists to the witness who appears in court, and through the courtroom expert the proponent of the witness offers them as exhibits; technical reports on the case supplied to the local expert by specialists in distant parts of the country; or affidavits of hearsay declarants.

In *State v. Williams*,[8] the latter sort of information was offered, and challenged. A defense expert relied on an affidavit to give his opinion. This was "perfectly proper," in the view of the reviewing court. However, the court rejected the defense argument that the expert should have been able to testify to the document's contents: "We reject the notion that the expert may be used as a conduit for the introduction of otherwise inadmissible evidence."[9]

It was a doctor testifying for the plaintiff who had admission into evidence of his hearsay bases challenged in *Gong v. Hirsch*.[10] During the testimony of a medical expert called by the plaintiff, the plaintiff sought to introduce a letter written about the patient by another physician. The letter contained observations about the patient's medical condition. The appellate court stated: "We also note that, even assuming that the letter was considered the type of evidence reasonably relied upon by experts, Rule 703 does not automatically mean that the *information itself* is independently admissible in evidence."[11]

III. Tradition Makes Sense

The common law approach to evidence commanded a trial judge to sustain a hearsay objection when a trial witness began to announce the opinions of another person. Make the other person appear before the tribunal and stand for cross-examination, the rule said. That common law approach continues to be an exercise in good sense, and is particularly needed when the full-scale possibilities of a contrary approach are considered.

IV. Abusive Possibilities

Were the rule otherwise — in other words, if a local expert could invoke the opinions of nontestifying experts at will — hardball lawyering would run amuck. Scenes like this might regularly occur. The plaintiff in an injury case calls his expert, Dr. Franklin. She states her training and background. She

---

[8] 549 So.2d 1071 (Fla. Dist. Ct. App. 1989).

[9] *Id.* at 1072.

[10] 913 F.2d 1269 (7th Cir. 1990).

[11] *Id.* at 1273. Other authorities have appreciated the difference between an expert's opinion and inadmissible underlying data. *See* Peter J. Rescorl, Comment, Fed. R. Evid. 703: *A Back Door Entrance for Hearsay and Other Inadmissible Evidence: A Time for a Change?*, 63 TEMP. L.Q. 543 (1990).

then lays out the foundation for her opinion. It consists of her hands-on treatment of the plaintiff *plus* her review of the report of three other examining specialists. Dr. Franklin then states her opinion.

At this point the plaintiff's attorney, in a sweep of generosity, announces: "Your honor, because Dr. Franklin relied on the reports of Dr. Lewis, Dr. Roca, and Dr. Stoneking, we move the admission into evidence of the reports of these three fine doctors."

Remarkably, objection is sometimes not lodged to the suggested procedure, and when this happens the plaintiff gets four experts for the price of one. Where an objection is made but the local court is inclined to allow the exhibits anyway, what does this bode for the future? One can expect dire consequences. Some opportunistic lawyers will reason: why not load up a single doctor with the reports of many? Why require several to testify when you can introduce all of the desired testimony through a single witness?

V. Ploys

Experience reveals that attorneys seeking to capitalize on the dazzling possibility of getting four doctors for one will sometimes attempt to disarm a discerning judge in a particular way. When the court expresses skepticism about the courtroom expert serving as a conduit for raw hearsay, this explanation might be heard. "Your honor, we are not offering the out-of-court report of Dr. Roca and the others for truth of the content of the reports. We are not using them as substantive evidence, but simply to illustrate the basis for Dr. Franklin's opinion. You can give an instruction to that effect." Can a limiting instruction meaningfully require the jury to distinguish between the hearsay's value as foundation for the expert's opinion and the truth of the matters which the hearsay asserts? Will the jury appropriately discount the conclusion of Dr. Roca about the severity of the injury, and the projected percentage of permanent disability? No. If the testifying expert who appears in the courtroom has recounted in great detail what another supposedly eminent specialist has said about a key issue in the case, it is asking too much to expect the jury to understand or observe that fine line. The better course is to stop the recitation or introduction of hearsay before it ever starts.[12]

VI. Exceptions: Cross and Redirect Examination

There are many rules of evidence which protect cross-examiners, but which they can waive. The doctrine explained by this Article, the rule

---

[12] R. Carlson, *Getting a Grip on Experts*, 16 Litigation No. 4, 36, 37 (Summer 1990), citing Imwinkelried, *The "Bases" of Expert Testimony: The Syllogistic Structure of Scientific Testimony*, 67 N.C.L. Rev. 1, 12 (1988); Carlson, *Collision Course in Expert Testimony: Limitations on Affirmative Introduction of Underlying Data*, 36 U. Fla. L. Rev. 234, 245 n.44 (1984).

prohibiting wholesale entry into evidence of an expert's hearsay basis, is one such rule. While prohibited on direct, the opposing party can delve into a hearsay report which would be otherwise inadmissible against him or her. Minnesota's recently revised Rule of Evidence 703(b) illustrates. Rule 703(a) in Minnesota mirrors the federal rule. Then this more recent innovation appears:

Minnesota Rule 703(b)

(b) Underlying expert data must be independently admissible in order to be received upon direct examination; provided that when good cause is shown in civil cases and the underlying data is particularly trustworthy, the court may admit the data under this rule for the limited purpose of showing the basis for the expert's opinion. Nothing in this rule restricts admissibility of underlying expert data when inquired into on cross-examination.[13]

Of course, once the cross-examination delves into the material, it may well open up new possibilities for the direct examiner on redirect. "Cross-examination on a part of a transaction enables the opposing party to elicit evidence on redirect examination of the whole transaction at least to the extent that it relates to the same subject."[14]

VII. Conclusion

It is the position of this Article that while a courtroom expert can state opinions based on out-of-court hearsay, an expert cannot spout the opinions of others in detail to the trial jury. A hearsay objection blocks this sort of abuse. Nothing in the recent *Daubert* case[15] suggests that judges should remove the bar of the hearsay rule from material which makes up expert's

---

[13] Minn Stat. Ann. § 50 (West Supp. 1993). The good cause exception in civil cases is noted in the Minnesota rule. Another exception applied in some courts is that for learned treatises and general points of scientific theory. They differentiate this sort of general background information from case-specific information drawn from tests, reviews, and examinations involved in the particular case at issue. Material in the latter category can be particularly damaging to the opponent and is most susceptible to an exclusionary objection. The distinction drawn here seems to be applied in United States v. King, 35 M.J. 337 (CMA 1992). The court recognizes that on direct an expert can explain the basis for his or her opinion, which may include properly authenticated business records of another party or, under federal rules, reference to learned treatises. Beyond the provisions of the business records and learned treatise exceptions, however, "experts are not licensed to ascend the witness stand and commence spouting hearsay generally." 35 M.J. at 341.

[14] Todd v Williams, 242 Va. 178, 409 S.E.2d 450 (1991), citing Briley v Commonwealth, 221 Va. 532, 540, 273 S.E.2d 48, 53 (1980).

[15] Daubert v Merrell Dow Pharmaceuticals, Inc, 509 U.S. ____ , 125 L.Ed.2d 469, 113 S.Ct. 2786 (1993).

underlying basis. In *Daubert*, the Supreme Court replaced *Frye*[16] with a reliability analysis.[17] Under the *Daubert* approach, the trial court determines whether the expert's underlying material supplies a valid basis for her conclusions. The emphasis by *Daubert* on the court's gatekeeping function has caused some to forecast that courts will tighten up Rule 703 as well, and that they will enhance safeguards imposed upon unexpurgated expert hearsay.

To this particular controversy should be added one more salient consideration, the Constitution's Confrontation Clause. That clause has sometimes escaped the attention of those who urge that judges should run their courts differently than the suggestions offered in this Article. Under the competing view, some urge judges to adhere to a "let it all in" philosophy. This writer contends that such a practice would decimate the tenets of the Sixth Amendment when that approach is applied in criminal cases. A "let it all in" methodology would authorize a local witness on the stand to read into the record or to give to the jury as an exhibit a number of questionable items, things like a nontestifying expert's written report about the defendant's sanity or conclusions drawn from a DNA test performed by someone else at a distant lab. Proponents of wide-open admission of underlying data seem to say that admission of such things are appropriate because the jury should know, in detail, the data that support the courtroom expert's opinion. But they say little about the case law which condemns the patent unconstitutionality of the practice they endorse.[18] The Confrontation Clause supplies the ultimate bar to application of the wide-open rule.

Similar principles need to be applied in the general run of civil cases as well. Whether in the civil or criminal arena, sound principles of judicial decision making demand rejection of unauthenticated expert hearsay.

---

[16] Frye v United States, 293 F. 1013 (D.C. Cir. 1923).

[17] Gianelli, *Daubert and Forensic Science*, 1 Shepard's Expert & Scientific Evidence Quarterly 457, 462 (1994).

[18] Carlson, *In Defense of a Constitutional Theory of Experts*, 87 Northwestern L. Rev. 1182 (1993), citing State v. Towne, 453 A.2d 1133 (Vt. 1982) (courtroom expert's recitation of the nontestifying doctor's opinion violated Sixth Amendment).

Discovery of Expert Witnesses —
Amendments to Rule 26

*James D. Toll**

The recent amendments to Rule 26 of the Federal Rules of Civil Procedure include some striking new requirements governing discovery of expert witnesses. If you practice in the federal courts, you must understand the nature and effect of these amendments.

Background

On April 22, 1993, the Supreme Court transmitted to Congress proposed amendments to the Federal Rules of Civil Procedure.[1] According to the Chief Justice, these amendments were designed "to secure the just, speedy and inexpensive determination of every civil action .... Judges and attorneys share the responsibility to see that the rules are utilized to achieve this objective."[2]

A good deal has been written about the amendments to Rule 26(a)(1) requiring mandatory pretrial disclosure in every civil action. The rationale for these changes — to avoid unnecessary motion practice, deter protracted litigation, and mitigate the "adversary hostility" permeating our current litigation system — is the same rationale underlying the amendments to the new expert witness discovery provisions.

These amendments became effective on December 1, 1993, and apply to all civil actions commenced thereafter, and to the extent "just and practicable," actions previously in progress.

The Substantive Changes

Rule 26(a)(2)(A) requires a party, without waiting for a discovery request, to disclose "to other parties the identity of any person who may be

---

* James D. Toll is a member of Sills Cummis Zuckerman Radin Tischman Epstein & Gross, Atlantic City, New Jersey, specializing in civil litigation, particularly product liability, construction litigation, and premises liability. Mr. Toll testified before the U.S. House of Representatives, Committee on the Judiciary, Intellectual Property and Judicial Administration Subcommittee, concerning the amendment to Rule 26.

[1] *See* Letter from Chief Justice William H. Rehnquist to the Honorable Thomas S. Foley, Speaker of the U.S. House of Representatives, dated April 22, 1993.

[2] *See Statement of James D. Toll* submitted to the U.S. House of Representatives, Committee on the Judiciary, Intellectual Property and Judicial Administration Subcommittee, June 16, 1993, at 6 (quoting Preliminary Draft of Proposed Amendments to the Federal Rules of Civil Procedure 1 (Aug. 19, 1991)).

used at trial to present evidence under Rules 702, 703 or 705 of the Federal Rules of Evidence."[3]

Rule 26(a)(2)(B) limits this disclosure to witnesses who are "retained or specially employed to provide expert testimony in the case or whose duties as an employee of the party regularly involve giving expert testimony."[4] These expert witnesses are also required to prepare written and signed reports containing:

> a complete statement of all opinions to be expressed and the basis and reasons therefor; the data or other information considered by the witness in forming the opinion; any exhibits to be used as a summary of or support for the opinion; the qualifications of the witness, including a list of all publications authored by the witness within the preceding ten years; the compensation to be paid for the study and testimony; and a listing of any other cases in which the witness has testified as an expert at trial or by deposition within the preceding four years.[5]

The Advisory Committee noted that a proposed draft of these rules (published in August 1991) would have:

> [r]equired that detailed written reports of parties' experts be exchanged during the discovery period and generally limit[ed] the direct testimony of such experts to the matters contained in those reports as may have been reasonably supplemented prior to trial. Several comments argue that this requirement would cause unnecessary additional expenses, discourage "real" experts from agreeing to testify, and create problems at trial. Requirements such as these have, however, been beneficially used in several courts for many years, and the Advisory Committee remains convinced that the concept is sound.[6]

However, the Committee "changed the language in subdivision (a)(2) to make clear that it applies only to specially retained or employed experts — and not, for example, *to treating physicians*."[7]

Under the prior rules, a party could often get away with serving a vague expert's report. The Advisory Committee noted that "[t]he information disclosed under the former rule in answering interrogatories about the 'substance' of expert testimony was frequently so sketchy and vague that it rarely dispensed with the need to depose the expert and often was even of

---

[3] Fed. R. Civ. P. 26(a)(2)(A).

[4] Fed. R. Civ. P. 26(a)(2)(B).

[5] *Id.*

[6] Advisory Committee on Civil Rules of Practice and Procedure of the Judicial Conference of the United States 8 (May 1, 1992).

[7] *Id.* (emphasis added).

little help in preparing for a deposition of the witness. Revised Rule 37(c)(1) provides an incentive for full disclosure; namely, that a party will not ordinarily be permitted to use on direct examination any expert testimony not so disclosed."[8]

The practitioner is well advised to study Rule 26(a)(2)(B) thoroughly. The expert's report now must include, among other things:

1. A statement of the expert's opinions and the bases for them
2. All data that the expert considered in forming the opinions
3. All exhibits used as a summary of or support for the expert's opinions
4. The expert's qualifications, including all of the expert's publications within the preceding ten years
5. The fees to be earned by the expert
6. The names of all other cases in which the expert *actually* testified as an expert, at trial or deposition, within the preceding four years[9]

The amendments are also designed to settle one long-standing dispute concerning the discoverability of materials that the expert *considered*, but did not rely on. The Advisory Committee concluded that, based on the new obligations of disclosure, "litigants should no longer be able to argue that materials furnished to their experts to be used in forming their opinions — whether or not ultimately relied upon by the expert — are privileged or otherwise protected from disclosure when such persons are testifying or being deposed."[10]

Rule 26(a)(2)(C) governs the *timing* of expert witness disclosure. Typically, the court will set a deadline in a scheduling order pursuant to Rule 16(b). If the court does not enter this type of order, and the parties do not agree (by stipulation) to abide by a particular schedule, then the disclosures must be made at least 90 days *before* the date the case is to be ready for trial.

However, if the expert's testimony is intended solely to contradict or rebut evidence on a subject matter identified by another party under paragraph 2(B), it must then be disclosed within 30 days of the first party's disclosure. This means that a defendant's expert report, in a typical case, will be due 30 days after receipt of the plaintiff's expert report.

Revised Rule 26(b)(4)(A) enables a party to depose the other side's expert *after* that expert's report has been served. The Advisory Committee felt that, with comprehensive expert reports, counsel would resort less often to depositions. Moreover, if the expert is deposed, the deposition should be

---

[8] Notes of Advisory Committee on Rules Re: Amendments to Rule 26 of the Federal Rules of Civil Procedure.

[9] Fed. R. Civ. P. 26(a)(2)(B).

[10] *Id.*

shorter (and hence more efficient) in view of the information that must previously be revealed in the expert's report.[11]

Finally, Rule 26(e)(1) mandates disclosure of any material change in the expert's opinions during the course of the action. The Rule provides that:

> [a] party is under a duty to supplement at appropriate intervals its disclosures under subdivision (a) if the party learns that in some material respect, the information disclosed is incomplete or incorrect and if the additional or corrective information has not otherwise been made known to the other parties during the discovery process or in writing. With respect to testimony of an expert from whom a report is required under subdivision (a)(2)(B), the duty extends both to information contained in the report and to information provided through a deposition of the expert.[12]

These requirements apply only to experts retained or specially employed to provide testimony in the case, or employees of a party whose duties regularly involve expert testimony. Treating doctors are *exempt* from this requirement. They can be deposed or called to testify at trial *without* a written report.

The requirement of a written report may be waived for particular experts or imposed on additional persons who may express opinions pursuant to Rule 702 of the Federal Rules of Evidence. These waiver provisions may arise by local rule, order, or written stipulation.[13]

Conclusion

The amendments to the rules governing discovery of expert witnesses will radically change the way that many practitioners have operated in the past. For others, perhaps, the changes are evolutionary, not revolutionary. In either case, the litigator (and the expert) must understand these new rules and comply with them. They will govern how we litigate expert and scientific issues in the federal courts for some time to come.

---

[11] *Id.*

[12] Fed. R. Civ. P. 26(a)(2)(B).

[13] *Id.*

Legal and Ethical Considerations in Using Expert Witnesses in Litigation

*Carol Henderson Garcia**

Introduction

As modern litigation becomes increasing complex, lawyers are routinely called upon to obtain and utilize specialized expertise in order to evaluate and litigate cases effectively. Complex litigation has spawned the proliferation of expert witnesses.[1] Since attorneys must increasingly rely upon experts,[2] attorneys need to be aware of their ethical obligations in dealing with them.

Not only do experts participate in many trials, but they often are the key focus at the trial.[3] The media have also influenced the public's expectations with regard to the use and strength of scientific evidence.[4] Jurors accord great

---

Professor of Law, Shepard Broad Law Center, Nova Southeastern University, Fort Lauderdale, Florida 33314. Professor Garcia is a former Assistant United States Attorney, a Fellow of the American Academy of Forensic Sciences (AAFS) and a past Chairperson of the AAFS Jurisprudence Section. This article contains material from the forthcoming Scientific Evidence in Civil and Criminal Cases by Moenssens, Starrs, Garcia, and Inbau which will be published by Foundation Press.

[1] *Expert Witnesses: Booming Business for the Specialists*, N.Y. Times, July 5, 1987, at 1, 13. Expert witness services, brokers, and clearinghouses are also growing. For example, The Technical Advisory Service for Attorneys (TASA), a Pennsylvania-based clearinghouse for experts, listed 10,000 experts in 4,000 categories in 1987. *Id.* In 1992, TASA offered 18,500 experts in 5,300 categories. Kates-Smith, *Opinions with a Price*, U.S. News & World Rep., July 20, 1992, at 64. *See also*, Greene, *Expert-Witness Industry Flourishing*, Chi. Daily L. Bull., Aug. 23, 1993, at 1.

[2] In 1983 the National Center for State Courts conducted a nationwide survey to determine the extent and nature of the use of expert testimony. Almost half of the attorneys responding to the survey encountered scientific testimony in a third of their cases. Saks & Van Duizend, The Use of Scientific Evidence in Litigation (1983). *See also* Gross, *Expert Evidence*, 1991 Wis. L. Rev. 1113, 1118 (describing more recent studies on the use of expert witnesses in American litigation).

[3] Note the attention upon the serological testimony in the William Kennedy Smith sexual battery case in West Palm Beach, Florida (State v. Smith, No. 91-5482 (Palm Beach Co. Cir. Ct. Dec. 11, 1991)) in 1991, and the psychiatric testimony in the Jeffrey Dahmer case (State v. Dahmer, No. F-9-12542 (Milwaukee Co. Cir. Ct. Feb. 12, 1992)) in Wisconsin in 1992.

[4] A study of 1,500 jurors regarding fingerprint evidence found that 71.9% of jurors' primary sources of knowledge of fingerprints comes from television and newspapers. Illsley, U.S. Dep't of Justice, Juries, Fingerprints and the Expert Fingerprint Witness 15 (1987). Unfortunately the media does not always accurately portray forensic evidence. An example is *The Naked Lie*, a made-for-TV movie in which a warrant for the arrest of a murderer is obtained based upon a single bloody hair and a voiceprint. In reality, neither would be positive indicator of the identity of a suspect. *See also* Jarvis, *Serial Killers and the*

weight to expert testimony, thus requiring attorneys to present the expert opinions fairly and accurately so as not to violate ethics rules.[5]

When selecting, preparing, and presenting expert testimony, an attorney must be aware, throughout the process, of his own ethical obligations as well as the ethical constraints upon an expert's behavior. This article addresses experts' ethics and attorneys' ethics in using expert witnesses, as well as the emerging cause of action, expert witness malpractice.

The Expert's Ethical Obligation

An attorney should become aware of experts' ethical obligations under the ethics codes of certifying bodies or professional associations.[6] For example, members of the American Academy of Forensic Sciences (AAFS) are prohibited from making material misrepresentations of their education or of the data upon which their professional opinions are based.[7] If an AAFS member is found to have violated the code, the ethics committee may impose sanctions, such as censure, suspension, or expulsion from the organization.[8]

Some courts have sanctioned experts for their unethical behavior. In *Schmidt v. Ford Motor Co.*,[9] the court banned the plaintiff's accident reconstruction expert from testifying in federal court in Colorado because he had conveyed intentionally misleading information in depositions and informal conversations with the defense expert. The expert also concealed his knowledge that one of the plaintiffs had tampered with the evidence.

Silver Screen: Mixing Up Fact and Myth, presented at American Academy of Forensic Sciences 41st Annual Meeting, Feb. 16, 1989 (expressing concern about the accuracy of forensic information as portrayed in serial killer movies).

[5] A recent poll taken by the *National Law Journal* and Lexis/Nexis found that jurors not only find experts generally credible, but the experts often influenced the outcome of the case. Overall, 71% of the jurors said the experts made a difference in the verdict. In criminal cases, 95% of the jurors thought the expert was very believable or somewhat believable. Cheever & Naiman, *The View from the Jury Box*, Nat'l L.J., Feb. 22, 1993, at S4. The survey found that experts were thought believable by 89% of the criminal and civil jurors.

[6] *E.g.*, National Association of Medical Examiners (N.A.M.E.) Bylaws, Article Ten, Ethics (1992) which provides that members of N.A.M.E. shall conform to the published ethics of the American Medical Association; The National Society of Professional Engineers Code of Ethics (1990) which sets forth fundamental canons, rules of practice, and professional obligations. The American Board of Criminalistics has promulgated rules of professional conduct with which applicants and diplomates must comply: Bylaws, Article IV.5 (1992).

[7] The American Academy of Forensic Sciences Bylaws Code of Ethics and Conduct, Art. II, Section 1 (1993).

[8] *Id.* at Art. II, Section 2.

[9] 112 F.R.D. 216 (D. Colo. 1986).

Attorney's Ethics in Dealing with Experts

Attorneys' ethical obligations are contained in each state's Rules of Professional Conduct or Code of Professional Responsibility. While no specific rule deals directly with attorneys and expert witnesses, some of the American Bar Association Model Rules of Professional Conduct are applicable. The Model Rules have been adopted in a majority of states.[10] Some of the model rules which have an impact on an attorney's use of expert witnesses are the following:

Rule 3.3 (Candor Toward the Tribunal) requires the attorney to investigate the background of witnesses to avoid putting on perjurious testimony.

Rule 3.8 (Special Responsibilities of a Prosecutor) specifies that the prosecutor's role as a *minister of justice* requires him or her to make timely disclosure of evidence or information that will negate evidence of guilt or mitigate guilt. Therefore, if fraud is uncovered relating to the expert's acts or knowledge, it must be disclosed.

Rule 5.3 (Responsibilities Regarding Nonlawyer Assistants) applies to experts as well as paralegals and extends to situations where the lawyer is in essence ratifying the unethical conduct of the expert.

Rule 8.3 (Reporting Professional Misconduct) requires attorneys to report unethical conduct of other attorneys. For example, if the opposing party's counsel knowingly uses an expert discovered to be a fraud, counsel is obligated to report the other lawyer to the appropriate authorities. A counsel in this situation who does not report is himself or herself in violation of the rule.

Rule 8.4(c) (Misconduct) states that it is professional misconduct: to violate the Model Rules; to commit a criminal act that reflects adversely on a lawyer's honesty, trustworthiness, or fitness; to engage in conduct involving dishonesty, fraud, deceit, or misrepresentation; or to engage in conduct that is prejudicial to the administration of justice.

Additionally, an attorney shall not fabricate evidence or counsel or assist a witness to testify falsely or offer an inducement to a witness that is prohibited by law or make frivolous discovery requests or intentionally fail to comply with a legally proper discovery request.[11] A lawyer shall not make false statements of material fact or law to a third person, such as an expert witness.[12]

---

[10] By November 1993, 37 states and the District of Columbia and the Virgin Islands had adopted the Model Rules.

[11] Model Rules of Professional Conduct Rule 3.4 (1993).

[12] Model Rules of Professional Conduct Rule 4.1 (1993).

Model Rules 1.1 (Competence) and 1.3 (Diligence) require an attorney to seek out expert services, if needed by the client. Failure by a defense counsel in a criminal case to obtain the services of expert witnesses may later be deemed by courts to have resulted in the ineffective assistance of counsel.[13] A civil or criminal practitioner may also be found liable for malpractice for failure to seek out expert services if they were warranted.

The prevailing general rule is that it is inappropriate to pay an expert a fee contingent on the outcome of the case,[14] nor may an attorney share fees with an expert.[15] An attorney has been held to have an ethical obligation to pay an expert's fees unless the expert gives an express disclaimer of responsibility.[16]

Attorneys have been sanctioned by the bar for abusing an expert witness on cross-examination. A prosecutor was suspended from the practice of law for 30 days for improperly eliciting irrelevant testimony from the defense's expert witness, a psychiatrist. The prosecutor insulted the witness, ignored the court's rulings on defense objections which were sustained, and inserted his personal opinions on psychiatry and the insanity defense into his questioning.[17]

The American Bar Association standards relating to the Administration of Criminal Justice also set forth standards for prosecutors and defense counsel to follow when working with expert witnesses in criminal trials. The standards provide that the attorney should respect the expert's independence, not dictate the formation of the expert's opinion, and that paying excessive or contingent fees is unprofessional conduct.[18]

---

[13] Proffitt v. United States, 582 F.2d 854 (4th Cir. 1978), *cert. denied*, 447 U.S. 910 (1980); Moore v. State, 827 S.W.2d 213 (Mo. 1992) (counsel ineffective for failing to request serological test); Loe v. United States, 545 F. Supp. 662 (E.D. Va. 1982) (counsel ineffective for failure to request examination of client by private psychiatrist).

[14] *See* Dupree v. Malpractice Research, Inc., 445 N.W.2d 498 (Mich. Ct. App. 1989). Florida has recently amended its Rules of Professional Conduct to state clearly that contingent fees for experts are prohibited:
A lawyer shall not:
            . . . .

> (b)fabricate evidence, counsel or assist a witness to testify falsely, or offer an inducement to a witness that is prohibited by law, except a lawyer may pay a witness reasonable expenses incurred by the witness in attending or testifying at proceeding, a reasonable, noncontingent fee for the professional services of an expert witness; and reasonable compensation to reimburse a witness for the loss of compensation incurred by reason of preparing for, attending, or testifying at proceedings.

Fla. Bar R. Prof. Conduct Rule 4-3.4(b) (1993).

[15] Sharing fees with nonlawyers violates Model Rules of Professional Conduct Rule 5.4(1) (1993).

[16] Copp v. Breskin, 782 P.2d 1104 (Wash. Ct. App. 1989) (the court cited Model Rules of Professional Conduct Rules 1.8(e) & 4.4 (1993)).

[17] Florida Bar v. Schaub, 618 So.2d 202 (Fla. 1993).

[18] ABA Standards Relating to the Administration of Criminal Justice, Standards 3-3.3 and 4.4.4 (3d ed. 1992).

Liability of the Expert Witness for Malpractice

In recent years, a new cause of actionhas been developing to hold expert witnesses, like doctors and lawyers, responsible for their negligent professional behavior. The law of expert witness negligence has developed largely in response to a recent recognition that such negligence is not uncommon.[19] Erroneous conclusions have been reported even within well-accepted scientific techniques such as fingerprint identification. In 1987, federal and state officials had to review 159 criminal cases in North Carolina after local authorities discovered what they determined to be questionable fingerprint identifications.[20] A similar situation arose in 1993 in New York.[21] Also in 1993, in the aftermath of the reversal of a rape conviction based largely on a serologist's evidence that was shown to be in error,[22] a state supreme court mandated an investigation of the effect the expert's potential errors might have had other cases in which the expert witness had testified. At the conclusion of the inquiry, the judge assigned to investigate the conduct of the expert rendered a detailed report to the Supreme Court of West Virginia concluding that:

> The overwhelming evidence of a pattern and practice of misconduct by Zain [the state police serologist] completely undermines the validity and reliability of any forensic work he performed during his tenure in the serology department of the state police crime laboratory. If the information which is now available concerning the pattern and practiceof misconduct by Zain had been available during the prosecution of cases in which he was involved, the evidence regarding the results of serological testing would have been deemed inadmissible.[23]

---

[19] Hilts, *Misconduct in Science Is Not Rare, a Survey Finds*, N.Y. Times [Nat.ed.], Nov. 12, 1993, at A-13; Starrs, *In the Land of Agog: An Allegory for the Expert Witness*, 30 J. Forensic Sci. 289 (1985) (Professor Starrs cites numerous instances of erroneous expert testimony). *See also* Moenssens, *Novel Scientific Evidence in Criminal Cases: Some Words of Caution*, 84 J. Crim. L. & Criminology 801 (1993) (this article contains numerous recent instances of expert incompetence, negligence, and intentional fraud).

[20] Bowden & Barret, *Fingerprint Errors Raise Questions on Local Convictions*, Fayetteville Times, Jan. 15, 1988, at 1A. The review was prompted by a fingerprint misidentification that resulted in the dismissal of two murder charges by the district attorney's office.

[21] The negligence that may have bordered on intentional misconduct of several fingerprint technicians of the New York State Police was disclosed on the CBS program *60 Minutes*. *See* Moenssens, *supra* note 19, at 816. *See also* Kutz, *Guest Editorial— A Mill Stone, Not a Milestone*, 43 J. Forensic Identification 1 (1993), and *Trooper's Wrongdoing Taints Cases*, A.B.A. J., Mar. 1994, at 22.

[22] State v. Woodall, 182 W. Va. 15, 385 S.E.2d 253 (1989).

[23] In the Matter of an Investigation of the West Virginia State Police Crime Laboratory, Serology Division, Civil Action No. 93-MISC-402, Report by The Hon. James O. Holliday, Senior Judge [hereinafter Report]. The report's recommendations included the statement that "[d]ue to the undisputed nature of the overwhelming evidence of misconduct on the part of Zain," prisoners and parolees in whose cases the serologist testified should be permitted to file petitions for post-conviction habeas corpus. This

3

Within the last year, pathologists have been shown to have either faked several hundreds of autopsies[24] or committed grievous errors[25] in determining the cause of death.

At present, the law does little to regulate the quality of expert testimony.[26] Solutions offered by the scientific and legal communities to curb expert abuses include: capping expert witness fees,[27] pre-screening experts, using only court-appointed experts, adherence to a strict code of ethics,[28] peer review,[29] and a science court.[30] Additionally, it has been suggested that fraudulent experts be prosecuted.[31] It has also been argued that the principal safeguard against errant expert testimony is the opportunity for opposing counsel to cross-examine.[32] The reality is that most lawyers do a woefully

---

applies to defendants in potentially 134 cases. Zain left the state police in 1989 and took a position as serologist with the Bexar County Criminal Investigative Lab in San Antonio, Texas. He was fired from that job for similar irregularities. *West Virginia Invalidates Blood Tests Results in Crimes*, N.Y. Times [Nat. ed.], Nov. 12, 1993, at A12; *Texas Investigator Says Zain More Than Careless*, Dominion Post, Nov. 7, 1993, at 4-A.

[24] Fricker, *Pathologist's Plea Adds to Turmoil*, A.B.A. J., Mar. 1993, at 24. The cases may result in the review of numerous convictions. In a related story, the pathologist was reported to have a "reputation for providing the type of forensic evidence prosecutors needed," though his conclusions were later deemed "impossible" by qualified reviewing medical examiners. *See* Fricker, *Reasonable Doubts*, A.B.A. J., Dec. 1993, 38, at 44.

[25] Nordheimer, *New Jersey Autopsy Misses Two Bullets in a Man's Head*, N.Y. Times [Nat. ed.], Oct. 20, 1993, at A1. The article mentions autopsies by county medical examiners in two different New Jersey counties and quoted the pathologist who had discovered the errors as stating that bad forensic medicine in New Jersey is more commonplace than the average citizen would dare imagine. It also mentions cases where a pathologist described bullet entrance and exit wounds, its track through the brain, in a case where it was later established that death was due to "blunt force injury" and that no evidence of a bullet wound 'existed. Further noted was a case where a medical examiner concluded that a woman died from alcohol poisoning and exposure, when a later autopsy at the request of the family established that the woman had been strangled and raped — a homicide.

[26] Peterson & Murdock, *Forensic Science Ethics: Developing an Integrated System of Support and Enforcement*, 34 J. Forensic Sci. 749 (1989).

[27] Florida Senate Bill 380 (1990), proposed capping expert fees at $250 an hour.

[28] National Forensic Center Summarized Code of Professional and Ethical Conduct, 1992.

[29] Burack, *Of Reliable Science: Scientific Peer Review, Federal Regulatory Agencies and the Courts*, 7 Va. J. Nat. Resources L. 27 (1987).

[30] *See Twenty-Five Year Retrospective on the Science Court: A Symposium*, 4 RISK — Issues in Health & Safety 95-188 (1993), containing a series of articles by advocates and detractors of the science court, including one by its "inventor." *See* Kantrowitz, *Elitism vs. Checks and Balances in Communicating Scientific Information to the Public*, 4 RISK — Issues in Health & Safety 101 (1993).

[31] Report, *supra* note 23.

[32] Trower v. Jones, 520 N.E.2d 297 (Ill. 1988); Sears v. Rutishauser, 466 N.E.2d 210 (Ill. 1984).

inadequate job in cross-examining experts.[33] One reason for this is improper preparation. Another may be that lawyers are often reluctant to incur the risks involved in challenging experts in their own fields. Many lawyers do not even avail themselves of the assistance of experts in preparing for cross-examination and are therefore unable to offer an effective challenge to statements made by experts. Finally, the vast majority of civil and criminal cases are settled or plea bargained prior to trial so that the expert may never be subjected to rigorous questioning during the adversary process.

To date, none of the solutions offered to curb expert abuses have succeeded in accomplishing their goal. Arguably, attempts at monitoring expert testimony may serve to deter some expert negligence and also result in experts being held personally accountable. However, such steps do not necessarily provide for compensation to individuals harmed by an expert's negligence.

The New Tort of Expert Witness Malpractice

In view of the inadequacy or unavailability of solutions to curb expert negligence, and the fact that professional sanctions against an expert do not make whole a person injured as a result of such misconduct, tort actions for damages against experts are on the rise. In the West Virginia serologist's case, a civil action for damages filed against the State resulted in a $1 million settlement.[34]

Only an expert witness malpractice cause of action will protect and compensate injured individuals, as well as deter future misconduct. It will ensure "quality control" of expert opinions by encouraging experts to be careful and accurate. The premise of the expert witness malpractice cause of action is that, first of all, expert witnesses owe a duty to their clients. However, the duty does not end there. Expert witnesses also owe a duty to any foreseeable plaintiff who may be affected by the expert's conduct and who are likely to suffer injury due to a negligently rendered opinion. These duties based upon their professional knowledge and skills are similar to those duties owed by a doctor to a patient and a lawyer to a client. The four elements of the expert witness malpractice action are: (1) the existence of a duty owed to the plaintiff arising out of the relationship between the expert

---

[33] Dowd, Book Review, 14 N. Eng. J. on Crim. & Civ. Confinement 169, 171 (1988) (reviewing Anderson & Winfree, Expert Witnesses: Criminologists in the Courtroom (1987)).

[34] Report, *supra* note 23, at 2. The Report discloses that the filing of the civil law suit by the released Woodall resulted in the preliminary discovery that the serologist's errors and other misconduct were a matter of common practice, and induced the state insurance carrier to recommend settlement for the policy's limit. This settlement then led to the mandate by the state supreme court to investigate all the past cases wherein the serologist gave expert testimony.

and the plaintiff; (2) a negligent act or omission by the expert in breach of that duty; (3) causation; and (4) injury.[35]

The standard of care for a forensic scientist is that of the reasonably prudent practitioner in the relevant scientific field. Standards of professional practice and ethical codes as promulgated by the discipline may be used to help define the duty of care. Most disciplines within the forensic sciences have adopted such standards of conduct. In order for a plaintiff to prevail, it must be determined that the expert did not adhere to the standard of a reasonably prudent expert in either rendering an opinion, conducting an examination, or giving testimony. Ordinarily, an independent evaluation by a disinterested expert skilled in the same field will be required to determine whether an expert deviated from the required standard of care.

A crucial element of the tort of malpractice is causation. Causation tests whether the defendant's actions were in fact connected by physical events to the plaintiff's injury, and whether the connection was close enough to allow compensation to the injured party. As stated by Richard S. Frank, a past president of the American Academy of Forensic Sciences, "[t]he impact of the forensic scientist's conclusions affords no room for error, because such an error may be the direct cause of an injustice."[36] In some cases, it will be readily apparent that an expert's testimony alone "caused" the wrong. This is especially true when the expert evidence is the only evidence presented in the litigation. Many studies have demonstrated that, despite jury instructions to the contrary, jurors give expert testimony greater weight than other evidence.[37] Thus, it is clear that financial injury to a potential plaintiff, or conviction and incarceration of a potentially innocent individual who is prosecuted on the basis of an expert's opinion evidence,[38] are reasonably foreseeable consequences of negligence, incompetence, or intentional misconduct by an expert.

Where a claim of expert witness malpractice is proved to have occurred in civil litigation, the measure of direct damages could include: the difference between a full verdict of proved loss and the reduced verdict resulting from the expert's testimony; the difference between a full settlement and the reduced settlement that resulted from the expert's misconduct; and/or the

---

[35] Keeton et al., Prosser and Keeton on the Law of Torts § 30, at 164-65 (5th ed. 1984).

[36] Frank, *The Essential Commitment For a Forensic Scientist*, 32 J. Forensic Sci. 5 (1987).

[37] Ludwig & Fontaine, *Effect of Witnesses' Expertness and Manner of Delivery of Testimony on Verdicts of Simulated Jurors*, 42 Psychol. Rep. 955 (1978).

[38] Courts have awarded plaintiffs damages of a certain amount per month for illegal confinement due to legal malpractice, rejecting the argument that estimating the value of a person's loss of liberty is speculative. *E.g.*, Geddie v. St. Paul Fire & Marine Ins. Co., 354 So. 2d 718 (La. App. 1978). *See also* Holliday v. Jones, 264 Cal. Rptr. 448 (Ct. App. 1989) (awarding damages for emotional distress as a result of wrongful incarceration due to professional malpractice).

cost in experts' and investigators' and attorneys' fees for responding to the expert's testimony and in proving the misconduct.

Expert witness malpractice causes of action are gaining momentum. Courts in New Jersey,[39] Texas,[40] California,[41] and Missouri[42] are among the growing number of jurisdictions that have allowed plaintiffs to sue experts for their malpractice. Only two jurisdictions, Washington[43] and Pennsylvania,[44] have clearly granted immunity to expert witnesses, stating that experts ought to be accorded absolute immunity and should be shielded through the testimonial privilege. Such limitations are rare, however, and the general recognition that such actions will be recognized by courts have induced defendants in malpractice suits to agree to settlements in many cases.

While no courts shielded erring expert witnesses from perjury charges for willful deceptions, or from damages actions where the expert's conduct involved intentional or grossly negligent conduct, a few courts have shielded experts from civil liability for damages in ordinary negligence cases. The courts have arrived at that result in one of two ways: (1) by holding that negligent mistakes or inaccuracies do not constitute perjury; or (2) by holding that testimony and reports provided to courts are privileged.[45] Some courts hold that the expert witness who gives opinion evidence is the court's witness, and therefore enjoys immunity against all post-trial damages claims whether sued by a party or nonparty to the action.[46] Two cases addressing such issues arose in California and Missouri. In *Mattco Forge, Inc. v. Arthur Young & Co.*,[47] the court held that the litigation privilege in the California Civil Code does not protect a negligent expert witness from liability to the party who hired the witness. In so holding, the court stated, "applying the privilege does not encourage witnesses to testify truthfully; indeed by shielding a negligent expert witness from liability, it has the opposite effect."[48] Also, in *Murphy v. Matthews*,[49] the Missouri Supreme Court held that witness immunity does not bar an action against a professional who agrees to provide litigation-related services for compensation if the professional is negligent in providing

---

[39] Levine v. Wiss & Co., 478 A.2d 397, 399 (N.J. 1984).

[40] James v. Brown, 637 S.W.2d 914 (Tex. 1982).

[41] Mattco Forge, Inc. v. Arthur Young & Co., 6 Cal. Rptr. 2d 781 (Ct. App. 1992).

[42] Murphy v. Matthews, 841 S.W.2d 671 (Mo. 1992).

[43] Bruce v. Byrne-Stevens & Assoc. Engineers, Inc., 776 P.2d 666 (Wash. 1989).

[44] Panitz v. Behrend, 632 A.2d 562 (Pa. Super. Ct. 1993).

[45] Saks, *Prevalence and Impact of Ethical Problems in Forensic Science*, 34 J. Forensic Sci. 772 (1989) (containing a summary of some cases involving litigation against expert witnesses).

[46] Bailey v. Rogers, 631 S.W.2d 784 (Tex. App. 1982); Clark v. Grigson, 579 S.W.2d 263 (Tex. App. 1978).

[47] 6 Cal. Rptr. 2d 781 (Ct. App. 1992).

[48] *Id.* at 788. The court stated, however, that the California litigation privilege would still shield experts that are court appointed, and would also shield expert witnesses from suit by opposing parties. *Id.* at 789.

[49] 841 S.W.2d 671 (Mo. 1992).

the agreed services. The court stressed, however, that its holding would not subject an adverse expert to malpractice liability because the expert owes no professional duty to the adversary. The court also stated that an expert retained by the court, independent of the litigants, would not be subject to malpractice liability.[50]

Witness immunity is an exception to the general rules of liability. The rule is traditionally limited to defamation cases and is extremely narrow in scope. Immunity was not meant to bar a suit against a professional who negligently performs services. The complaint is not with the testimony provided in court, it is with the out-of-court work product which was negligently produced. By testifying, the expert is merely publishing his or her negligence in court. Therefore, no absolute immunity should be afforded experts; they are neither judges nor their adjuncts, but merely third-party participants in litigation. And the courts, the legal profession, and the forensic disciplines recognize that the trend is firmly toward permitting claims for damages resulting from negligent testimony by experts.

Some concern may be voiced over whether the growing recognition of a cause of action for expert malpractice will have a chilling effect on the willingness of persons to serve as forensic experts in litigation. The emergence of such a cause of action may in fact result in the disappearance of some experts who are habitually negligent or incompetent, but this is of course a salutary by-product of the legal trend. But even if the existence of a cause of action for expert malpractice has an effect on the availability of a number of experts, or results in an increase in the fees charged for their services, these results are not so compelling as to justify a public policy against recognizing causes of action for expert witness malpractice. The very existence of the cause of action will ensure that experts are held accountable for their opinions. The full and accurate development of evidence in civil and criminal litigation is not served by protecting the negligent, incompetent, or dishonest expert witness. The justice system as a whole benefits when such causes of actions are permitted. The forensic sciences themselves will enjoy greater respect and admiration when it is known their practitioners are accountable for misdeeds and that the professions favor eliminating the unworthy among them.[51]

---

[50] The *Matthews* holding is limited to pre-trial, litigation support activities.

[51] The President of the International Association for Identification wrote a letter to CBS' *60 Minutes* after the program about the New York State Police fingerprint experts who fabricated evidence aired on March 28, 1993. In it, he states, *inter alia*: "The IAI strongly condemns the manipulation of any type of physical evidence or sworn testimony which influences the fair outcome of an investigation or legal proceeding. Nothing undermines the integrity of scientific evidence more severely than fabrication [of evidence] by an individual." The writer also assured CBS that the organization scrutinizes very carefully all cases where any examiner's misconduct or incompetence is questioned and said "the forensic disciplines are quick to discipline and criminally prosecute those responsible." *See Letter from President Shane to CBS '60 Minutes'*, reprinted in Chesapeake Examiner, Aug. 1993, at 20.

A Lawyer's Pathway
to Medical and Scientific Information:
New Options for Bridging the Gap (Part I)

Victor Miller*
Lawrence Callahan**

Introduction

The Supreme Court's decision in *Daubert*[1] requires attorneys to bring science directly into the courtroom. With this landmark ruling, the Court made the quest for reliable scientific information an essential one.

Although most lawyers obviously know how to perform *legal* research, many regard medical and scientific research as an awesome task far beyond their capabilities. Lawyers are often unsure of *what* information they ought to be searching for, *where* to find the information, and *how* to comprehend and utilize it.

Part I of this article addresses the following questions:

- *What resources are available to members of the legal community (including the judiciary) who need medical or scientific information?*
- *What are the most efficient ways to obtain this type of information?*
- *What would it cost?*

In Part II of this article — to be published in the next issue of SESEQ — we will address how lawyers may personally interpret and utilize medical and scientific information.

I. Sources of Medical and Scientific Information

Medical and scientific information, encompassing areas like toxicology, epidemiology, and the environment, is housed in different forms and locations. There are, of course, lists of specialized libraries covering discrete subjects, like medicine, engineering, and physics.

---

* Victor Miller, a pharmacist/toxicologist and information specialist, is Director of the Center for Research Information located in the Washington, D.C. area (301) 641-0653 or (301) 585-2745.

** Lawrence Callahan, a Ph.D. in Chemistry, has been employed as a research scientist at the National Institutes of Health, the Food and Drug Administration, and the United States Pharmacopeial Convention.

[1] Daubert v. Merrell Dow Pharmaceuticals, Inc., 509 U.S. ____ , 125 L.Ed.2d 469, 113 S.Ct. 2786 (1993).

Whether you need to review primary sources (textbooks, journals, or official government publications) or secondary sources (computerized databases, abstracting services, and indexing services), it is essential to understand the differences between these sources and where best to obtain them.

A. Primary Sources

Primary sources mainly encompass new material, particularly papers describing the results of original research. New works often undergo a process of comment, modification, and evaluation, known as *the refereeing process,* before they are published. Although this process often eliminates poor studies, it does not ensure that any given work is scientifically valid or reliable.

Journals or periodicals are among the most effective ways to obtain current information and an excellent source for practitioners to keep "up-to-date." The Appendix to this article provides an overview of some of the most prominent scientific journals covering the areas of public health, epidemiology, medicine, health care administration and policy, and occupational and environmental health. (Electronic journals, a new concept that has arisen in the past decade, have yet to gain popularity.)

Scientific periodicals often contain the first detailed accounts of new work. They should provide sufficient detail to *interpret* the observations, *replicate* the experiments, and *evaluate* the theories.

When searching for an article published in an obscure journal, you might use an excellent guide to journals known as *Ulrich's International Periodicals Directory* (published by R.R. Bowker in 5 volumes). It is usually available in public libraries and university libraries. This directory may be used to determine the names of libraries that have holdings of a particular journal.

The National Library of Medicine ("NLM"), headquartered in Bethesda, Maryland, has one of the best collections of journals worldwide. You may gain access to this collection through any one of six regional centers located at universities throughout the country.

Textbooks and official government publications are also good reference sources. Textbooks may come in different formats, including reference works, handbooks, conference proceedings, and government reports. Some may contain secondary information sources: anthologies, year books, glossaries, and dictionaries. Three online databases that contain useful information regarding textbooks are CATLINE, BOOKS IN PRINT, and TACO LINE, a database in which it is possible to search for information within the table of contents of scientific and medical textbooks.

One useful technique is to identify an author of a well-known reference source (or the author of a chapter in a reference text) and contact the individual to obtain additional information.

B. Secondary Sources

Secondary sources refer to materials (online databases, printed bibliographies, etc.) prepared to disseminate information that has already appeared in another form, particularly in a primary source.

1. Abstracts, Indexes, Bibliographies

For more than a century, there has been a proliferation of books and journals devoted to specific medical and scientific subjects. Thus, the indexing of medical and scientific publications has become vital.

Indexes, catalogues, and book lists provide details of publications without elaborating on their contents. Currently, the most widely used index is *Index Medicus*, published by the NLM, a bibliographic listing of references to current articles from approximately 3,000 of the world's medical journals, in 36 languages.

Abstracts and reviews of articles go beyond titles and provide summaries of contents. A good example is *Excerpta Medica*, a European publication, divided into 41 specialized subject sections, covering more than 3,500 journals, from over 110 countries. Other examples, such as *Chemical Abstracts* and *Biological Abstracts*, may be very useful.

The NLM publishes approximately 15 bibliographies per year on topics chosen for their current popular interest. These are known as *Current Bibliographies in Medicine*. Subjects published in 1993 include *Morbidity and Mortality of Dialysis; Orthotics, Prosthetics and Mobility Aids*; and *Health Care for Women: Access, Utilization and Outcomes*.

Library of Congress Tracer Bullets are produced in Washington, D.C., by the Library of Congress' Science and Technology Division, Science Reference Section. These guides are designed to help a reader begin to locate published materials on a scientific topic. Examples include Electromagnetic Fields — Physiological and Health Effects, Alzheimer's Disease, and Asbestos.

These guides include a weighted list of subject headings to be used in searching a card, book, or computer catalog; lists of basic texts, bibliographies, state-of-the-art reports, conference proceedings, and government publications; a list of abstracting and indexing services useful in finding journal articles and technical reports; and the names and addresses of organizations to contact for additional information.

2. Electronic Databases

From the universe of the printed word, society has now progressed to electronic information retrieval. With only a personal computer and a modem, a lawyer can access vast collections of medical and scientific information.

There are now more than 70 "online databases" covering the life sciences and related areas in the United States, Europe, and Japan. These include the world's leading databases of medical and pharmaceutical information, such as *Medline, Biosis Previews*, and *Embase* (a European database renowned for its coverage of drug-related literature).

There are two primary types of computer files: bibliographic and data files. The former includes references or citations to published literature and the latter contains actual data in a structured format. The producers of these files make them available to vendors, including DIALOG and STN

International (a scientific and technical network providing access to more than 160 scientific and technical databases). The vendors in turn provide online services to end-users.

Often a database is offered by several hosts and in CD-ROM format. This makes the choice difficult. You must consider cost, convenience, frequency of use, and familiarity of the search language.

User-friendliness is an important criterion. A software program developed by the NLM, known as *Grateful Med*, allows the user to run a search on Medline without any expert knowledge. There are also databases tailored to the individual with no basic training in science or technology. One example is the *Health Periodicals Database*.

There are also some microcomputer software packages, such as *Toxicology and Public Health: Understanding Chemical Exposure,* that give the user the equivalent of a continuing education course, covering the principles of toxicology with examples from over 200 toxic materials.

II. Effective Approaches to Accessing Information

Accessing scientific and medical information for effective use in legal cases is now more crucial and in many ways easier than ever.

While the on-line databases are quite useful, they are not quite sufficient. Given the scope and sheer volume of scientific data, a complete search can seldom be accomplished with only computer terminals. You must often go to the library. (There are over 30,000 different scientific journals, and most computer-accessible scientific databases do not contain full-text articles.)

There is no doubt too that an attorney's research skills are critical in the search for scientific information. All too frequently a lack of basic scientific knowledge can cause an attorney to bypass relevant data or depend on unreliable expert witnesses. Therefore, it is often essential for an attorney to have a basic understanding of the science involved in a case from the very beginning.

There are many good sources of background information. *Deadly Doses: A Writer's Guide to Poisons* (Writer's Digest Books, Cincinnati, Ohio, 1990, edited by S.D. Stevens and A. Klarner) is an example of a well-written text explaining basic toxicological principles in easy-to-read language. It was written for mystery crime writers who devise elaborate plots to "poison" their victims.

At the opposite end of the spectrum is the well-known text, *Casarett and Doull's Toxicology: The Basic Science of Poisons* (Pergamon Press, New York, 1991, 4th ed.). It is written primarily for graduate students in toxicology. This comprehensive text is well written, and the accompanying index is a useful guide to detailed aspects of the discipline.

Frequently, legal arguments revolve around issues of (1) causation —did exposure to the chemical cause the cancer or another debilitating physical or mental sickness; (2) patents —had the compound been synthesized previously; (3) treatment protocols —was the physician's treatment within generally accepted medical standards.

Encyclopedias are often the best places to start in the quest for this type of medical or scientific information. *Encyclopedia Britannica,* which is now divided into a 12-volume micropaedia and a 29-volume macropaedia, often provides good background information. It is available on CD-ROM, which permits fast electronic searches.

More detailed scientific information is available in the 20-volume *McGraw-Hill Encyclopedia of Science and Technology,* and the *Kirk-Othmer Encyclopedia of Chemical Technology,* a particularly good, comprehensive encyclopedia that specializes in chemical technology. Both are available on WESTLAW.

In the medical field, the *Penguin Medical Encyclopedia* explains diseases, organs, and human physiology in straightforward, nontechnical language. The *British Medical Association Complete Family Health Encyclopedia* is clear, well illustrated, comprehensive, and informative.

Another often overlooked source of basic scientific information is the popular magazine. *Scientific American, Science News, Chemical and Engineering News, Journal of the American Medical Association, Science, Nature,* and the *New England Journal of Medicine* all contain excellent review articles in many diverse areas. All are available in a full-text format on either WESTLAW (MAG-ASAP) or NEXIS.

Newspapers are also excellent sources of information on fast-breaking developments. Indeed, newspapers often contain the *first* reports of significant developments. NEXIS and WESTLAW (PAPERS, NEWSABS, NEWSEARCH) are particularly useful databases for relevant newspaper articles. The *New York Times* and the *Washington Post* each provide extensive medical and scientific coverage.

Textbooks are also commonly used to acquire basic understanding. Each scientific or medical field has at least one or two textbooks that are generally considered to be "classics" or "bibles" within those fields. The *Oxford Textbook of Medicine* is comprehensive and one of the few medical textbooks available on CD-ROM. *Cecil's Textbook of Medicine* (Saunders), *Harrison's Principles of Internal Medicine* (McGraw-Hill), *Davidson's Principles and Practice of Medicine* (Churchill Livingstone), and *The Principles and Practice of Medicine* (Appleton and Lange), are all standard general medical texts. All are updated regularly and are generally available in many public libraries.

Other texts that are classics in their fields, updated regularly and of particular value in legal matters, include: *Goodman and Gilman's The Pharmacological Basis of Therapeutics* (Macmillan), *Textbook of Adverse Drug Reactions* (Oxford), *Anderson's Pathology* (Mosby), *Hutchison's Clinical Methods* (Bailliere Tindall), *Oxford Textbook of Public Health, Brain's Diseases of the Nervous System* (Oxford), *Danforth's Obstetrics and Gynecology* (Lippincott), *Williams' Obstetrics* (Prentice-Hall), *Casarett and Doull's Toxicology* (Macmillan), *Epidemiology in Medicine* (Little Brown), *Hunter's Diseases of Occupations* (Hoder & Stoughton), *Andrew's Diseases of the Skin* (Saunders), *Occupational Skin Disease* (Saunders), *Diagnostic Imaging* (Blackwell Scientific), *Current Surgical Diagnosis and Treatment* (Prentice-Hall), *Cancer: Principles and Practice of Oncology* (Lippincott), *Immunology* (I.M. Riott,

Churchill Livingstone), *Immunological Diseases* (Little Brown), *Arthritis and Allied Conditions* (Lea & Febiger), *Comprehensive Textbook of Psychiatry* (Williams and Wilkins), *Essentials of Dental Surgery and Pathology* (Churchill Livingstone), *Principles of Biochemistry* (McGraw Hill), *Textbook of Clinical Chemistry* (Saunders), *Wintrobe's Clinical Hematology* (Lea & Febinger), *Clinical Microbiology* (Arnold), *Microbiology* (Davis et al., Lippincott), and *Simpson's Forensic Medicine* (Edward Arnold).

There are several caveats to remember when using textbooks. They are frequently out of date, even as they roll off the presses. The are also typically filled with conventional wisdom and technical jargon. Nevertheless, textbooks are best used to achieve a basic understanding of what is "generally accepted."

Handbooks can also be very useful, particularly in providing information on medical treatment, diagnosis, or drugs. The following are of particular value and are updated on a regular basis: *Conn's Current Therapy* (Saunders), *Current Medical Diagnosis and Treatment 1994* (Appleton & Lange), *Merck Manual of Diagnosis and Treatment, Martindale Extra Pharmacopoeia* (Pharmaceutical Press), and the *USP Dispensing Information* (United States Pharmacopeial Convention).

In medicine and science, as in most fields, you must understand some of the technical jargon. Therefore, it is often important to have several good specialized dictionaries available and to use them when necessary.

Most fields of medicine and science have specialized dictionaries that contain reliable, precise definitions. *Butterworths Medical Dictionary* and *Churchill's Illustrated Medical Dictionary* are the two most comprehensive medical dictionaries. *Dorland's Illustrated Medical Dictionary, Stedman's Medical Dictionary*, and *Gould Blakiston's Medical Dictionary* are also reliable and widely available. *Hawley's Condensed Chemical Dictionary* (Van Nostrand Reinhold), the *McGraw-Hill Dictionary of Scientific and Technical Terms*, the *Dictionary of Toxicology* (Macmillan), and the *Macmillan Dictionary of Immunology* are useful guides to the technical jargon in their respective fields.

For an overview of recent developments in a well-defined medical field, an excellent resource would be any of the following electronic medical databases: MEDLINE, EMBASE, or BIOSIS PREVIEWS. All are available on WESTLAW. MEDLINE is also available on MEDIS (LEXIS).

MEDLINE (MEDlars Online) indexes over 3,200 journals published in the United States and 70 other countries in every field of biomedicine. Coverage of previous periodicals (coverage dates back to 1966) is provided by backfiles that total almost 6 million references. It is produced by the NLM, through whom it can be accessed at a much reduced rate and easily searched using the *Grateful Med* Software.

A particularly useful feature of the NLM databases is that each article is analyzed and indexed using Medical Subject Headings (MeSH), a 16,000-term medical language thesaurus. This thesaurus is available when using *Grateful Med* and can greatly assist you in searching for relevant literature.

EMBASE, a European database produced by Elsevier Science Publishers in the Netherlands, consists of abstracts and citations from over 3,500 biomedical journals from 1974 onwards. It focuses on international literature and is particularly renowned for its coverage of drugs. It is available in the United States through DIALOG.

BIOSIS PREVIEWS provides the most comprehensive worldwide coverage of research in the life sciences. It covers over 9,000 primary journals and monographs as well as symposia, reviews, preliminary reports, and selected institutional and government reports and other secondary sources. BIOSIS is produced in Philadelphia with coverage dating back to 1969. Most of the records contain no abstract and the primary usefulness of this database may be to uncover information on difficult-to-find research topics.

There are a number of other databases that can be particularly informative in their respective fields.

Three databases available from NLM are very useful for gathering toxicological information. TOXNET provides valuable data on hazardous chemicals. It consist of nine files, including CCRIS (Chemical Carcinogenesis Research Information System). It is a scientifically evaluated, fully referenced database, developed by the National Cancer Institute, that contains carcinogenicity, tumor promotion, and mutagenicity test results on over 3,000 chemicals; HSDB (Hazardous Substance Data Bank) is a factual, non-bibliographic database that focuses on the toxicology of potentially hazardous chemicals and contains records on over 4,500 chemical substances.

RTECS (Registry of Toxic Effects of Chemical Substances), maintained by the National Institute of Occupational Safety and Health (NIOSH), contains data on the toxic effects of over 100,000 chemicals; TRI (Toxic chemical Release Inventory) contains annual estimated releases of toxic chemicals to the environment and the amount transferred to waste sites by industrial facilities, dating back to 1987 (based on data submitted to the EPA as mandated by the Emergency Planning and Community Right to Know Act); EMIC (Environmental Mutagen Information Center) and ETIC (Environmental Teratology Information Center) contain bibliographic information dating back to 1950 on genotoxic agents.

TOXLINE, which is also available on WESTLAW, contains extensive bibliographic coverage of the toxicological, pharmacological, biochemical, and physiological effects of drugs and chemicals. Information is derived from secondary sources that do not require royalty charges. Therefore, it is a relatively inexpensive source of information. TOXLINE dates back to 1965 and can also be searched using MeSH vocabulary.

TOXLIT is derived from Chemical Abstracts and contains information from a wider variety of sources than TOXLINE, including patent literature. TOXLIT is significantly more expensive than TOXLINE and there is a good deal of overlap. TOXLIT should be used when a comprehensive search is desired or when the information cannot be found in TOXLINE.

AGRICOLA is the database of the National Agricultural Library and provides comprehensive coverage of worldwide literature on agriculture and related subjects from 1970. It is available on WESTLAW and in CD-ROM from several vendors.

CAB ABSTRACTS is also a comprehensive database on agriculture and biological information produced by the Commonwealth Agricultural Bureaux in Great Britain. It is also available on WESTLAW and covers material from 1972 onwards.

CA SEARCH is produced by the Chemical Abstracts Service and includes citations to over 10,000 journals covering the worldwide patent literature. It has extensive coverage in all areas of chemistry and chemical engineering and dates back to 1967. It is available from DIALOG and STN International. COMPENDEX PLUS is the computer database version of Engineering Index and is produced by Engineering Information. It covers over 4,500 journals from 1970 onwards and is available on WESTLAW.

DIOGENES is a database that contains information relating to the US Food and Drug Administration (FDA) and is prepared by FOI Services. The database contains news stories and unpublished documents relating to the United States regulation of pharmaceuticals and medical devices. It includes documents obtained from the FDA under the Freedom of Information Act, newsletters, enforcement reports, medical device report incident summaries, press releases, and talk papers from the FDA.

CATLINE is the National Library of Medicine's Catalogue on Line (CATLINE) containing records of over 660,000 monographs, reports, and first issues of periodicals published since 1801. The file is updated weekly.

BOOKS IN PRINT ONLINE, produced by R.R. Bowker, contains bibliographic descriptions and ordering information for more than 1.9 million books currently in print or declared out of print (from July 1979 to date) and soon to-be-published titles from some 22,000 publishers.

OUT-OF-PRINT SCIENTIFIC, MEDICAL AND TECHNICAL BOOKS ONLINE (produced by John P. Coll Books) contains bibliographic descriptions of more than 3,000 out-of-print books in the fields of physical and biological sciences, engineering, and medicine. Citations are searchable by personal author, corporate author, exact title, title words, or subject category.

DIRLINE, the Directory of Information Resources online, contains records of mainly U.S. professional societies, voluntary associations, government agencies, institutions, libraries, self-help/support groups, health information centers, poison control centers, and similar sources.

REPROTOX provides up-to-date information and summaries of articles dealing with industrial and environmental chemicals and their effects on human fertility, pregnancy, and fetal development. It is available online from the Reproductive Toxicology Center at the Columbia Hospital for Women in Washington D.C. Updates are continuous and new agents are added weekly.

ALLIED AND ALTERNATIVE MEDICINE is a unique online database, produced in the UK, providing coverage of the wider areas of clinical medicine such as acupuncture, herbal medicine, homeopathy, holistic treatment, and other areas of "complementary" medical practice. It is available in the U.S. through DIALOG.

NAPRALERT (Natural Products Alert) is an online database that contains bibliographic and factual data on natural products and covers the pharmacology, biological activity, taxonomic distribution and chemistry of plant, microbial, and animal (including marine) extracts. It is available through STN International.

IBIS (Interactive BodyMind Information System) represents a truly unique database. It is a medical database program referencing 282 common medical conditions, and offering treatments from more than 12 systems of conventional and natural therapies. (Examples include the subjects of nutrition, botanical medicine, Chinese herbs, acupuncture, homeopathy, physical medicine, and psychospiritual therapies). IBIS is written in hypermedia format to allow fast and flexible access to complex information. Discs are available for use on Macintosh computers.

These information resources reflect only a *portion* of the scientific information that is available.

III. Costs and Account-Related Matters

The information industry unfortunately has no standard way of pricing its products. A number of parameters are explained below that may be of assistance in evaluating the costs of searches:

1. Connect-hour charges: most vendors charge for each minute during which the searcher is connected to the system. The actual connect time charge varies with each database.

    Other vendors quote a basic system connect rate, a database royalty rate, and telecommunications (packet switching network) costs. (Packet switching networks are special telephone circuits designed to carry only computer data, including Tymnet, Telenet, and Sprintnet). To determine the actual costs, all these components must be added together.

2. Some vendors quote a connect hour rate that includes a number of different components. Prime-time premium/off hours discount: for vendors such as Data-Star a premium is paid to access a vendor's system during regular business hours. A discount is given if the search is conducted after business hours or late in the evening.

3. Some vendors quote a connect hour rate that includes a number of different components. Display charges: these charges come in several varieties and depend upon how much of a given record is viewed.

    (a) Offline print charge: databases that have display charges usually give the option of having a record or parts of a record printed offline at the vendor's computer facility and the hard-copy printout is then mailed to the end-user.

(b)   Display formats: vendors such as Dialog give the user various options with respect to the format of the bibliographic citation. For example, a "full" format display of each record in Embase costs $0.90.

Examples of different formats include bibliographic citation and abstract or the full text of articles. To make matters more complicated, the cost for displaying each format *varies* with the database, and the actual information displayed in each format *varies* with the database.

All online hosts produce lists of the databases they offer for searching, and most provide detailed information about the size and scope of each file, the structure of its records, and the costs of accessing them.

APPENDIX

ACADEMIC MEDICINE
AMERICAN JOURNAL OF ROENTGENOLOGY
AMERICAN FAMILY PHYSICIAN
AMERICAN HEART JOURNAL
AMERICAN JOURNAL OF CARDIOLOGY
AMERICAN JOURNAL OF CLINICAL NUTRITION
AMERICAN JOURNAL OF CLINICAL PATHOLOGY
AMERICAN JOURNAL OF DISEASES OF CHILDREN
AMERICAN JOURNAL OF THE MEDICAL SCIENCES
AMERICAN JOURNAL OF MEDICINE
AMERICAN JOURNAL OF NURSING
AMERICAN JOURNAL OF OBSTETRICS AND GYNECOLOGY
AMERICAN JOURNAL OF OPHTHALMOLOGY
AMERICAN JOURNAL OF PATHOLOGY
AMERICAN JOURNAL OF PHYSICAL MEDICINE AND
   REHABILITATION
AMERICAN JOURNAL OF PSYCHIATRY
AMERICAN JOURNAL OF PUBLIC HEALTH
AMERICAN JOURNAL OF SURGERY
AMERICAN JOURNAL OF TROPICAL MEDICINE AND
   HYGIENE
AMERICAN REVIEW OF RESPIRATORY DISEASE
ANESTHESIA
ANESTHESIA AND ANALGESIA
ANESTHESIOLOGY ANNALS OF EMERGENCY MEDICINE
ANNALS OF INTERNAL MEDICINE
ANNALS OF OTOLOGY, RHINOLOGY AND LARYNGOLOGY
ANNALS OF SURGERY
ANNALS OF THORACIC SURGERY
ARCHIVES OF DERMATOLOGY
ARCHIVES OF DISEASE IN CHILDHOOD
ARCHIVES OF ENVIRONMENTAL HEALTH
ARCHIVES OF GENERAL PSYCHIATRY
ARCHIVES OF INTERNAL MEDICINE
ARCHIVES OF NEUROLOGY
ARCHIVES OF OPHTHALMOLOGY
ARCHIVES OF OTOLARYNGOLOGY—HEAD AND NECK
   SURGERY
ARCHIVES OF PATHOLOGY AND LABORATORY MEDICINE
ARCHIVES OF PHYSICAL MEDICINE AND REHABILITATION
ARCHIVES OF SURGERY ARTHRITIS AND RHEUMATISM
BLOOD
BRITISH MEDICAL JOURNAL
BRAIN
BRITISH HEART JOURNAL
BRITISH JOURNAL OF OBSTETRICS AND GYNECOLOGY

BRITISH JOURNAL OF RADIOLOGY
BRITISH JOURNAL OF RHEUMATOLOGY
BRITISH JOURNAL OF SURGERY
CA: A CANCER JOURNAL FOR CLINICIANS
CANADIAN MEDICAL ASSOCIATION JOURNAL
CANCER
CHEST CIRCULATION CLINICAL ORTHOPAEDICS AND
    RELATED RESEARCH
CLINICAL PEDIATRICS CLINICAL PHARMACOLOGY AND
    THERAPEUTICS
CRITICAL CARE MEDICINE
CURRENT PROBLEMS IN SURGERY
DIABETES
DIGESTIVE DISEASES AND SCIENCES
DISEASE-A-MONTH
ENDOCRINOLOGY
GASTROENTEROLOGY
GERIATRICS
GUT HEART AND LUNG HOSPITAL PRACTICE (OFFICE
    EDITION)
HOSPITALS AND HEALTH NETWORKS
JOURNAL OF THE AMERICAN MEDICAL ASSOCIATION
    (JAMA)
JOURNAL OF ALLERGY AND CLINICAL IMMUNOLOGY
JOURNAL OF THE AMERICAN COLLEGE OF CARDIOLOGY
JOURNAL OF THE AMERICAN DIETETIC ASSOCIATION
JOURNAL OF BONE AND JOINT SURGERY.
AMERICAN VOL. JOURNAL OF BONE AND JOINT SURGERY.
BRITISH VOL. JOURNAL OF CLINICAL ENDOCRINOLOGY
    AND METABOLISM
JOURNAL OF CLINICAL INVESTIGATION
JOURNAL OF CLINICAL PATHOLOGY
JOURNAL OF FAMILY PRACTICE
JOURNAL OF GERONTOLOGY JOURNAL OF IMMUNOLOGY
JOURNAL OF INFECTIOUS DISEASES
JOURNAL OF LABORATORY AND CLINICAL MEDICINE
JOURNAL OF LARYNGOLOGY AND OTOLOGY
JOURNAL OF NERVOUS AND MENTAL DISEASE
JOURNAL OF NEUROSURGERY
JOURNAL OF NURSING ADMINISTRATION
JOURNAL OF ORAL AND MAXILLOFACIAL SURGERY
JOURNAL OF PEDIATRICS
JOURNAL OF THORACIC AND CARDIOVASCULAR SURGERY
JOURNAL OF TOXICOLOGY
CLINICAL TOXICOLOGY
JOURNAL OF TRAUMA
JOURNAL OF UROLOGY

LANCET
MAYO CLINIC PROCEEDINGS
MEDICAL CLINICS OF NORTH AMERICA
MEDICAL LETTER ON DRUGS AND THERAPEUTICS
MEDICINE
NEUROLOGY
NEW ENGLAND JOURNAL OF MEDICINE
NURSING CLINICS OF NORTH AMERICA
NURSING OUTLOOK
NURSING RESEARCH
OBSTETRICS AND GYNECOLOGY
ORTHOPEDIC CLINICS OF NORTH AMERICA
PEDIATRIC CLINICS OF NORTH AMERICA
PEDIATRICS PHYSICAL THERAPY
PLASTIC AND RECONSTRUCTIVE SURGERY
POSTGRADUATE MEDICINE
PROGRESS IN CARDIOVASCULAR DISEASES
PUBLIC HEALTH REPORTS
RADIOLOGIC CLINICS OF NORTH AMERICA
RADIOLOGY SOUTHERN MEDICAL JOURNAL
SURGERY
SURGERY, GYNECOLOGY AND OBSTETRICS
SURGICAL CLINICS OF NORTH AMERICA
UROLOGIC CLINICS OF NORTH AMERICA
WESTERN JOURNAL OF MEDICINE

Reaction to *Daubert v Merrell Dow*

Carl F. Cranor*

The U.S. Supreme Court in *Daubert v. Merrell Dow Pharmaceuticals, Inc.*[1] clearly rejected the *Frye*[2] test for the admissibility of scientific evidence in toxic tort cases, holding that it had been superseded by the Federal Rules of Evidence. It further held that the Federal Rules, especially Rule 702, contemplate some degree of regulation of "the subjects and theories about which an expert can testify."[3] Thus, a trial judge, the court said, "must ensure that any and all scientific testimony or evidence is not only relevant, but reliable."[4] Moreover, there must be a "grounding in the methods and procedures of science," the knowledge "must be derived by the scientific method" to establish evidentiary reliability, and the knowledge must be "relevant" to the facts of the case.[5] This ruling entails a preliminary assessment "of whether the reasoning or methodology underlying the testimony is scientifically valid and of whether that reasoning or methodology can be applied to the facts in issue."[6] In *dicta* the Court suggests several factors that *may be* relevant to this inquiry, but also notes that none of them is decisive nor is the list exhaustive: the theory or technique's testability, whether it has been subjected to peer review, its known or potential error rate, and its acceptance within a particular part of the scientific community.[7] And, quite importantly, "[t]he focus, of course, must be solely on principles and methodology, not on the conclusions they generate."[8]

Finally, the court addressed both plaintiff and defense concerns about its decision. To the defense who claimed that abandoning the *Frye* test would lead to a " 'free-for-all' in which befuddled juries are confounded by absurd

---

*Carl F. Cranor is Professor of Philosophy and Interim Dean of the College of Humanities and Social Science at the University of California, Riverside. He has served as the principal investigator of the Carcinogen Risk Assessment Project (University of California, Riverside), a project funded in part by the National Science Foundation, and has served on California's Proposition 65 Science Advisory Panel and as Co-Chair of California's Comparative Risk Project.

1 ____ U.S. ____ , 113 S.Ct. 2786, 125 L.Ed.2d 469 (1993).

2 Frye v. United States, 293 F. 1013 (D.C. Cir. 1923).

3 *Daubert*, 113 S.Ct. at 2795. The dissenting opinion concurred in rejecting the Frye rule and concurred that scientific testimony must be relevant, but argued that the majority had overreached itself in arguing for the "reliability" of evidence as part of Rule 702.

4 *Daubert*, 113 S.Ct. at 2795.

5 *Id.* 2795-96.

6 *Id.* 2796.

7 *Id.* 2796-97.

8 *Id.* 2797.

and irrational pseudoscientific assertions," it responded that this view is "overly pessimistic about the capabilities of the jury, and of the adversary system generally."[9] Instead, "[v]igorous cross-examination, presentation of contrary evidence, and careful instruction on the burden of proof" as well as directed verdicts and summary judgments serve as corrections to "scintilla" of evidence sufficient for admission, but insufficient for a verdict.[10] As to plaintiff's concerns that acknowledging a screening role for judges will sanction a "stifling and repressive scientific orthodoxy and will be inimical for the search for truth," the Court acknowledges the possibility that in practice even a flexible gatekeeping role for the judge, "inevitably on occasion will prevent a jury from learning of authentic insights and innovations."[11]

I

Several observations are in order about this decision. First, in articulating its test for admissibility, the Court "of course" focuses on the "principles and methodology" that scientists use, not on their "conclusions."[12] Conclusions should be a matter of scientific opinion based upon valid "methodology and procedures." Thus, there is a clear statement that judges should evaluate the scientific procedures and methodology, but not use a scientist's *conclusions* as the reason for excluding testimony. Some might suggest that just because an expert uses a sound methodology, e.g., a stethoscope, he or she could infer a bad conclusion from it. While such an invalid inference or misuse is possible, the court addressed the issue, noting that the expert testimony must be relevant and assist the trier of facts in the case.[13] The distinction between the principles and methodology an expert uses and the conclusions he or she reaches is both important and subject to debate. It is subject to debate because the defense bar is likely to favor judges evaluating conclusions while the plaintiffs' bar favors a focus only on principles and methodology. It is important because, if judges had the authority to weigh the credibility of the conclusions that qualified experts reach, this authority would tend to usurp the function of the jury.[14] Moreover, it is precisely the conclusions of experts that are likely to be at issue, especially if they are inconsistent with those of other experts. In such cases it should be the finder of facts who decides the issue — as long as, in light of *Daubert*, the methodology is correct. In addition, some might suggest that an expert's entire chain of reasoning should be subject to judicial examination for admissibility. This would substitute an admissibility hearing for trials, would necessitate judicial inquiry into every

---

[9] *Id.* 2798.

[10] *Id.*

[11] *Id.* 2798-99.

[12] *Id.* 2797.

[13] *Id.* 2795-96.

[14] Kenneth J. Cheesbro, *Taking Daubert's 'Focus' Seriously: The Methodology/Conclusion Distinction*, 2 Mealey's Litigation Reports: Toxic Torts 16.

inference, and would necessitate judges becoming scientists and logicians in order to evaluate inferences. And the judge would supplant the jury in judging all links in the inference chain. Moreover, the Court notes the traditional remedies of cross-examination for exposing poor reasoning.

Second, with respect to the four factors that bear on "whether the reasoning or methodology underlying the testimony is scientifically valid," none is decisive or determinative of the validity of reasoning or methodology and as a group they are not exhaustive.[15] Thus, the four factors or considerations should not become a *four-factor test* because the Court clearly does not intend this. Moreover, it is easy to see why several of these factors should not be determinative. Peer review typically does not determine valid reasoning or procedures; it may improve the work and help to clarify it or to check it, but if the work is well done, it is typically well done independent of the peer evaluation. Moreover, publication "does not necessarily correlate with reliability . . . and in some instances well-grounded but innovative theories will not have been published . . . [and some results] are too particular, too new or of too limited interest to be published."[16] In addition, general acceptance is no guarantee of valid reasoning or procedures since one can both reason validly about scientific matters even though one's views have not been generally accepted in the scientific community[17] and have invalid reasoning or procedures accepted by some appropriate part of the scientific community at least for some period of time. Thus, acceptance is neither logically nor pragmatically necessary or sufficient for the validity of reasoning. Both peer review and general acceptance provide checks on inferences to scientific conclusions, but neither is determinative. Finally, even testability, which seems to be an obvious criterion of what constitutes a defensible scientific principle, may not always be possible for a given theory. The Office of Technology Assessment has noted that some of the models used to provide evidence of the carcinogenic effects of substances have not yet been tested (although they potentially could be); that some, at least in the present state of knowledge, cannot be tested because of experimental limitations; and that some should not be tested because of moral concerns.[18] Indeed, some theories in physics, perhaps the paradigm science for many, are even known to be false.[19]

Third, the Court clearly recognizes a distinction between the "scintilla" of evidence sufficient to carry the burden of production and the amount of evidence sufficient for carrying the burden of persuasion. This is noteworthy

---

[15] *Daubert*, 113 S.Ct. at 2796. The factors are described at *id.* 2796-97.

[16] *Id.* 2797.

[17] Cranor, Regulating Toxic Substances: A Philosophy of Science and the Law 68 (New York: Oxford University Press, 1993).

[18] The U.S. Congress, Office of Technology Assessment, Identifying and Regulating Carcinogens 25 (Washington, D.C.: U.S. Government Printing Office, 1987).

[19] Nancy Cartwright, a 1993 MacArthur Fellow, argues this in How the Laws of Physics Lie (Oxford: The Clarenden Press, 1983) at 3 and throughout.

because some commentators place such great weight on the judicial screening of scientific testimony that this becomes the focus of attention. Plaintiffs merely need the appropriate quality and amount of evidence (the "scintilla") necessary to carry the production burden for admissibility, not the amount and persuasiveness of evidence to win the case. Yet some commentators and defense briefs in *Daubert* suggest that before evidence is *admissible* it must be not only accepted in the scientific community, but published in the peer-reviewed literature. Since in some toxic tort cases a few major pieces of evidence determine the outcome of a case, e.g., one or two epidemiological studies are quite important, evidence sufficient to survive such stringent requirements for major pieces of evidence hardly seems like a "scintilla." Thus, it seems that "scintilla" at the least should refer not only to the contribution a piece of evidence would make to an overall case (small), but also to the likelihood of its truth (not high as the discussion of demanding substantive standards of admissibility suggest). In short, if the substantive requirements for admissibility are too demanding, this will be inconsistent with the claim that there need only be a scintilla of evidence to satisfy the requirement.

II

Both the defense and the plaintiff's bar are striving for the appropriate "spin" on the Court's opinion in *Daubert* in order to help shape future trial court cases and appellate opinions. And, of course, the spin can have substantial effects on the development of the law. However, rather than discuss detailed points of interpretation, perhaps a more useful contribution is to put some of the technical-interpretative issues into a broader context. These broader issues in general cluster around the science-law interface, conceptions of science, the substantive burdens that must be satisfied in order to carry the burden of production and science-law policy issues. However, all of these are framed by background considerations of the legal/regulatory environment in which toxic tort cases must be decided.

Many, perhaps most, potentially toxic substances have come into commerce as products or into the environment as byproducts of production, as contaminants or as pollutants without extensive legally required testing for their effects on human health and the environment. Some *products* have been tested under premarket approval statutes such as the Food, Drug and Cosmetic Act (FDCA), the Consumer Products Safety Act (CPSA), or the Federal Insecticide, Fungicide, and Rodenticide Act (FIFRA), of course, but many of these were in commerce before extensive testing was required.[20] And even when testing has been required as a result of legislation of the

---

[20] For example, in 1987 there were about 600 pesticides that had been in the market prior to 1970 that had not been adequately tested. Even many registered since 1970 lack full toxicity testing. OTA, Identifying and Regulating Carcinogens 118-26.

1970s, it is not clear how good that premarket screening has been.[21] Even when substances have been subjected to testing under the FDCA, CPSA, or FIFRA, there are political and commercial pressures to move them into commerce which may result in their not being fully tested for diseases that have long latency periods, that have more subtle effects, or that are unusual or unexpected. For substances that have been permitted into the environment since the Toxic Substances Control Act was enacted in 1976, it is not clear how carefully they have been screened under that premarket approval procedure.[22] Moreover, typically the pollutants, contaminants, and byproducts of production are not subject to premarket evaluation. And, under most regulatory statutes, substances cannot be withdrawn from commerce, or exposures to pollutants or contaminants regulated, without the government bearing the burden of proof (which varies by statute) to establish that the substances are harmful at current exposure levels.[23] Of course, tort law remedies which have both deterrent and "regulatory" effects are not available to plaintiffs until they carry both the burden of production to the satisfaction of a judge and the burden of persuasion to the satisfaction of a jury.

Related to the above point is the relation between the regulatory law and the tort law. It may be that in principle the regulatory law is the appropriate institution to judge the risks and benefits from exposures to potentially toxic substances, but frequently this "in principle" attractiveness is undermined by agencies being "captured" by the regulated industry.[24] Thus, on the one hand, if one sees the regulatory system as more protective of human health in these areas than the tort system or as providing a better balance of the affected interests, then one might well be less concerned about how stringent tort law burdens of proof and admissibility rules should be. On the other hand, if one sees the tort system as a partial backup for the failures of the regulatory system (even when premarket approval statutes are in issue), then cumbersome production burdens would substantially frustrate the backup function of the tort law. And, if one sees the tort law as a kind of last-ditch insurance scheme against uncompensated harms probably caused by others, this might argue for less demanding burdens of production and admissibility rules.

In this legal environment, scientists must provide evidence of harm before a substance can be regulated more stringently or before a tort suit is successful. Consequently, the more stringent are the tort law admissibility standards, the harder it is for plaintiffs to carry their production burden, the

---

[21] OTA, Identifying and Regulating Carcinogens 3-20, esp. 18.

[22] *Id.* 14, 126-34.

[23] *Id.* 199-200.

[24] *See* Barry Mitnick, The Political Economy of Regulation (N.Y.: Columbia University Press, 1980), Kenneth Meier, Regulation: Politics, Bureaucracy, and Economics (N.Y.: St. Martin's Press, 1985), and Michael Reagan, Regulation: Politics and Policy (Boston: Little Brown, 1987).

harder it is for plaintiffs to receive compensation for any injuries suffered, and the harder it is for the tort law to have any deterrent or regulatory effects or to serve a backup role to the regulatory system. This, by itself, is not an argument for one set of admissibility standards versus another, but it is a reminder that, because plaintiffs have both the production and the persuasion burden because they seek to change the legal status quo, these combined with scientific standards of evidence can have substantial effects on the outcome of cases and their wider legal and social effects. Moreover, in the tort law overall a plaintiff's risk of losing should not be much greater than defendant's risk of losing. However, if scientific standards of evidence are much more demanding than legal burdens of proof (on which more below) and if they determine the evidentiary standards for admissibility, this will substantially distort the traditional balance of interests at stake in the tort law.[25] In recent years there has been widespread discussion urging that even more scientific information should be legally required to document that substances are harmful before tort action is permitted. Given the current legal/tort environment and the typically more stringent burdens of proof in science, such demands will decrease successful meritorious tort suits. The coincidence of scientific and legal burdens of proof may have gone unnoticed, but these two together can have profound consequences for protecting human health.

Thus, one's views of the legal/regulatory environment, the relationship between the tort and the regulatory law, and the relationship between substantive burdens of proof in science and the law may substantially shape one's views about the degree to which judges should screen scientific evidence in the tort law. These background points are raised because frequently they are not articulated and the discussion is merely focused on technical-interpretive issues which may conceal crucial issues.

Both the plaintiffs' and defendants' bars offer somewhat different views of what science is and the role it has to play in tort cases. The defense bar tends to see science as a "cumulative process in which scientists build on each other's work."[26] Such views emphasize the publication of results that have been subjected to peer review and continual challenge which leads to a convergence of reasoned explanations. The plaintiffs' bar tends to characterize science as a "field of constant discovery and advance in reasoning . . . [in which] breakthroughs inevitably take time to gain general acceptance."[27] Plaintiffs' *amici* develop this view arguing that scientific theories are

---

[25] Regulating Toxic Substances 55, 77, 156.

[26] Bert Black and John Andrew Singer, *Focus on: Daubert v. Merrell-Dow Pharmaceuticals, Inc.*, 1 Shepard's Expert & Scientific Evidence Quarterly 19, 29 (1993), citing defense *amicus* briefs by the American Association of Science and the National Academy of Science.

[27] Petitioners' Brief 33 n. 62.

"imaginative visions superimposed on . . . facts."[28] Science "lies not in discovering facts, but in discovering new ways of thinking about them."[29]

What is important for the interpretive debate about *Daubert* is not that one conception of science versus another must be chosen by the courts, because that would freeze into law a particular interpretation of what science is, a concern expressed by the *Daubert* minority.[30] Rather, the courts and commentators should recognize, as the *Daubert* Court has, that both conceptions of the vast array of intellectual activities we call "science" have truth to them,[31] and that room in the law must be made for the differing views of science and the variety of activities engaged in under that rubric. That is, some of the activities we call science are indeed cumulative, building carefully on the work of others. Other activities are substantial reconceptions of what has gone before (one need only read the work of Thomas Kuhn and sociologists of science to see this point). And there has been considerable recent work arguing that because the facts "underdetermine" the theories which seek to explain them, the theories are not only "imaginative visions superimposed on . . . facts" as the Plaintiffs' *amicus* briefs claim, but that they are artifacts of society and culture more generally.[32] Moreover, it may be that both characterizations are appropriate for both "normal" and revolutionary science if one looks closely enough.[33] That is, since facts typically underdetermine the theories to explain them, even in normal or routine science, disagreements between scientists may constitute reconceptions of the facts or substantial departures from the work of others. And from a historical perspective, even revolutionary advances may appear to add cumulatively to the stock of scientific knowledge. It should not be the role of the law to take a position on complex interpretive views of what science is, views in dispute both within the scientific community and within the community of commentators on science, in order to adjudicate issues in the tort law. The evidentiary house of the law should be large enough for different *respectable* conceptions of science and the insights which the different views have to offer for particular disputes. Neither the defense nor plaintiff community has a corner on the whole truth about what science is and neither view should dominate the discussion or dictate the "proper" interpretation of *Daubert*. Much is

---

[28] Physicians, Scientists and Historians of Science Brief in Support of Petitioners 7-8.

[29] *Id.* 11.

[30] *Daubert*, 113 S.Ct. at 2799-800 (Rehnquist, CJ, concurring in part and dissenting in part).

[31] *Daubert*, 113 S.Ct. at 2798.

[32] Thomas Kuhn, The Structure of Scientific Revolutions 7 (Chicago: The University of Chicago Press, 1970) and Stephen Jay Gould, The Mismeasure of Man 322 (Cambridge: Harvard University Press, 1981), as well as numerous sociologists of science who have gone beyond Kuhn's views.

[33] A University of California, Riverside, philosophy doctoral student, Dennis Deets, is currently conducting research on this issue.

contested and unclear about the nature of science and scientific reasoning that has not been addressed in discussions about the use of science in the tort law.[34]

Thus, judges should be reluctant to endorse any particular conception of science offered by the contending parties, because, as indicated above, both defense and plaintiffs' *amici* call attention to important features of science. If this view is correct, then for purposes of admissibility, judges should adopt more permissive rather than less permissive admissibility rules in so far as these are based on a *respectable* view of what science is, because otherwise they may be resting their admissibility decisions on narrow conceptions of science that are both mistaken as to a correct view of scientific activities and prejudicial to one side or another in the legal disputes at issue.[35]

A second contested notion resulting from the *Daubert* decision is the role of who should decide on the evaluation of scientific evidence for admissibility.[36] Since both judges and juries will have to evaluate the persuasiveness of science, one issue is whether judges or juries should have a proportionately greater role in assessing it. On one extreme judges should let all scientific evidence in as long as the expert has the appropriate professional credentials and let the jury decide how persuasive the admitted evidence is. On the other extreme, judges should screen out all scientific evidence that has not been published in peer-reviewed literature and should keep the jury from considering all but the most persuasive peer-reviewed evidence.

It is important to notice how the issues are framed. Some in the defense bar suggest that the issue is mainly one of competence: are judges or juries more competent to judge admissibility of scientific evidence? And, of course, the answer is that judges are more competent because they are used "to dealing with abstruse and esoteric concepts."[37] However, this only partially characterizes the issue. While relative competence is *a consideration* in

---

[34] Also, one should note that scientists may not be the best commentators on their activities. While scientists are good at doing research, we have much to learn from historians, philosophers, and sociologists of science about characterizations of what science is. Thomas Kuhn, trained as a physicist, but whose research has been in the history of science, is a prime example.

[35] Much of the "science" that is at issue in typical toxic tort cases is likely to be on the margins of the bulk of the scientific activity. The development of products for commerce is not a core activity of the scientific community — it is the development of a technology or a product, such as Bendectin, asbestos fireplace logs, or asbestos-insulated hair-dryers, which typically applies an aspect of the scientific research of others and may not involve much research that we typically think of as scientific. Thus, we should be careful about attributing too many characteristics of basic science to product development. Many such activities are marginal for understanding the biological, physical, chemical, or geological aspects of the world. The Court may be recognizing this point when it notes in discussing peer review that some scientific "propositions . . . are too particular, too new or of too limited interest to be published." *Daubert*, 113 S.Ct. at 2797.

[36] Black & Singer, Focus on: Daubert 37.

[37] *Id.* 39.

evaluating who is the appropriate party to judge scientific issues, it is not the only one, possibly not the most important one, and certainly not necessarily the decisive one, taking all the relevant considerations into account. Focusing on competence may appeal to the judiciary, for with judges deciding who is the appropriate party to decide, will not most judges decide that they themselves are better at judging the science than the jury? Other considerations, however, bear on this issue. Partly it may be an issue of whether juries or judges are more likely to make the "correct" decision (a normatively laden concept, if there ever was one). Partly it is a matter of time management — if judges have an extensive role to play in evaluating evidence, then judges would hear some or much of the evidence twice: once in a preliminary hearing and again in presentation to the jury (the only time-saving on this view occurs when the judge decides to exclude evidence). Finally, partly it is a matter of "broader political philosophical point[s] about democracy."[38]

> Juries tend to represent the community's concerns, as the democratic appliers of the law, whereas judges tend to be the government's representative as providers of the "orderly supervision of public affairs." Judicial power to exclude juries from considering the factual issues of toxic exposure deprives the more democratic body from participating in that aspect of the decision ... given the normative aspects of assessing and controlling toxic risks, public input via jury decisions seems quite important.[39]

The point here is not to settle the issue or even to explore it in detail, but to bring attention to some of the broader policy issues that should rightfully bear on the discussion and to get away from a narrow focus only on competence.

Third, one of the most important topics to be addressed in the future arising from *Daubert* decision is the relationship between the substantive standards of evidence in science and the law. There was some discussion of the issue in the *Daubert* briefs, but the Court did not consider it. Elsewhere I have noted the importance of this issue and argued that typical substantive standards of *scientific* evidence resemble the criminal law's "beyond a reasonable doubt" burdens of persuasion.[40] To the extent that this resemblance holds, then, everything else equal, requiring that tests of statistical significance or other scientific burdens of proof measure up to such demanding standards for admissibility will substantially distort the burden of production and thus the tort law balance of interests. This will make it quite difficult for plaintiffs to introduce evidence, especially evidence on the frontiers of medical knowledge, regarding the toxic effects of substances.

Related to the above are concrete concerns about tests of statistical significance. The plaintiffs in *Daubert* argued that the required level of

---

[38] Cranor, Regulating Toxic Substances 70.

[39] *Id.* 70.

[40] *Id.* 76-78.

statistical significance need not be at the 5 per cent level, but that the chances of false positive results could be higher.[41] Some *amici* disagreed about the appropriate test of statistical significance or whether there should be such tests at all. Some argued for the 5 per cent level[42] while others argued that significance tests are misleading and fail to provide full information about the underlying facts.[43] Moreover, we should note two crucial features of stringent 5 per cent level tests. For subtle biological effects, if the 5 per cent level is maintained, this may lead to a false negative result[44] simply because the study is too insensitive to detect the harm under study. In addition, everything else equal, the lower the false positive rate (thus, the "better" the science), the higher are the odds of a false negative (failing to detect a harmful substance). In such cases the goals of research science are inconsistent with the compensatory and deterrence aims of the tort law.[45] Thus, substantive admissibility standards should not be so stringent that they become equivalent of the criminal law's "beyond a reasonable doubt" burden of persuasion or that they prevent discovery of the very harms the tort law is designed to protect us against.[46]

III

This brief comment has called attention to a variety of science-law policy issues. I characterize these as science-law policy issues because the interaction the law and science is so critical in cases like *Daubert*. In the few issues considered above one can take a technical/interpretive view of the *Daubert* decision or place the issues in a wider policy context. I have followed the latter course because this helps to provide the significance of the narrower debates. The context should remind us of some of the background and goals of the tort law and how the technical issues should serve them. For instance, the aim of the tort law is not to ensure the purity of science, but to use science in the service of doing justice between parties and seeing to it that those who are wrongly harmed are compensated for their injuries. Thus, admissibility rules should serve the overall goals of torts and not necessarily ensure that none but the best peer-reviewed science is admitted. The admissibility burden can impose particular hardships on plaintiffs since they bear the burden of production. However, if this threshold hurdle is too high — because of misconceptions of what science is, because of an inappropriate

---

[41] Plaintiffs' Brief (contrasting the scientific "quest for certainty" with the legal "more likely than not" standard). Of course, statistical significance (or the equivalent in confidence intervals) is not all that is pertinent to evaluating scientific research; experimental design and other methodological issues are relevant as well.

[42] Professor Alvan R. Feinstein Brief in Support of Respondents 16.

[43] Professors Kenneth Rothman, Noel Weiss, James Robins, Raymond Neutra and Steven Stellman, Brief in Support of Petitioners 4.

[44] That is, a statistical study that shows there is no toxic effect when there is one.

[45] Cranor, Regulating Toxic Substances 71-78.

[46] *Id.* 80-81.

conception of the relationship between the regulatory law and torts or a misconception of about the difficulty to removing toxic substances from our lives, because of substituting the much more demanding scientific standards of evidence for tort standards — this will substantially change the balance of interests in tort cases that have to use scientific evidence. Some commentators have argued that while the substantive rules of the tort law favor plaintiffs, the procedural rules tend to favor defendants. However, while examining the tort law in the face of defense bar criticism, Gillette and Krier conclude that on balance there is no need to greatly reform the law to make it more favorable to defendants.[47] If they are correct, as it appears they are, then many suggestions to make tort law admissibility rules more demanding, by means of a narrow conception of science, by means of more stringent substantive standards of admissibility, or by means of a too intrusive role for judges, will make procedural hurdles even greater for plaintiffs and substantially distort the presently desirable balance of tort law interests between plaintiffs and defendants. In interpreting and applying *Daubert*, lower courts should keep these concerns in mind and not inadvertently and drastically change the tort law.

---

[47] C.P. Gillette & J.E. Krier, *Risk, Courts and Agencies*, 138 Univ. Pa. L. Rev. 1027 (1990).

Review of Recent Literature Addressing Expert and Scientific Evidence

Bert Black *

1. **Boston, *A Mass Exposure Model of Toxic Causation: The Content of Scientific Proof and the Regulatory Experience*, 18 Colum. J. Envtl. L. 181 (1993).**

This book-length article (it is over 200 pages long) distinguishes between mass toxic exposure cases and single or isolated cases. The article also provides an excellent review of causation theory, epidemiology, and toxicology. Professor Boston's primary thesis is that courts have generally been far more demanding in their review of scientific evidence when multiple rather than single cases are at issue. He takes the Agent Orange litigation, in which Judge Jack Weinstein held the plaintiffs' expert testimony inadmissible, as the paradigm mass exposure case. The paradigm isolated exposure case is *Ferebee v. Chevron Chemical Co.,*[1] in which Judge Abner Mikva of the District of Columbia Circuit ruled that expert testimony was admissible if the expert was willing to testify.

In dealing with mass exposure cases, Professor Boston suggests that courts can draw on the regulatory model for resolving scientific issues. The lesson from regulatory agencies, he says, is not whether they would require labels or warnings, but rather the methodology they use to assess risks. The kinds of evidence that are probative of a relationship between a toxic chemical and a disease, and the statistical methodologies used to evaluate such evidence, should carry over into the litigation context. Professor Boston also argues that one justification for adopting rigorous scientific standards in tort litigation is that courts have been able to exercise relatively close judicial oversight of administrative agency risk assessment decisions, which demonstrates judicial capacity to examine scientific data and methodology.

The article concludes that with regard to the substantive content of scientific evidence bearing on causation, courts have at least tacitly acknowledged that mass exposure cases differ from isolated exposure cases. They also

---

* Bert Black is the partner in charge of the Environmental Practice Group at the Baltimore Law Firm of Weinberg and Green.

[1] 736 F.2d 1529 (D.C. Cir.), *cert. denied*, 496 U.S. 1062 (1984).

have demonstrated sophistication in distinguishing between generic causation and individual causation, have almost universally demanded particularistic proof, and have been increasingly willing to scrutinize scientific evidence offered by parties. The article also concludes that with regard to the approach courts take in assembling the information they need, the regulatory model should serve as a very useful guide. Again, strict scrutiny of the parties' evidence should be required, and the explanatory theory or rationale linking the evidence in a case with an expert's conclusion should be demonstrably scientific.

2.   Brennan, *Environmental Torts,* 46 Vand. L. Rev. 1 (1993).

Professor Brennan writes that environmental tort litigation is a burgeoning area lying somewhere between traditional tort law and environmental law. Under traditional tort theory, he says, one would not expect to see many environmental tort cases, because they should be hard to win. In fact, lawyers take such cases because the law has proven flexible enough to accommodate them. Information on environmental exposures has become more readily available as a result of environmental statutes, and people are more and more willing to bring suit when they feel they have been harmed. Strict liability has in many cases done away with the need to prove negligence, and courts have not readily accepted regulatory compliance as a defense. Also, the combination of probabilistic causation with medical monitoring has helped to overcome problems in establishing causation. Professor Brennan tentatively concludes that more litigation of this type is advisable from a deterrence point of view.

3.   Fischer, *Proportional Liability: Statistical Evidence and the Probability Paradox,* 46 Vand. L. R. 1201 (1993).

A number of commentators have suggested that one way to accommodate tort law to probabilistic evidence in toxic exposure cases would be to pay damages proportionately. For example, if 25 per cent of the risk of a certain kind of disease was attributable to a defendant, then that defendant would pay 25 per cent of the damages suffered by the plaintiff. In another version of the theory, the plaintiff might even recover prospectively, or compel the defendant to purchase insurance against the ultimate occurrence of the disease.

In this article, Professor Fischer argues that proportional liability is a bad idea from a deterrence perspective because it paradoxically encourages activities that increase risk. The paradox is that the more background risk that exists, the less incentive there is a for a prospective defendant to reduce risk. Thus Professor Fischer concludes the traditional common law may do a better job. He recognizes that the traditional tort system may prevent plaintiffs from recovering because they cannot prove causation, and he suggests that to the extent a solution is required, a statutory approach would be best.

4. Sanders, *From Science to Evidence: The Testimony on Causation in the Bendectin Cases*, 46 Stan. L. Rev. 1 (1993).

Professor Sanders starts from the premise that by the time science becomes evidence, it is greatly changed, and that juries have trouble comprehending it as a science. He believes that the law, in the first instance, creates this problem by demanding of science more than it can deliver, and then distorts the work of scientists to fit legal requirements. He points out that persuasiveness is not necessarily a useful indicator of scientific validity, and that trial procedures often minimize the jury's understanding of scientific issues. In the Bendectin cases, for example, the juries seemed often to undervalue the epidemiologic evidence. The article suggests possible changes in three areas: admissibility, how evidence is presented, and who the fact finder is. It concludes by recommending more use of court appointed experts and bifurcated trials.

5. *Symposium on Scientific Evidence*, 84 J. Crim. L. & Criminology 1 (1993).

This symposium, published shortly after the decision in *Daubert*, provides an excellent collection of articles on scientific evidence in criminal cases. Andre A. Moenssens wrote a forward on novel scientific evidence in criminal cases. Professor William C. Thompson, a criminologist who holds both a PhD. and a law degree, contributed an excellent piece on DNA identification techniques. Rockne P. Harmon, the prosecutor who has been perhaps the most militant advocate of DNA typing, wrote a piece questioning why the methodology should be so controversial, it being his position that the evidence in most cases is merely duplicative of other evidence of guilt. Peter J. Neufeld, one of the most active defense lawyers in the DNA area, responded. In addition to these articles, Professor Paul C. Giannelli wrote a piece on "junk science" in criminal cases, and Professors Gary M. Ernsdorff and Elizabeth F. Loftus wrote a piece on techniques used to enhance and elicit repressed memories. Finally, the symposium issue includes a comment on the horizontal gaze nystagmus sobriety test.

BOOK REVIEWS

Uncommon Sense: The Heretical Nature of Science, Alan Comer*

Reviewed by
Bert Black**

Where and why did science begin, and how reliable and certain is the knowledge it produces? Alan Cromer's book, *Uncommon Sense: The Heretical Nature of Science*, comes up with some surprising and controversial answers to these questions. Science, he tells us, would never have developed had the ancient Greeks not sown the cultural seeds of skepticism, debate, logic, and objectivity. Without Greece, there would have been no Newton or Einstein. Cromer, who is a professor of physics at Northeastern University, also argues that science can produce absolute truth and certainty, which puts him at odds with most modern philosophers of science.

Few would quarrel with the importance of the Greeks, or with the ability of science to provide very accurate and reliable descriptions of phenomena, and explanations of why they occur. But *Uncommon Sense* unnecessarily exaggerates these features of science. Cromer overemphasizes the special role of Greece to bolster his view that science is counterintuitive and difficult to teach, and he overemphasizes the certainty and truth of scientific knowledge to highlight why it should be taught. Along the way he lambastes Western religion as antiscientific, and he exalts the psychological theories of Piaget as the best way to increase scientific literacy in the United States. The result is a hodgepodge of not very thoroughly developed ideas thrown together with the goal of reforming education and the teaching of science in this country.

Fixing on the Greeks as absolutely necessary for the development of science is both futile and unscientific. Whether science originated solely with the Greeks, or from the confluence of several cultures, is not really a meaningful question. One might ponder what would have happened without Greece, but there is no way to test the hypothesis of "no Greece, no science." And such speculation is unnecessary to an understanding of how modern science works in practice. Indeed, Cromer's fascination with the Greeks seems more motivated by his desire to demonstrate the difficulty of teaching science than it is by a serious effort to explore its historical roots.

---

* Oxford University Press 1993.

** Bert Black is the partner in charge of the Environmental Practice Group at the Baltimore law firm of Weinberg and Green.

The attack on Thomas Kuhn's relativist view of science is similarly off target. Kuhn, and the more radical Paul Feyerabend, took issue with the logical positivist view of science as an engine for producing certainty. They argued that a philosophically rigorous definition of science, shorn of any value-ladened preconceptions, is impossible. Feyerabend, in a particularly illustrative — and amusing — flight of hyperbole, once argued that there is no rational basis for distinguishing modern medicine from witchcraft. Of course, there is. Scientific medicine wiped out smallpox. Witchcraft never could have. And virtually all educated people know the difference between the two. One does not have to return to the absolute truth of logical positivism, however, to address the relativist view that Feyerabend and Kuhn espouse. While there may be no "absolute certainty," science does let us sort out more certain from less certain knowledge, and at the extremes to accept some ideas, and reject others, with little doubt that we are right.

Indeed, even *Uncommon Sense*, despite its exaggerated positions, in many ways presents a relatively balanced picture of science. The book is well written and eminently readable, and its discussions of historical examples should prove very useful to lawyers and judges trying to develop a better sense of how science works in practice. Chapter 8, entitled "Science and Nonsense" is particularly helpful. This chapter begins with the surprising (for Cromer) nonabsolutist recognition that while a concise description of science is elusive, most scientists agree on what is and is not scientific. Cromer adopts John Ziman's idea of science as public knowledge, a search for consensus based on publication and review. Though he spends too much effort trying to tie Ziman back to the tradition of Greece, he still does a good job explaining why we can be so sure about the "truth" of scientific ideas like Newtonian mechanics, at least for most purposes.

Chapter 8 also gives examples of how wild speculation can pose as science. Cromer discusses the fascinating case of Immanuel Velikovsky, who in 1950 published a book that purported to explain many biblical miracles as a result of near collisions between Earth and other planets. No scientific journal would publish this nonsense, but Velikovsky had a large following. As Cromer puts it, "[w]ell written pseudoscience, with its exciting generalizations and lack of mathematics, can always find a bigger audience than carefully crafted, but necessarily tedious, rebuttals."[1] In addition to Velikovsky, *Uncommon Sense* debunks parapsychology. The book tells the story of J. B. Rhine, who claimed he had run tests with cards in which the subject had been able to name what was on a card without looking at it. Data supporting this claim were sloppy and questionable, and could not be replicated by other scientists.

Its initial claims about the absolute truth of science notwithstanding, *Uncommon Sense* also gives an excellent example of how accepted ideas sometimes get overturned. It describes how the assumption that the laws of

---

[1] Uncommon Sense, at 151.

physics are indifferent to position, orientation, and handedness was toppled when experiments confirmed a number of questions that had been raised by two theorists. The lesson is not that science is a matter of taste, but rather that good solid theoretical and experimental work is required to replace a generally accepted idea with something else.

A contrasting example, also discussed in Chapter 8, is cold fusion. When Stanley Pons and Martin Fleischmann announced to the press in early 1989 that they had achieved fusion in a small electrolytic cell, they attracted worldwide attention. If they were right, their discovery would mean a limitless and environmentally safe source of energy. The only catch was that they had gone public before going through the normal review process of science, and close scrutiny quickly revealed that their claims were simply impossible. Had they generated the amount of heat they claimed, the related generation of neutrons would have killed them.

Chapter 8 closes with an excellent discussion of "pathological science," a term originally used by the Nobel Prize winning chemist, Irving Langmuir, in 1953. Langmuir had visited Rhine and was shocked to learn that Rhine had essentially discarded data that tended to disprove his theories of parapsychology. Langmuir also told the story of P. R. Blondlot, a member of the French Academy of Sciences, who in 1903 announced that he had discovered "N-rays," which were generated by heating a wire inside an iron tube. The rays did not pass through the iron, but they would pass through aluminum, and they were supposedly detectable by eye. Blondlot, however, continued to see N-rays even when the generating device, without his knowledge, had been removed. In reality, there was nothing to be seen.

Langmuir found that such cases of "pathological science" had some commonly recurring characteristics. "They are generally claims, based on a weak or marginal effect, of fantastic phenomena contrary to all experience. There are conflicting reports from independent investigators. Reasonable explanations of the data, based on known science, are rejected. Interest rises rapidly for a time and then gradually fades away."[2]

If only for its concise and well-written examples from the history of science, *Uncommon Sense* is worth reading. Even its inordinate excursions on the Greeks, absolute certainty, and Piaget's psychology are entertaining, if not convincing. While not a "must read" for devotees of science and the law, the book will reward readers with new insights into the fundamental question of how to identify valid scientific knowledge.

---

[2] *Id.* at 167.

Court-Appointed Experts:
Defining the Role of Experts Appointed under Federal Rule of Evidence 706,
Joe S. Cecil & Thomas E. Willging*

Reviewed by
*Bert Black***

The Supreme Court's decision in *Daubert*[1] has focused attention on how trial courts can best access scientific knowledge and understand it. *Court-Appointed Experts: Defining the Role of Experts Appointed Under Federal Rule of Evidence 706* ("*Court-Appointed Experts*") by Joe S. Cecil and Thomas E. Willging should prove very useful in developing procedures to address this question. It reports on a study the authors conducted under the auspices of the Federal Judicial Center to find out why Rule 706 of the Federal Rules of Evidence is employed so infrequently. It also discusses alternatives to the appointment of experts, and possible changes to Rule 706.

The study was based on a questionnaire sent to all active federal district court judges, and follow-up telephone interviews with judges who had used Rule 706. The authors also contacted judges who had not appointed experts, to allow them to explain their viewpoint. The results of the survey were quite interesting. The 537 questionnaires that were mailed out yielded responses from 431 judges, a response rate of about 80%. Of the judges who responded, 345 had never used Rule 706, and of those who had, more than half had used it only one time. Indeed, fewer than 3 per cent of the responding judges had used court-appointed experts five or more times.

When the authors followed up with the judges who had used experts to determine what kinds of expertise they most often sought, medicine was cited most frequently, along with engineering experts (appointed in patent and trade cases) and accounting experts in commercial cases. Medical experts were used most often in medical malpractice cases, but also in defective products and toxic exposure cases. The judges gave two principal reasons for appointing experts. The most common reason was to assist in understanding technical issues. Some judges, however, suggested that use of court-appointedexperts might help to bring about settlement. The reasons for not appointing experts fell into six general categories:

---

* Federal Judicial Center 1993.

** Bert Black is the partner in charge of the Environmental Practice Group at the Baltimore law firm of Weinberg and Green.

[1] Daubert v. Merrell Dow Pharmaceuticals, Inc., 113 S.Ct. 2786 (1993).

1. Infrequency of cases requiring extraordinary assistance
2. Respect for the adversarial system
3. Difficulty identifying an expert suitable for appointment
4. Securing compensation for an expert
5. Lack of early recognition that appointment is needed
6. Lack of awareness of the procedure

Though the judges generally expressed a preference for appointing experts early on during the course of litigation, there were a number of instances reported in which an expert had been appointed immediately before or during the course of an ongoing trial. Most of the last-minute appointments occurred in cases involving bench trials, which permit a court far more flexibility in terms of scheduling.

In the vast majority of cases, the court, rather than one of the parties, suggested use of a court-appointed expert, but on a few occasions one or both parties made such a suggestion. Usually the parties did not oppose the use of a court-appointed expert, at least formally. There were, however, a few cases in which formal opposition was mounted.

Finding experts for court appointment was one of the biggest issues identified. In some cases, judges have abandoned the effort because no suitable person was willing to serve. It is apparently more common for judges to appoint experts they have identified and recruited, typically based on previous personal or professional relationships, than for courts to have the parties nominate experts. Sometimes judges would contact local institutions for assistance in identifying suitable experts.

Court-Appointed Experts also discusses at length the way in which experts communicate with the court and with the parties after their appointment. It notes that court-appointed experts are deposed in relatively few cases, and that they serve a variety of functions in addition to testifying at trial. The published opinions indicate that court-appointed experts fill nontestimonial roles more than they actually give testimony.

Perhaps the most interesting chapters of *Court-Appointed Experts* are the last two, which consider alternatives to court appointment, on the one hand, and improving the use of court-appointed experts on the other. The alternatives suggested include more active judicial screening of the party appointed experts at trial, endeavoring to narrow the issues between the party-appointed experts, the use of special masters, and taking steps to make it easier for juries to understand the testimony of the parties' experts. The latter approach often may involve court questioning of an expert, and in some cases even jury questioning, usually in the form of questions submitted in writing to the judge for screening.

The authors report that the vast majority of judges who had used court-appointed experts were very satisfied with the result, which raises the question again as to why Rule 706 is not invoked more frequently. When asked for changes that would make it easier to use the Rule, the most commonly raised problems were compensation and controlling ex parte communications. Several judges suggested better coordination between the Federal Rules of Civil Procedure and the Federal Rules of Evidence, in particular integration of the special master provisions of the Rules of Civil Procedure with the court-appointed expert provisions of the Rules of Evidence. The authors suggest pretrial procedures based on early identification of issues likely to require expert testimony, specification of disputed issues, and pretrial screening of the parties' experts regarding admissibility. These procedures need not necessarily lead to court appointment, but should in any event clarify the issues for trial.

Court-Appointed Experts concludes that appointment of experts will very likely remain a rare procedure, suited only to the most demanding cases. The authors, however, still see Rule 706 as an important alternative source of authority to deal with the kind of complex scientific issues that can arise in modern litigation.

Succeeding As An Expert Witness, Feder

Reviewed by
Marc S. Klein

The *law of unintended consequences* generally holds that, for each intentional act, we may also expect some unintended (and unanticipated) consequence. This law operated with the adoption of the new Federal Rules of Evidence (in 1975) governing expert and scientific evidence. While these rules were designed to improve the quality of adjudication, they also gave rise to a lucrative new profession: expert witnessing.[1]

When a new profession emerges, "how to" books often follow. In that regard, Harold Feder has hit a home run with *Succeeding As An Expert Witness*.[2]

I must admit that I was skeptical when I first opened the book. I expected another collection of nostrums and war stories. Feder's book is not that sort of work. It is, instead, a fine text (written by an accomplished plaintiffs' trial attorney) for those who want to succeed as an expert witness.[3]

I. Nature of the Book

Feder's book is not an academic treatise. It is a practical guide for the forensic expert. To use an analogy, it is not a work about the history and

---

[1] Expert witnesses have been around, of course, for hundreds of years. But many commentators have noted the tremendous increase in their prominence and use since the adoption of the new federal rules. *See, e.g.*, Samuel R. Gross, *Expert Evidence*, 1991 Wis. L. Rev. 1113, 1118-20, 1131-32 (1991) (discussing the current frequency of expert testimony and the new phenomenon of "professional witnesses"); Marc S. Klein, *Expert Testimony in Pharmaceutical Product Liability Actions*, 45 Food Drug Cosm. L. J. 393, 394 (1990) ("Modern evidence rules liberalized the use of expert testimony to promote rational decisionmaking in the resolution of increasingly complex litigation. Unfortunately, their liberal thrust has also led to widespread abuse ..."); Peter W. Huber, Liability: The Legal Revolution and its Consequences 43-44 (1988) (With the liberalization of the rules governing this area, "[e]xperts lined up in hordes, on both sides of the courtroom, to educate juries on the finer points of designing a morning sickness drug, a crashworthy car, or a safer playground swing").

[2] Tageh Press, PO Box 401, Glenwood Springs, CO 81602.

[3] Harold A. Feder is a trial lawyer with more than 34 years of experience in the courtroom. He is a member of the American Academy of Forensic Sciences, the Association of Trial Lawyers in America, and past president of the Colorado Trial Lawyers Association.

theory of warfare; rather, it is a soldier's manual on how to survive and win on the battlefield.[4]

The book walks the expert through the entire process, from a potential retainer through the conclusion of the case. It includes, of course, points along the way of interest solely to the expert, like how he or she can ensure payment for services rendered and generate new business in the process.

The book includes many useful checklists.[5] It also includes a wealth of information in a comprehensive set of appendices.[6]

II. A Laudable Emphasis on Ethics

Throughout the book, Feder stresses the importance of ethics. At the very beginning of his work, Feder declares that his objective is to "emphasize *professionally correct and ethical methods* to be followed by expert witnesses through the mileposts of a forensic undertaking . . . ."[7] He devotes an entire chapter to "Ethical and Interprofessional Problems and Solutions."[8]

Feder's discussion involves the practical stuff of everyday litigation. Every expert with real professional standards (or a conscience) should be prepared to confront ethical dilemmas inherent in the profession. Experts must consider the goals of the lawyers and clients — and experts will naturally desire to please them. But, Feder emphasizes, experts should not sell their souls in the process. There are times when the expert must say no.

Thus, Feder wisely advises the expert that, "[b] *efore* deciding to take on a case, you must examine your conscience and your professional and technical experience for conflicts of interest or professional inabilities."[9] Later, Feder warns, the honest expert must be prepared for some unpleasantry when he or she renders a *preliminary verbal report*:

> Some clients and attorneys may terminate your services upon receipt of an adverse preliminary verbal report. They may believe that your conclusions are heading in the wrong direction or your methods are inordinately impartial. . . . Continue to follow the method and standards

---

[4] Feder's book is primarily geared for the novice expert witness in the routine case — the bread and butter of litigation. But experts in high-stakes toxic tort or product liability cases can profit from many of its lessons.

[5] *See, e.g., Feder,* at 93 (checklist of proper contents of expert's final report).

[6] *See, e.g., Feder,* at 191 (Appendix A: *Things to Do List* for the expert); *id.* at 194 (Appendix C: criteria for evaluating an expert's performance); *id.* at 227 (Appendix L: *Guidelines for Deposition and Trial Testimony*); and *id.* at 230 (Appendix M: *Deposing an Expert Witness* (a generic outline)).

[7] *Feder,* at xi (emphasis added).

[8] *See id.,* Chapter 22, at 171.

[9] *Id.* at 34 (emphasis added).

that you know to be correct. *If your preliminary report seems to suggest dissatisfaction with your methods or conclusions, it may be best for all concerned to terminate the assignment.*[10]

Feder makes it clear that, for his money, he wants an honest expert. Most lawyers do. It is a healthy perspective for both professions, the judicial system, and society at large.

III. Some Interesting Points

You will find a number of interesting observations and techniques in Feder's book of value to both the expert and the lawyer:

A. Expert Witnessing is an Ancient Practice

After presenting a concise overview (in Chapter 1) of the expert's role in litigation, Feder then reviews the expert's role in the history of human dispute resolution:

> . The tribal councils of ancient societies frequently sought guidance from designated magicians, sorcerers, and tribal wisemen. These persons did not possess divine gifts or supernatural powers. Rather, they had the ability for keen observation of nature, physical facts, animal behavior, contents of roots, plants and herbs, and uniformity of times, tides and seasons. By focusing attention on this body of data, they were able to correctly predict a number of future events. This gave them a position of superiority in primitive society. On analysis, we have not really come that far. Today [expert witnesses] are, for similar reasons, considered to hold a special place in the dispute resolution process.[11]

Feder properly encourages experts to understand that their profession is an ancient and noble one. The modern forensic setting may be different, but humanity has relied on experts to resolve disputes ever since the beginning of recorded time.

B. Why Experts Must Keep Current

Feder properly emphasizes that experts have a clear obligation "to stay current in [their] profession. [Experts] cannot rely on outdated and outmoded theories, methods, concepts, or equipment."[12]

How does Feder effectively make this point? He does so with a little-known, albeit staggering, fact about our modern information revolution:

---

[10] *Id.* at 78 (emphasis added).

[11] *Id.* at 10.

[12] *Id.* at 28.

Humankind's collective knowledge in the last fifty years equals perhaps one-half of our knowledge accumulated during recorded history. It is therefore awe-inspiring to consider the amount of new knowledge we will witness in the next twenty-five years.[13]

Feder lists "eight categories" of activity through which experts can remain current in their fields. These include:

1. Reading professional literature
2. Being active in the field
3. Continuing education/certification
4. Research and publishing
5. Teaching, lecturing, and consulting
6. Attending seminars
7. Attending professional conferences
8. Engaging in peer review[14]

On this score, Feder hits the nail right on the head. In fact, judges and lawyers have often used these same categories — or some close variants of them — to determine whether a witness is truly an expert in his or her field.[15]

C. How to Prepare

Feder stresses the value of good demonstrative evidence.[16] He devotes nearly an entire chapter, moreover, to the importance of ensuring the *validity* of this type of evidence. Thus, "the expert must give meticulous care to the source of the data and methods of combination. Unbiased techniques of enlargement and enhancement are combined with fundamental fact gathering details such as date, time, and place of initial data gathering."[17]

---

[13] *Id.*

[14] *See id.* at 28-33.

[15] *See, e.g.*, Smith v. Hobart Mfg. Co., 185 F. Supp. 751, 756 (E.D. Pa. 1960) (expert not qualified because, among other things, he was not a "member of at least one organization or society dedicated to the improvement of that profession"); Hartke v. McKelway, 526 F. Supp. 97, 101 (D.D.C. 1981) (physician's "reading of literature and conferring with other physicians on the eve of trial did not qualify her to testify"), *aff'd*, 707 F.2d 1544 (D.C. Cir.), *cert. denied*, 464 U.S. 983 (1983); *see generally* Marc S. Klein, *Expert Testimony in Pharmaceutical Product Liability Actions*, 45 Food Drug Cosm. L.J. 393, 407-08 (1990) (cataloging numerous indicia of expertise).

[16] *See, e.g., Feder*, at 57 ("Experts tell us we learn 15 percent from what we hear and 85 percent from what we see. Therefore, you must translate complex principles into visual presentations.")

[17] *Id.* at 59. Feder's advice on this score is borne out by Judge Bright's recent decision in Robinson v. Missouri Pacific R.R. Co., 16 F.3d 1083, 1089 (10th Cir. 1994) ("[U]nder Rule 702, we suggest that as 'gatekeeper' the district court carefully and meticulously

Feder also cautions the expert about the grave implications of unautho-rized *destructive testing*. (Spoliation caused by destructive testing, among other things, is now a hot topic in several areas, particularly products liability.) Feder properly emphasizes that an expert should not, under any circum-stance, perform *any* destructive test until he or she has "consult[ed] with [the] attorney and client first."[18] As Feder correctly warns: "Disastrous results can result from destructive testing which has not been [conducted] in accordance with these guidelines."[19]

D. Discoverability of Material Considered by the Expert

Feder properly advises experts that:

> Recent case decisions and rules of evidence generally provide that the information on which you rely to help you form opinions may be inquired into through the discovery process. *That means that any communication with the attorney, client, witnesses, or other experts, or any part of your investigative field process which in any way formulates a basis for your opinion can be viewed and inquired into by the opposition.*[20]

This is sound advice (albeit a little superficial in its treatment of the legal issues). The discoverability of material considered by an expert has been the subject of controversy in the past.[21] The new version of Rule 26, however, clearly tilts in favor of discoverability.[22] Consequently, the expert (and lawyer) should at all times remember this golden rule: "[I]n most cases both your file and your opinions will be subject to discovery. That being the case, test everything you write, note, report, or say against the probability that it may fall to the opposition or may be introduced at trial."[23]

E. How to Educate the Lawyer

Feder shares his wisdom and experience about regular features of the relationship between the lawyer and expert.

---

make an early pretrial evaluation of scientific expert opinions and films or animations illustrative of such opinions"). For an interesting discussion of some issues concerning virtual reality in the courtroom, *see* Arielle Emmett, *Simulations on Trial*, Tech. Rev., May/June 1994, at 30.

[18] *Feder*, at 84.

[19] *Id.* at 84.

[20] *Id.* at 96 (emphasis added).

[21] *See, e.g.*, Marc S. Klein, *Two Year Review of Developments in the Law of Expert Testimony*, Sci. Evid. Review — Monograph No. 1, 15-16 (ABA 1992) ("Sometimes counsel must be concerned about the information that his or her own expert has reviewed in forming an opinion. If the expert considered some inadmissible information, and it is even arguably inconsistent with his or her opinion, an adversary may be able to use that information to impeach the expert's credibility").

[22] *See* James Toll's article on the recent amendments to *Fed. R. Civ. P.* 26 in this issue of *SESEQ*.

[23] *Feder*, at 102.

For example, many lawyers invariably ask their experts for copies of the most important works in their fields. Feder mentions this common practice and takes it one step further (by encouraging experts to help lawyers who fail to ask): "Most technical, professional, and scientific fields boast a text or series of books which constitute 'the Bible' for that field. Experienced trial lawyers will regularly ask you for such texts. Failing that request, take the initiative and make that information available to the attorney."[24]

F. Discovery is a Defensive Exercise

Feder reminds the expert of something that many good litigators stress: you cannot win the case in your deposition, but you sure can lose it. Play defense. Thus, Feder writes:

> There is a fundamental rule in discovery matters which you probably already know. Your client may not win the case during discovery, but the case could well be lost at that time. Talking too much in discovery, revealing more than is required, waxing eloquent or acting egotistical, telling all you know about the subject: all can be detrimental to the case.[25]

Feder does not limit his discussion of this key point to exhortation. He provides some very good examples of "good and bad answers to deposition questions" that effectively make the point.[26]

G. How to Handle Direct and Cross-Examination

Feder includes some important information about effective direct and cross-examination. He writes about how to organize the direct, including some "do's and don'ts."[27] These include "an example of doing it wrong on direct,"[28] and, most important, Feder explains how and why the expert should simplify complex issues for the jury on direct examination.[29]

Most of Feder's advice is well taken. Feder emphasizes, for instances, that experts — like good trial lawyers and negotiators — should not try to sell past closing:

> The usual admonition for cross-examining counsel is to stop when you're ahead, use restraint, and not overplay. The same admonitions are equally true for you as the expert witness undergoing cross-examination. Do not overplay the expert role. Do not overemphasize

---

[24] *Id.* at 91.

[25] *Id.* at 119.

[26] *See id.* at 125.

[27] *Id.* at 151.

[28] *Id.* at 156.

[29] *Id.*

your superior knowledge. Be accurate with the facts. Be firm without being an advocate. *Maintain control of the situation.*[30]

This is easier said than done. But there is no excuse for not endeavoring to "maintain control of the situation."

IV. Conclusion

The new judicial activism licensed by *Daubert* will help drive junk science from the courts. Judicial education will also help.[31] But many scholars have recognized that the legal system cannot do it alone. Thus, forensic experts must also contribute to any solution of this problem:

> Apart from the debate over systemic change in the legal system, there is much that experts can do to achieve improvements within the structure of existing rules. No amendment of the rules is required for professions to articulate their own standards of good practice for members who offer expert testimony. No amendment of the rules is required for experts to refuse to testify to material that lacks sufficient scientific basis. And, no amendment to the rules is required for experts to refuse to work with lawyers who will not permit experts to set forth their findings accurately and completely.[32]

The necessity of responsible expert testimony is a point that Feder stresses in his book. For this alone, it is laudable. In terms of technique and practice, moreover, Feder's book is quite valuable for experts and lawyers alike. I certainly intend to buy some additional copies and send them to my experts.

---

[30] *Id.* at 170 (emphasis added).

[31] *See, e.g.*, Science and Technology in Judicial Decision Making: Creating Opportunities and Meeting Challenges 51 (Carnegie Comm. on Science, Tech. & Gov't 1993) (stressing the necessity of judicial education on science and technology issues).

[32] Daniel W. Shuman, Elizabeth Whitaker, & Anthony Champagne, *An Empirical Examination of the Use of Expert Witnesses in the Courts — Part II: A Three City Study*, 34 Jurimetrics J. 193, 208 (Winter 1994). *See also* Barry L. Shapiro & Marc S. Klein, *Epidemiology in the Courtroom: Anatomy of an Intellectual Embarrassment*, in Pharmacopidemiology I 87, 110-13 (S. Edlavitch ed. 1989) (discussing the particular measures that the scientific and medical communities can undertake themselves "to combat junk science in the courtroom").